A Social History of the Deccan, 1300–1761

In this fascinating study, Richard Eaton recounts the history of southern India's Deccan plateau from the early fourteenth century to the rise of European colonialism in the eighteenth. He does so, vividly, by narrating the lives of eight Indians who lived at different times during this period, and whose careers illustrate particular social processes of the region's history. In the first chapter, for example, the author recounts the tragic life of maharaja Pratapa Rudra in order to describe the demise of regional kingdoms and the rise of interregional sultanates. In the second, the life of a Sufi shaikh is used to explore the intersection of Muslim piety, holy-man charisma, and state authority. The book's other characters include a long-distance merchant, a general, a slave, a poet, a bandit, and a female commander-regent.

Woven together into a rich narrative tapestry, the stories of these eight figures shed light not only on important social processes of the Deccan plateau across four centuries, but also on the complex relations between peoples and states of north India and those to the south of the Narmada River. This study of one of the least understood parts of South Asia is a long-awaited and much-needed book by one of the most highly regarded scholars in the field.

RICHARD M. EATON is one of the premier scholars of precolonial India. His many publications include *The Rise of Islam and the Bengal Frontier, 1204–1760* (1993), *India's Islamic Traditions, 711–1750* (2003) and *Temple Desecration and Muslim States in Medieval India* (2004).

D1648650

THE NEW CAMBRIDGE HISTORY OF INDIA

General editor GORDON JOHNSON
President of Wolfson College, Cambridge

Associate editors C. A. BAYLY
Vere Harmsworth Professor of Imperial and Naval History, University of Cambridge,
and Fellow of St Catharine's College

and JOHN F. RICHARDS
Professor of History, Duke University

Although the original *Cambridge History of India,* published between 1922 and 1937, did much to formulate a chronology for Indian history and describe the administrative structures of government in India, it has inevitably been overtaken by the mass of new research over the past seventy years.

Designed to take full account of recent scholarship and changing conceptions of South Asia's historical development, *The New Cambridge History of India* is published as a series of short, self-contained volumes, each dealing with a separate theme and written by one or two authors, and published within a four-part structure.

The four parts are as follows:

I The Mughals and their Contemporaries

II Indian States and the Transition to Colonialism

III The Indian Empire and the Beginnings of Modern Society

IV The Evolution of Contemporary South Asia

*A list of individual titles will be found
at the end of the volume.*

THE NEW CAMBRIDGE HISTORY OF INDIA

I · 8

*A Social History of
the Deccan, 1300–1761
Eight Indian Lives*

RICHARD M. EATON

University of Arizona

CAMBRIDGE
UNIVERSITY PRESS

CAMBRIDGE UNIVERSITY PRESS
Cambridge, New York, Melbourne, Madrid, Cape Town, Singapore, São Paulo

Cambridge University Press
The Edinburgh Building, Cambridge CB2 2RU, UK

Published in the United States of America by Cambridge University Press, New York

www.cambridge.org
Information on this title: www.cambridge.org/9780521716277

© Cambridge University Press 2005

First published 2005
First paperback edition published 2008

Printed in the United Kingdom at the University Press, Cambridge

A catalogue record for this book is available from the British Library

Library of Congress Cataloguing in Publication data
Eaton, Richard Maxwell.
A social history of the Deccan, 1300–1761: eight Indian lives / Richard M. Eaton.
p.   cm. – (The new Cambridge history of India; I, 8)
Includes bibliographical references and index.
ISBN 13: 978 0 521 25484 7 (hardback)
ISBN 10: 0 521 25484 1 (hardback)
1. Deccan (India) – History.   2. Deccan (India) – Biography.
I. Title.   II. Series.
DS436 .N7 1987 pt. 1, vol. 8   [DS485.D25]
954′.8 – dc22

ISBN-13   978-0-521-25484-7 hardback
ISBN-13   978-0-521-71627-7 paperback

For my sister and brother-in-law
BETH AND ROSCOE SWARTZ

Celebrating fifty years of marriage

CONTENTS

COLOR PLATES

MAPS

GENEALOGICAL TABLES

TABLES

ACKNOWLEDGMENTS

Historians, to paraphrase the classical proverb, merely stand on the shoulders of their predecessors. In my own case, I must acknowledge many shoulders, and not only those of my distinguished predecessors, some of whom date to the fourteenth century. There is also a host of contemporary colleagues and friends who, in various ways, generously assisted me in my journey into the rich field of Deccani history. These include Balasubramanya, V. K. Bawa, Ninad Bedekar, Dilip Chitre, Devin Deweese, Anne Feldhaus, Stewart Gordon, Jo-Ann Gross, Sumit Guha, Syed Shah Khusro Hussaini, Pervaram Jagannatham, Rochelle Kessler, Gijs Kruijtzer, Sunil Kumar, M. S. Mate, R. S. Morwanchikar, N. S. Ramachandra Murthy, Gail Omvedt, Aloka Parasher-Sen, Jaisingrao Pawar, Helen Philon, S. Fiaz and Frauke Quader, Velcheru Narayana Rao, M. Pandu Ranga Rao, Lee Schlesinger, David Shulman, Carla Sinopoli, Susan Stronge, Cynthia Talbot, Mahesh Tendulkar, Phillip B. Wagoner, and Eleanor Zelliot. To all I express my indebtedness and gratitude. However, I alone bear responsibility for any shortcomings in the study.

The idea for the book took shape in 1995–96 when I was a fellow at the Woodrow Wilson Center for Scholars in Washington DC. Much of the text was drafted in the autumn of 2000 when I was a fellow with Tucson's Udall Center for Public Policy, and I completed the work in the academic year 2003–04 during a sabbatical leave from the University of Arizona. I wish to thank the officers of those three institutions for affording me the time and facilities to conduct the research for the study.

Most of the volume's color illustrations were made from photographs I took while touring the Deccan in June and July 2001. Despite the trip's several mishaps,[1] that monsoon journey was immeasurably enriched by the generosity of the many knowledgeable colleagues I was fortunate to meet along the way. I wish to thank Anne Feldhaus for going many miles out of her own way to take the photographs for Plates 4 and 5. For permission to reproduce the other illustrations in this volume, I wish to thank the Victoria and Albert Museum (London), the Chester Beatty Library (Dublin), and the American Council for Southern Asian Art (Ann Arbor). Finally, I thank Lois Kain for preparing the volume's six maps.

---

[1] These include dropping my camera in the Arabian Sea at Janjira, getting suspended mid-air in Raigarh's cable car because of a power outage, and being stranded in Bidar owing to lack of funds.

INTRODUCTION

There is properly no history; only biography.

Ralph Waldo Emerson (1841)

In early January 1996, a fierce blizzard had just blanketed Washington DC in snow. Icy winds howled outside the narrow, Gothic windows that encircled my tiny study, perched high up in one of the fairytale towers of the Smithsonian Castle. While I tried to stay warm in that dilapidated but charming relic of the nineteenth century, my mind was a world away. I was pondering "the social history of the Deccan" on a cold day, part of a year spent as a fellow with the Woodrow Wilson Center for Scholars.

I first had to resolve some knotty conceptual problems, one of which was geographic in nature. Most historians of India write about, or simply presume, coherent core regions – that is, areas characterized by stable, long-term political and cultural institutions. Like magnets, nucleated political cores attract armies, scholars, foreign visitors, long-distance merchants, and crucially, court chroniclers. Ultimately, owing to the considerable data left behind by such groups, these regions also attract modern historians. This might explain why core areas like north India, Bengal, or the Tamil south are comparatively well covered in the historical literature.[1]

But the Deccan is a relatively understudied region, partly because it has no enduring political or cultural center. To be sure, one finds sporadic periods of imperial rule from capital cities like Kalyana under the Chalukyas, Bidar under the Bahmanis, or Vijayanagara under its first three dynasties. But in history's larger sweep, this dry and mainly undifferentiated upland plateau never possessed a single, perennial political core, no lasting hub of imperial rule on the order of Delhi or the Kaveri delta.

---

[1] Such centers also have an internalized conception of themselves as lying at the heart of cultural and/or political space, indeed, as having created such space. One need only think of the many chroniclers who wrote their histories while, as it were, peering out from the ramparts of Delhi's Red Fort, or from any of the other great forts of the Mughal heartland.

1

Indeed, this begs the nettlesome question of just what defines the Deccan and where exactly it is located. North Indians popularly conceive it as lying vaguely to the south of the Indo-Gangetic Plain, while Tamils and Malayalis just as vaguely locate it to the north of their native regions. Geographers have given precise-sounding definitions by using indices like rainfall, vegetation, soil type, and the like, or by citing prominent natural features such as the Narmada River or the Sahyadri Mountains (i.e., Western Ghats).[2] Ultimately, though, I settled on the reasoning of one of India's foremost chroniclers, Muhammad Qasim Firishta (d. 1611), himself a longtime resident of Bijapur. Ignoring physical geography altogether, Firishta mapped the region in terms of its vernacular languages, using for this purpose the metaphor of kinship. One of the four sons of India ("Hind"), he wrote, was "Dakan," who in turn had three sons: "Marhat, Kanhar and Tiling" – that is, areas native to speakers of Marathi, Kannada, and Telugu. "Presently, these three communities (*qaum*) reside in the Deccan."[3] For Firishta, as indeed for twenty-first-century residents when queried on the matter, the Deccan comprises the territory today constituted by three linguistically defined states: Maharashtra, Karnataka, and Andhra Pradesh.

There still remained the question of how to write a social history of a region lacking an enduring geo-political center. For without such a center, the Deccan also lacks a unified and coherent master narrative of the sort often told for north India, with its neat sequence of Delhi-based empires. What, then, would hold together a social history of the Deccan?

The question followed me as I left my Castle tower one wintry day and walked across Washington's Mall to the National Gallery, where the paintings of the Dutch artist Johannes Vermeer (d. 1675) were on special exhibit. As I joined the throngs of people who stood outside, shivering in the cold and waiting in what seemed an endless queue for admission, I wondered why Vermeer's art was attracting such avid interest. A solution suggested itself when, once inside the crowded galleries, I realized that most of the artist's work consisted of portraits of anonymous folk plucked from everyday life – a milk maid, a music teacher, a lace-maker, a student. It was not his several landscape paintings that drew most onlookers, but these finely crafted portraits with their distinctive

---

[2] On the problem of defining the geographical boundaries of the Deccan, see S. M. Alam, "The Historic Deccan – a Geographical Appraisal," in *Aspects of Deccan History*, ed. V. K. Bawa (Hyderabad, 1975), 16–31.

[3] *Dakan bin Hind-ra sih pisar ba vujud amada, mulk-i Dakan-ra ba ishan qismat numud. Va ism-i anha Marhat va Kanhar va Tiling bud. Va aknun ki in sih qaum dar Dakan maujud-and.* Muhammad Qasim Firishta, *Tarikh-i Firishta*, 2 vols. (Lucknow, 1864–65), 1:10.

play of light. In them, Vermeer seemed to have captured features and moods that, while true to the individuals he painted, were also instantly recognized as belonging to a shared, universal humanity. This, in turn, allowed viewers to identify with the artist's subjects in a direct and compelling way. It was as though, when examining his portraits, viewers were peering into mirrors, seeing themselves reflected in the fabric of other times, other people.

It also occurred to me that when he conceived and executed his portraits, Vermeer, though he wielded a brush and not a pen, was actually tapping into the power of biography. For, simply put, people are profoundly drawn to the personalities and life-stories of others, a truth known to any parent who has been asked repeatedly by a child, "read that story to me again." Wandering through the exhibit, I recalled how a student of mine once reacted to a text I much admire and had assigned – Eric Wolf's *Europe and the People without History*. Noting the absence of any life-narratives in the book, my student wickedly remarked that the book should have been entitled *Europe and the History without People*.

That indictment points to the very different histories of biographical writing in the popular and the academic worlds. In popular culture, fascination with life-narratives has never diminished. In one form or another the genre has endured across the planet and throughout time, impervious to the fickle fashions of the academic world. For India, one has only to think of the *Amar Chitra Katha* comic book series, Bollywood's blockbuster films, radio or television melodramas, or the standard fare available at bus, railway, or airport bookstalls. But in the academic world biography, though one of the oldest genres of history-writing, has had a more tortuous career. Just eighteen years after Emerson penned the dictum cited as the epigraph to this Introduction, Karl Marx signaled a virtual death sentence for the academic writing of biography. In 1859 he declared, "It is not the consciousness of men that determines their existence, but on the contrary it is their social existence that determines their consciousness."[4] Ushering in the advent of social history as a new and exciting subfield within the broader discipline of history, this manifesto encouraged many to explore the past not by tracing the lives of individual actors, but by studying vast socio-economic forces.[5] For more than a century, most social

---

[4] Karl Marx, *A Contribution to the Critique of Political Economy* (1885; repr. Chicago, 1918), preface, 11–12.

[5] Focussed as it was on class analysis and modes of production, Wolf's *Europe and the People without History* (Berkeley, 1982) fits squarely within the tradition that had its roots in Marx. It is in no way a disparagement of Wolf's enormous achievement to observe that his insights might have been made more poignant, and accessible, had they been illustrated with life-stories.

historians would view biography with a degree of suspicion; even today, the genre is seldom found in doctoral dissertations submitted to departments of history.

But by the end of the twentieth century a new trend became visible. In the 1980s and '90s some scholars had begun to view biography not as a genre inherently antithetical to social history, but as a vehicle that could be recovered and mobilized for writing precisely such history.[6] Prompted by the truth of Emerson's dictum and the genius of Vermeer's art, I came to the same conclusion. Soon after returning from the Vermeer exhibit to my tower in the Castle, I resolved to write the present volume through the lives of several carefully chosen men and women.

There was yet another reason for embarking on this approach. By foregrounding the biographies of some of India's precolonial figures, one could also reclaim for history subject matter that, having been largely abandoned by professional historians, has been eagerly appropriated by politically motivated myth-makers. "One of the remarkable features of the recent spectacular burst of creativity among Indian writers," notes writer William Dalrymple,

has been that few writers are drawn either to serious biography or narrative history. Though Indian historians produce many excellent specialist essays and numerous learned journals, it is impossible, for example, to buy an up-to-date biography of any of India's pre-colonial rulers.

Here perhaps lies one of the central causes of the current impasse. It is not just up to the politicians to improve the fairness and quality of India's history. Unless Indian historians learn to make their work intelligible and attractive to a wider audience, and especially to their own voraciously literate middle class, unhistorical myths will continue to flourish.[7]

There are, in short, compelling reasons why responsible historians should restore biography and narrative to their craft.

But how to do it? The aim in the present volume is to use the lives of vivid personalities as instruments to investigate and illuminate social processes fundamental to the history of the Deccan between the early fourteenth and mid-eighteenth centuries. Such processes include, among others, colonization,

---

[6] See, for example, Carlo Ginzburg, *The Cheese and the Worms: the Cosmos of a Sixteenth-century Miller* (Baltimore, 1980); Natalie Zemon Davis, *The Return of Martin Guerre* (Cambridge, MA, 1983); Natalie Zemon Davis, *Women on the Margins: Three Seventeenth-century Lives* (Cambridge, MA, 1995); Paul E. Johnson and Sean Wilentz, *The Kingdom of Matthias* (New York, 1994); Orlando Figes, *A People's Tragedy: the Russian Revolution, 1891–1924* (New York, 1996). For recent examples in South Asian history, see David Arnold and Stuart Blackburn, eds., *Telling Lives in India: Biography, Autobiography, and Life History* (New Delhi, 2004), and Vijaya Ramaswamy and Yogesh Sharma, eds., *Biography as History: Indian Perspectives* (Mumbai, forthcoming).

[7] William Dalrymple, "India: the War over History," *New York Review of Books* 52, no. 6 (April 7, 2005), 65.

factional strife, élite mobility, slavery, inter-caste relations, and social banditry. It is not that the people whose lives I have chosen to highlight were the movers or the *causes* of such social processes. To argue in that manner would bring back the ghost of Great Man Theory, a kind of history-writing that one hopes is safely past. But individuals do embody microcosms of at least some, if not many, aspects of the social macrocosms in which they live. And since the individuals foregrounded in this volume lived through, and were thoroughly immersed in, particular historical processes, the aim has been to examine their lives with a view to elucidating those processes in a manner more tangible and accessible than is found in conventional social histories.

One should be clear, however, about the meaning of biography. Contemporary notions of the genre are shaped largely by positivist methodologies inherited from nineteenth-century Europe. The professional biographer of that era would have carefully assembled original sources – letters, memoirs, newspaper accounts, etc. – in an attempt to reconstruct a factual narrative of a person's life from birth to death. The product would be coherent, linear, tidy, and above all, "objective." Accounts of precolonial Indian figures, on the other hand, are in many cases not recorded or preserved by professional biographers, but live in the collective memory of communities. That is, they are socially constructed, meaning that a figure's life might be shaped to conform to a particular community's values or interests. When constructing a narrative of such a figure, then, one is to some extent also reconstructing the culture of the community that had preserved his or her memory.

Some might regard the recorded lives of precolonial Indians as hagiographies and not biographies, on the grounds that the lives of such figures have been, and continue to be, popularly mythologized, even sanctified.[8] But it would be wrong to neatly pigeon-hole the source material respecting the people discussed in this volume as belonging to either category to the complete exclusion of the other. It is perhaps best to view biography and hagiography as genres occupying opposite ends of a continuum. Plotting the eight persons highlighted in this volume along such a continuum, those discussed in chapters 1, 2, 6 and 7 – i.e., Pratapa Rudra, Gisu Daraz, Tukaram, and Papadu – would likely fall toward the hagiographical end, since much of what we know of their lives has been socially constructed. By contrast, those discussed in chapters 3, 4, 5, and 8 – i.e., Mahmud Gawan, Rama Raya, Malik Ambar, and Tarabai – would occupy

---

[8] For example, the very name of the popular comic series *Amar Chitra Katha* suggests that figures drawn from Indian history are in some sense immortal (*amar*), rather than finite characters firmly rooted in specific historical contexts.

points closer to the biographical end, inasmuch as much of what we know of their lives derives from sources independent of a community's collective memory. But they all would share at least some elements of each type.

The time period covered in the study is informed by one over-arching theme. As noted, the Deccan has no master narrative of its own. But it did have intense interaction with the peoples, cultures, and states of north India, which during our period became a sort of alter-ego for societies south of the Narmada River. Individuals, communities, and whole states defined their identity with respect to this colossus of the north, sometimes in opposition to it, sometimes in imitation of it. Indeed, the chronological limits of the study, 1300 and 1761, are defined by two profoundly important moments in the history of this interregional interaction: the ascendency of the Delhi Sultanate in Deccani affairs, and the defeat of the Marathas in the Third Battle of Panipat. Between these two moments there occurred a range of interactions between north India and the Deccan, but through it all, the preponderance of influence flowed from north to south, rather than the reverse. In fact, the careers of fully five of the eight figures in this study were defined by their relations with Delhi. Only that of Gisu Daraz served to connect Delhi with the Deccan in a creative way. The other four – Pratapa Rudra, Malik Ambar, Papadu, and Tarabai – all suffered invasions from the north, which for two of them proved disastrous.

Several considerations guided the selection of the figures whose careers are foregrounded in the volume. The first was that they represent as wide a spectrum of the total society as the source materials would permit: a maharaja, a Sufi shaikh, a long-distance merchant, a generalissimo, a slave, a poet, a low-caste rebel, and a dowager. Second, that they represent different subregions of the Deccan; there are two from Andhra, and three each from Karnataka and Maharashtra. Third, that their lives be distributed across the entire four-and-a-half centuries covered in the volume; at least one of the eight was alive during any given year between 1300 and 1761 (excepting several decades in the mid-seventeenth century). But the most important consideration was the degree to which their life-stories could shed light on some particular social process. These processes form the subject-matter of the eight chronologically arranged chapters.

The first chapter discusses the settling of the interior plateau by pioneering cultivators who, between the twelfth and early fourteenth centuries, displaced or incorporated indigenous pastoral groups. It then analyzes the diffusion into the Deccan of a new sort of state system, the transregional sultanate, which arrived with the conquest of the region by armies of the Delhi Sultanate in the early fourteenth century. Following that conquest, Sultan Muhammad bin Tughluq attempted to colonize the Deccan with immigrants transplanted from Delhi. Chapter 2 explores that process, together with the roles played by Sufi shaikhs in providing an ideological and juridical rationale first for Tughluq colonialism in the Deccan, and later, for the successful revolt against Tughluq rule led by those same colonists and their descendants. That rebellion led to the establishment of an independent Deccani sultanate, the Bahmani kingdom.

Chapter 3 examines the incorporation of the Deccan into global regimes of commerce in the fifteenth century, especially the networks that connected the Deccan with the Iranian plateau. The negative side of this early form of "globalization" was the emergence of a rift between "Deccanis" – i.e., descendants of north Indian migrants who had been born and raised in the Deccan – and chauvinistic "Westerners," mainly Iranians, who hailed from points beyond the Arabian Sea. This rift would lead to the disintegration of nearly every Deccani sultanate between the fifteenth and seventeenth centuries.

Our knowledge of the southern Deccan has vastly increased in recent decades, thanks to the profusion of recent monographs on the state of Vijayanagara. But these studies tend to view that state in isolation from the rest of the Deccan plateau, in this respect following more than a century of Orientalist and Indian nationalist scholarship that walled off the study of the southern from the northern Deccan. Implicitly or explicitly, scholars writing within those traditions assumed that the state of Vijayanagara represented a Hindu bulwark against an expansive Muslim north, and that prior to the Battle of Talikota (1565) the peoples of the northern and southern plateau inhabited separate socio-cultural worlds. Investigating the processes of élite mobility and the diffusion of Persian culture across the plateau in the fifteenth and sixteenth centuries, Chapter 4 questions the validity of these assumptions. In this way it urges the academic reintegration of the Deccan's northern and southern halves, which have experienced more than a hundred years of scholarly apartheid.

Chapter 5 takes up the badly understudied topic of Afro-Indian relations, and more specifically, Africa's role in the rise and fall of military slavery in the Deccan between the mid-fifteenth and mid-seventeenth centuries. Tracing the career of a single slave from Ethiopia to Baghdad to Ahmadnagar, the chapter asks how the commercial system of the Arabian Sea basin, combined with the political system of the Deccan sultanates, supported the trafficking of military labor from Africa to India. It also examines why that trade began when it did, why it ended when it did, and what ultimately happened to the many military slaves imported to the Deccan.

Chapter 6 looks at the social base of non-Brahmin devotional cults, in particular the Varkari movement centered on Pandharpur, Maharashtra. In part, the aim here is to use the work of the devotional poet Tukaram to explore relations between Brahmins and non-Brahmins in the early seventeenth century. Beyond that, the chapter focuses on how vernacular devotional literature and the sultanates' use of vernacular records in their revenue and judicial systems contributed to the formation of linguistic communities. For in the Marathi-speaking western Deccan, precisely such processes helped lay the groundwork for the appearance of a new political entity – Shivaji's Maratha kingdom.

Chapter 7 shifts attention to Telangana, focusing on the brief and stormy career of a low-caste toddy-tapper who turned brigand during the chaotic aftermath of the Mughal conquest of Bijapur and Golkonda. This episode, it is argued, illustrates a phenomenon some historians have called "social banditry." Moreover, inasmuch as examples of subaltern resistance to larger regimes of power are seldom documented before the nineteenth century, the case affords a rare glimpse of a precolonial counter-hegemonic movement. Along the way, it reveals much about caste, class, and communal relations at the micro-level of Telangana society.

The volume's final chapter traces the rise of coastal Brahmins in the central institutions of the Maratha state founded by Shivaji, as well as the changing meaning of the term "Maratha" – and the social groups included within that category – during the seventeenth and eighteenth centuries. Both of those phenomena were related to the eruption of Maratha armies into the heart of the decaying Mughal empire in the eighteenth century – a movement that reversed a pattern of more than four centuries of north Indian pressure on the Deccan. The book closes with the culmination of that movement, the Third Battle of Panipat, which proved to be a turning point for both regions.

The debacle at Panipat also coincided with the growth of European power in South Asia, a phenomenon that would open up another, but not the last, chapter in the social history of the Deccan.

CHAPTER 1

PRATAPA RUDRA (R. 1289–1323): THE DEMISE OF THE REGIONAL KINGDOM

> With all these people of various skills serving him, and surrounded by five thousand atten-
> dants who showered him with gold and riches and sprinkled him with scented water from
> golden bottles, Prataparudra sat in the great assembly and ruled the kingdom, considering
> the petitions of the local lords and entertaining the requests of ambassadors.[1]
>
> *Prataparudra Caritramu* (early sixteenth century)

THE RAJA'S NEW CLOTHES – AND TITLE

A broad geo-cultural axis stretches along the spine of South Asia from Lahore
to Delhi to Hyderabad in the central Deccan plateau, with extensions running
from Delhi east to Patna and southwest to Ahmadabad (see Map 1). Forged
by ancient trade and migration corridors linking South Asia with the Iranian
plateau, this axis facilitated the flow of cultural currents that greatly accelerated
over the course of the past millennium. As a result, there emerged along these
corridors a set of related traits that have persisted down to the present: Persian
styles of architecture, music, art, dress, technology, cuisine; and a history of
the Persian language used for administrative purposes, often followed by forms
of spoken Urdu. Not least, new ideas of political and social organization were
carried along the corridors of this Indo-Persian axis.

The story of Pratapa Rudra, the last sovereign of the Kakatiya dynasty in
the eastern Deccan (1163–1323), forms in a sense the first chapter in the
larger story of the extension of this axis from Delhi to the Deccan plateau.
For this king's extraordinary career, and tragic fate, bridges the appearance
of two very different kinds of state system in Deccani history. One of these
was the "regional kingdom," the sort of polity found on the Deccan between
c. 1190 and 1310, and represented by the Kakatiyas under Pratapa Rudra and
his dynastic predecessors. The other was the "transregional sultanate," a type of

---

[1] From Phillip B. Wagoner, "Modal Marking of Temple Types in Kakatiya Andhra: Towards a Theory
of Decorum for Indian Temple Architecture," in *Syllables of Sky: Studies in South Indian Civilization, In Honour of Velcheru Narayana Rao*, ed. David Shulman (Delhi, 1995), 465. Wagoner's
translation.

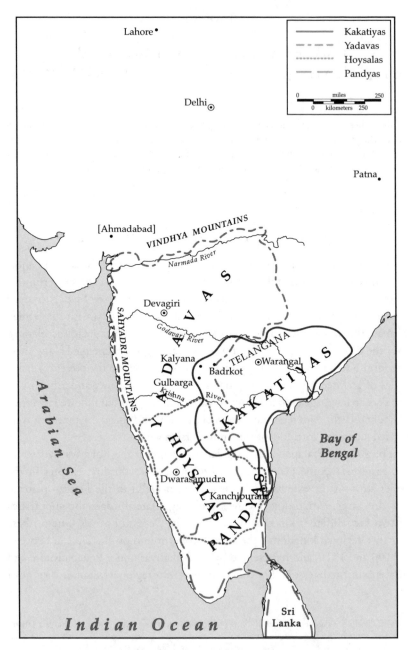

Map 1. Regional kingdoms of the Deccan, 1190–1310.

polity that, newly introduced to the Deccan along the Indo-Persian axis from north India during Pratapa Rudra's reign, would remain the Deccan's dominant form of state system until the coming of British power in the eighteenth century. It is fitting, then, that this study should begin with an exploration of this transition. It is equally fitting that, in order to understand how it occurred, we train our attention on a man who had, as it were, one foot in each of these two political worlds.

On a clear morning in 1318 Pratapa Rudra, his citadel at Warangal completely surrounded by a host of invaders from north India, found he had reached the end-game in the chessboard of South Asian politics. The army confronting him had marched about a thousand miles in order to punish the Kakatiya sovereign for failure to pay tribute owed the sultan of Delhi. Facing far superior war machinery deployed around the stone walls and moat that encircled his citadel, his last line of defense, the king realized the futility of further resistance. Representatives of the two sides sat down to negotiate a settlement, according to which the king would cede to the Delhi Sultanate a single fortress, Badrkot, and deliver to Delhi as an annual tribute a substantial quantity of gold and jewels, 12,000 horses, and a hundred war elephants "as large as demons." The negotiations over, the Kakatiya sovereign now ascended the eighteen steps leading up to the parapets of the citadel's stone wall (see Plate 1). There, standing on top of the ramparts, in full view of both his fellow Telugu warriors and the invading northerners, the king turned his face in the direction of the imperial capital of Delhi. Bowing slowly, he kissed the rampart's surface in a gesture of humble submission.[2]

Although this was not the first time Pratapa Rudra submitted to Delhi – nor would it be the last – the Persianized symbols and conceptions of authority that accompanied his submissions were deeply significant, since they represented the very first links in the Indo-Persian axis that would connect the Deccan with north India and, beyond that, the Iranian plateau. For as he stood atop the ramparts of Warangal, the king wore a robe of investiture presented to him by representatives of the army from Delhi. This robe now entered Deccani ceremonial usage, just as the Arabic word for the garment, *qaba*, would enter the Telugu language. The king was also given a new title by the officers of the invading army – *salatin-panah*, "the refuge of kings."[3] Inasmuch as the title contained a form of the word "sultan" – the Turko-Persian term for supreme

[2] Amir Khusrau, *Nuh Sipihr*, in *History of India as Told by its Own Historians*, ed. and trans. H. M. Elliot and John Dowson (Allahabad, 1964), iii:558–61.

[3] Ibid. 'Abd al-Malik 'Isami, *Futuhus-salatin*, ed. A. S. Usha (Madras, 1948), 363. *Futuhu's Salatin*, ed. and trans. Agha Mahdi Husain (London, 1967), ii:561–62.

sovereign – Pratapa Rudra was in effect being assimilated into a Perso-Islamic lexical and political universe that had already diffused through the Middle East, Central Asia, and north India. There is no evidence that Pratapa Rudra ever referred to himself as "sultan"; in the eyes of his subjects he doubtless was still a "raja," even "maharaja." Yet within a generation of his reign, amidst the political convulsions that accompanied first the imposition of Delhi's authority in the Deccan, and then the evaporation of that authority, upstart rulers styling themselves "sultan" would spring up all over the plateau. Pratapa Rudra's new title and new clothes, given him as he solemnly bowed toward Delhi from atop his citadel's ramparts, were only two of many elements in this semantic transfer, as ever more quarters of the plateau would become ideologically integrated into the still larger world of Perso-Islamic civilization.

THE FRONTIER SOCIETY OF THE KAKATIYA STATE

Age-old stereotypes die hard. The image of precolonial India as a static, caste-ridden social order, thoroughly mired in a timeless "tradition" dominated by Brahmanical ideology, derives in part from classical Sanskrit literary and legal texts, many of which project a vision of a tidy, law-abiding, and reverent society – an image, in short, of India as it ought to have been, at least to the Brahmin ideologues who authored or sponsored such texts. While texts of this sort certainly served the political purposes of British administrators who saw themselves as projecting a dynamic and progressive impulse into a stubbornly stagnant India, they are of little help to social historians who want to know how earlier social orders actually operated, and how they changed over time.

A very different picture emerges, however, if one turns from such norma-tive texts to the mass of vernacular stone inscriptions that, found in much of precolonial India, recorded day-to-day business transactions, such as transfers of fixed or movable property. Although comparable research on two of the Deccan's major subregions, Karnataka and Maharasthra, has yet to be under-taken, Cynthia Talbot's recent study of the Andhra region under the Kakatiyas casts considerable light on what social actors actually did, at least in this corner of precolonial India, as opposed to what classical texts say they were supposed to do. Moreover, the social horizon of these inscriptional data – which encom-passes merchants, landed peasants, herders, warrior chiefs, and women – far exceeded that of Brahmanical texts. As a result, in place of the stereotyped picture of a static or even stagnant precolonial India, this kind of evidence reveals a number of dynamic processes.

First, the inscriptions reveal the gradual but unmistakable emergence of Andhra as a distinct and self-conscious cultural region during the several centuries prior to Pratapa Rudra's reign. As early as 1053, the term *andhra bhasa,* "the language of Andhra," was being used synonymously for Telugu, indicating that people were mapping language onto territory, whether consciously or not. Nor was Andhra alone in being locally understood as a linguistically defined region. A Marathi religious text dating to the late thirteenth or early fourteenth century enjoined its devotees to stay in Maharashtra and not to go to the Telugu or Kannada countries[4] – a sentiment suggesting that in Maharashtra, too, region and language had become conceptually fused. In Andhra, a new phase began when chieftains, and later monarchs, began mapping political territory onto those parts of the Deccan where Telugu dominated as the vernacular language. In 1163, when the chiefs of the Telugu-speaking Kakatiya clan declared their independence from their Chalukya imperial overlords, inscriptions in areas under their control – which at that time included only parts of Telangana in the interior upland – switched from Kannada to Telugu, indicating official recognition of Telangana's vernacular language. By the time of Pratapa Rudra's reign, Kakatiya officials were issuing Telugu inscriptions in all areas under their rule, which then included fully three-quarters of modern Andhra Pradesh. In short, the clear trend was for political territory to be thought of as "naturally" corresponding to cultural territory, inasmuch as the Kakatiya state mapped itself onto a linguistically defined region.

Driving this process was the emergence of warrior groups which, in various parts of the Deccan's semi-arid interior in the twelfth and thirteenth centuries, had formed themselves into petty states whose ruling chiefs began patronizing the vernacular tongues of their own regions, as opposed to either the vernaculars of political superiors in other regions, or the prestigious, pan-Indian vehicle of discourse, Sanskrit. For Andhra, a crucial moment in this process was the 1230s, when Pratapa Rudra's great-grandfather, Ganapati (1199–1262), launched a series of campaigns from his power-base in Telangana and annexed to the Kakatiya state the rich and densely settled coastal littoral between the Krishna and Godavari deltas. This marked the first time that Telugu-speakers of the coast had become politically unified with those of the interior. Similarly, in thirteenth-century Maharashtra the Yadava dynasty of rulers consolidated their authority over that region's predominantly Marathi-speaking population, while in Karnataka the Hoysalas did the same among Kannada-speakers. Not

---

[4] Anne Feldhaus, "Maharashtra as a Holy Land: a Sectarian Tradition," *Bulletin of the School of Oriental and African Studies* 49 (1986): 534–35.

only did these ruling houses favor the official use of the spoken languages of their respective realms at the expense of either Sanskrit or the vernaculars of neighboring polities. By legitimating the sorts of transactions that forged expanding networks between social groups of different classes and regions, these states, as Talbot notes, catalyzed processes of supralocal identity formation and community building.[5] In a word, the rulers of all three states promoted the fusion of language, linguistic region, and dynastic authority (see Map 1).

Also revealed in these stone inscriptions is the dynamic character of the Kakatiya state, specifically its capacity to transform both the land and the people brought under its political authority. Before the eleventh century, much of the Deccan's dry interior had been only sparsely inhabited by pastoral groups or shifting cultivators. But the undulating landscape of Telangana, the Kakatiyas' political heartland, was perfectly suited for the construction of reservoirs, or "tanks," formed by stone or mud embankments built across rain-fed streams. By storing water for use in irrigation systems, the hundreds of tanks that dot the inland Deccan opened up a relatively unproductive frontier zone to both wet and dry farming. It is estimated that warrior families subordinate to the Kakatiyas built about 5,000 tanks, most of which are still in use today.[6] Indeed, two of Andhra's largest reservoirs – Ramappa tank with its embankment 2,000 feet long and 56 feet high, and Pakala lake with its one-mile embankment, both in Warangal district – were built by Kakatiya subordinate chiefs.[7] Such tanks formed the basis of a new economy that gradually assimilated former herders or shifting cultivators into a predominantly agrarian society.

The dynamic of a moving economic and social frontier is also reflected in the different kinds of temples patronized in the Kakatiya period. Along the densely populated Andhra coast of Pratapa Rudra's day, large and venerable temples that had predated the Kakatiya period received multiple endowments and attracted donors from distant lands. Long-distance merchants patronized such major temples with a view to extending the geographic reach of their networks of alliances, while herders appear to have done so in order to retain grazing rights in heavily cultivated coastal regions where there was little room for pastures. Distinct from these great institutions of the Andhra coast were the more numerous smaller temples that appeared mainly in the Deccan's dry interior. These temples were datable only to the Kakatiya period, and their

[5] Cynthia Talbot, *Precolonial India in Practice: Society, Region, and Identity in Medieval Andhra* (Oxford, 2001), 214.

[6] Conversation with Prof. M. Pandu Ranga Rao, Chairman, New Science Degree College, Hanumakonda, June 28, 2001.

[7] Talbot, *Precolonial India*, 97–98.

sponsoring clientele had a far more restricted geographical reach than did those of the coastal temples.

Although smaller and less venerable than their coastal counterparts, the newly founded temples of the interior uplands played a crucial role in expanding agrarian society since their endowments often included the building and maintenance of tanks, which in turn helped make Andhra's dry uplands physically arable. They also played pivotal roles in the politics of the Andhra interior. Whereas the larger temples of the coast integrated diverse peoples across great distances, the smaller temples forged vertical alliances between local superiors and subordinates. In fact, most of these temples were patronized *not* by kings of the ruling dynasty, but by subordinate chiefs and military leaders who, in making gifts in land, consolidated their power bases among residents of those lands while affirming ties to their political superiors. In sum, records issued between 1163 and 1323 reveal a robust frontier society in which emergent leaders forged new political networks amidst an expanding agrarian society.

Such findings run counter to one of the favorite tropes of South Asian scholarship, that of "the south Indian temple," understood as a monolithic, ahistoric institution that rather elegantly bound together king, kingdom, and cosmos in harmonious symmetry. Central to this understanding is the notion that south Indian kings both established and continuously patronized temples, owing to their alleged need to stress their association with the gods, from whom they derived their earthly sovereignty. In the Kakatiya inscriptions, however, when kings were mentioned at all, it was not their piety or devotion to the gods that was stressed, but their boasts of smashing earthly enemies.

Finally, as is typical in frontier zones undergoing rapid change, an egalitarian social ethos seems to have pervaded upland Andhra in Kakatiya times. The largest block of property donors in this period were warrior-chiefs termed *nayaka*, a title that could be acquired by anybody, regardless of social origins. Birth-ascribed caste rankings were notably absent in the inscriptional record. Warrior groups in Andhra made no pretensions to *kshatriya* status; in fact, they proudly proclaimed their *sudra* origins. Even the Kakatiya kings, with only one exception, embraced *sudra* status. Nor do named subcastes (*jati*) – another pillar of an alleged "traditional Indian society" – appear as memorable features of people's identity, further pointing to a social landscape remarkably unaffected by Brahmanical notions of caste and hierarchy. Rather than caste rank, or *varna*, what seemed to have mattered, precisely because it was so often specified in the inscriptional record, was occupational status – i.e., Vedic Brahmin, secular Brahmin, royalty or nobility, chief or military leader, warrior-peasant, merchant or artisan, and herdsman. But even these categories were fluid. Fully 30 percent of the Kakatiya inscriptions that named both fathers and sons show the two as having *different* occupations, suggesting that social status in interior Andhra was to a great extent earned, not inherited.

The open nature of the Kakatiyas' frontier society is seen above all in the rising political prominence of officers of humble origins, at the expense of an older, hereditary nobility. In the early 1200s, hereditary nobles comprised nearly half of all individuals who recognized Kakatiya overlordship, while non-aristocratic officers comprised only a fourth of that class. By the time of Pratapa Rudra, however, the proportion of non-aristocratic officers had risen to 45 percent of the total, while the nobility had declined to just 12 percent, pointing to the growing ability of Kakatiya monarchs – and especially the last two, Rudrama Devi and Pratapa Rudra – to break the entrenched power of landed nobles by placing men of their own choice on lands of former nobles.

In sum, the contemporary Kakatiya inscriptions analyzed by Talbot add much to what we know about Pratapa Rudra from contemporary Persian chronicles. The latter generally depict the Telugu monarch as either Delhi's unwilling tributary, occasional ally, or staunch opponent during the most aggressive phase of the sultanate's southward expansion. The inscriptional evidence, on the other hand, reveals a man who personified the egalitarian ethos of upland Andhra of his day: he never claimed *kshatriya* origins or took on lofty titles like "king of kings" (*maharajadhiraja*), he never founded royal temples in the manner of the classic imperial *raja*. Nor did he patronize the settlement of Brahmin villages, or *agrahara*s. Of all the monarchs of his line, moreover, Pratapa Rudra had the fewest landed nobles serving him, and the largest number of officers elevated from humble origins.

Such a portrait confirms information found in the king's earliest biography, the early sixteenth-century *Prataparudra Caritramu*, which praises Pratapa Rudra for his having recruited a community of the finest Telugu warriors, or *nayaka*s, in his service.[8] His fierce loyalty to the warriors he is said to have recruited and promoted is certainly consistent with the last known fact concerning the king's life – namely, his tragic end.

ON THE RAMPARTS OF WARANGAL'S CITADEL

Today hardly more than a dusty provincial town, Pratapa Rudra's capital, Warangal, is largely bypassed by the main communication arteries of modern

---

[8] Cynthia Talbot, "Political Intermediaries in Kakatiya Andhra, 1175–1325," *Indian Economic and Social History Review* 31, no. 3 (1994): 261–89.

India. What strikes the visitor is the city's well-preserved defensive fortifications, in particular its several concentric circular walls.[9] An earthen wall, one-and-a-half miles in diameter and surrounded by a moat some 150 feet wide, was built by Rudrama Devi (1263–89) and in Kakatiya times formed the city's outer wall (see Plate 2). Protecting the citadel is a formidable inner wall some three-quarters of a mile in diameter and made of huge blocks of dressed granite, irregular in size but perfectly fit without the use of mortar. Built originally by Ganapati and heightened by Rudrama Devi to over twenty feet, this wall is also surrounded by a wide moat. Forty-five massive bastions, from forty to sixty feet on a side, project outward from the wall and into the waters of the moat. On the inward side of this wall an earthen ramp fit with eighteen stone steps rises at a gentle slope up to the ramparts (see Plate 1). Encircling the entire core of the capital, these steps enabled warriors from any part of the citadel to rush quickly, if necessary, to the top of the ramparts. These were the eighteen steps that Pratapa Rudra climbed in 1318 before donning his *qaba* and bowing down toward the Delhi sultan.

Among the Kakatiya kings, only Pratapa Rudra had to face invasions by north Indian armies. Free from such disruptions, his predecessors had steadily expanded the kingdom's frontiers until these nearly matched the frontiers of the Telugu-speaking Deccan. They established their capital at Warangal in 1195, just several years before the long reign of the kingdom's greatest builder, Ganapati (1199–1262). It was this king who built the city's original stone walls, established royal temples, and most importantly, pushed his kingdom's frontiers in all directions, including to the coastal tracts along the Bay of Bengal. There he actively promoted his kingdom's commercial contacts with the world beyond India's shores. Lacking sons, however, Ganapati named his daughter Rudrama Devi (1262–90) to succeed him, and when she also had only daughters the old king expressed his wish that Rudrama adopt her grandson as her own son and heir to the throne. Such was how, in 1289, Pratapa Rudra rose to the Kakatiyas' "lion throne," there to reign during an era that later chroniclers would hail a Golden Age.

But in 1309, twenty years into the maharaja's reign, Delhi's Sultan ʿAla al-Din Khalji sent his slave general Malik Kafur into the Deccan with orders to invade the Kakatiya state. Since its founding in 1206, the Delhi Sultanate had already absorbed the entire Indo-Gangetic plain of north India, forming the largest and most powerful state India had ever seen to that point. Now it was

---

[9] Some time after the mid-sixteenth century, a third concentric wall was added, an earthen rampart nearly eight miles in diameter.

looking across the Vindhya Mountains to the wealthy states of the Deccan plateau. But outright annexation of the Deccan was not on Delhi's mind, at least not yet. Malik Kafur was instructed neither to annihilate nor to annex the Kakatiya state, but rather to incorporate Pratapa Rudra as a subordinate monarch within Delhi's expanding circle of tributary kings.[10] It was an ancient Indian strategy.

Arriving before Warangal's outer walls in mid-January 1310, Malik Kafur rained showers of arrows on Kakatiya defenders for a full month. In mid-February, Delhi's forces having breached the city's outer, earthen walls and invested the stone walls of the citadel, Pratapa Rudra sued for peace, sending a gift of twenty-three elephants to the northern general. In return, the latter sent the king a robe (khil'at). Inasmuch as such robes in Perso-Islamic culture symbolized political overlordship, wearing one implied Pratapa Rudra's incorporation within Delhi's "circle of kings." Following his master's orders, Malik Kafur sent to the citadel a messenger who advised Pratapa Rudra that, having submitted to Delhi, he would soon receive a parasol (chatr) as a further sign of his incorporation under the sultanate's imperial shadow. The king was also instructed to bow, while remaining in his palace in the citadel, in the direction of Sultan 'Ala al-Din Khalji in Delhi. A month later, Malik Kafur began his march back to Delhi, his pack trains laden with the spoils of victory, and for several years Pratapa Rudra dutifully paid Delhi a heavy annual tribute.

These new arrangements profoundly altered the Kakatiya raja's position in the Deccan's political order. No longer occupying the pinnacle of a political hierarchy, Pratapa Rudra now found himself sandwiched between the sultan of Delhi and his own vassals, while some of the latter, especially those in unruly southern Andhra, seized on the king's preoccupation with Delhi to declare their own independence. But alliance with the north cut two ways. In 1311, when Sultan 'Ala al-Din Khalji solicited the Kakatiya king's help in invading the Pandya kingdom in the Tamil country to the south, Pratapa Rudra used the opportunity to suppress the rebellions of his former vassals in the Nellore region. And it was in his double role as Kakatiya sovereign and subsidiary ally of Delhi that he personally led his armies against the Pandyas at Kanchipuram.

---

[10] Said the sultan to his general, "I charge you to march towards Telingana with a large army and move swiftly doing one stage a day; on your arrival in the suburbs of Telingana, you should subject the whole area immediately to effective raids. Afterwards, you should lay siege to the fortress and shake it to its foundations. Should the Rai of Telingana [Pratapa Rudra] submit and present wealth in money and elephants, you should reinstate him under my sovereignty and restore his dominion; you should give him a robe studded with jewels and promise him a parasol on my behalf with due regards. This done, you should return to the capital in good cheer." 'Isami, Futuhu's Salatin, trans., II:464–65.

In 1318, however, the king had become remiss in sending up his annual tribute, and so the Delhi sultan sent down another general, Khusrau Khan, to collect the overdue payments, by force if necessary. Halting just three bow-shots from Warangal's outer walls, the northerners camped within sight of the city's fountains and mango orchards. Having engaged the Kakatiya cavalry along the city's perimeters, the invaders captured the principal bastion of Warangal's outer wall; they also captured Pratapa Rudra's principal general. By the end of the next morning they had advanced clear to the city's formidable, innermost fortification, which they now invested. An account of the battle that ensued, as recorded by the most famous poet of the age, Amir Khusrau, shows that the Telugu warriors defending Warangal's citadel had to face the deadliest and most advanced military technology to be found anywhere in the world – a new sort of siege equipment that had already been introduced to north India from the Iranian plateau. The implements deployed by the northerners included huge stone-throwing engines (technically counter trebuchets, or *manajiq*), smaller siege engines (or tension-powered ballistas, '*arrada*), wooden parapets (*matars*), stone missiles (*ghadban*), great boulders used as missiles (*guroha*), small machines for hurling stones ('*arusak*), and, what proved especially effective, a 450-foot-long earthen ramp (*pashib*) that led to and across a filled-up portion of moat, enabling the besiegers to breach the citadel's stone walls.[11]

Aware of the larger armies and superior technology arrayed against him, Pratapa Rudra sent messengers to the invaders, protesting lamely that whereas he had intended to send his tribute to Delhi, he had to keep the matter in abeyance "since the distance is great and the roads are infested with miscreants." Serious negotiations now ensued, at the conclusion of which Pratapa Rudra dispatched a hundred elephants and 12,000 horses to the northerners' camp, further agreeing that thenceforth this would constitute his annual tribute to Delhi. A staged political ritual was once again enacted, and again the Delhi Sultanate's commanding general bestowed upon Pratapa Rudra symbolically charged royal paraphernalia: a mace, a bejeweled robe (*qaba*), and a parasol. And on this occasion, as narrated at the outset of this chapter, the king, instead of bowing toward Delhi from inside his citadel as he had done nine years earlier, ascended the stone ramparts of the city's inner walls, faced the imperial capital of Delhi, and bowed to the rampart's surface.

---

[11] Amir Khusrau, *Nuh Sipihr*, ed. Mohammad Wahid Mirza. Islamic Research Association series no. 12 (London, 1950), 111–14.

Soon after these events, in 1320, a political revolution in Delhi replaced the ruling Khalji dynasty with the Tughluq house, and Pratapa Rudra, taking advantage of the chaos in the north, once again neglected to pay his tribute. So in 1321 Delhi's new ruler, Sultan Ghiyath al-Din Tughluq, sent his son, Ulugh Khan, south to recover the arrears. For a third and final time, a north Indian army arrived before Warangal's two concentric walls. On this occasion the Tughluq general – the future Sultan Muhammad bin Tughluq (r. 1325–51) – subjected the city to a six-month siege, protracted in part by dissensions between Khalji and Tughluq factions within his army. Unable to bring the siege to a successful conclusion, Ulugh Khan retreated to Devagiri, the former capital of the Yadava dynasty in Maharashtra, now annexed to Delhi and used by Tughluq governors and commanders as a staging site for invasions further south. Meanwhile, Pratapa Rudra, supposing the northerners had left for good, threw open the public granaries for a grand public feast. But such celebrations proved premature, for whereas the Sultanate's armies had left the Warangal region, they had not yet left the Deccan as a whole. In 1323, after spending several months resting and strengthening his forces in Devagiri, Ulugh Khan returned to Warangal with 63,000 mounted archers[12] and surprised the unsuspecting Pratapa Rudra, whose supplies and provisions were by now too depleted to enable his capital to survive another sustained siege.

Upon breaching both of the city's walls, Ulugh Khan's forces subjected the capital to unchecked plunder and destruction. This time there were no negotiations with the Kakatiya monarch, no attempts to intimidate or chastise him into obedience to a superior overlord. Rather, the Kakatiya dynasty would be annihilated and its territories formally annexed to the Delhi Sultanate. Accordingly, following inherited Indian practice, Ulugh Khan did what rulers and officials of the Delhi Sultanate typically did whenever annexing territory formerly controlled by a defeated Hindu raja. In order to deprive a defeated monarch of the most visible and public emblem of his former legitimacy, conquerors normally desecrated the temple housing the image of the "state-deity" that had protected the former king.[13] Accordingly, Ulugh Khan ordered the demolition of the great Svayambhusiva temple, whose remains still lie scattered about the heart of Warangal's fort area. Soon thereafter, Tughluq authorities built an enormous mosque (since demolished) to one side of the

---

[12] Vilasa Inscription, dated 1330, cited in B. D. Chattopadhyaya, *Representing the Other? Sanskrit Sources and the Muslims* (New Delhi, 1998), 58.

[13] See Richard M. Eaton, "Temple Desecration and Indo-Muslim States," in *Beyond Turk and Hindu: Rethinking Religious Identities in Islamicate South Asia*, ed. David Gilmartin and Bruce B. Lawrence (Gainesville FL, 2000), 246–81.

site of the former temple, and a sumptuous audience hall, known today as the "Khush Mahal" (see Plate 3), some 175 yards west of the temple site.[14] Finally, a governor was appointed, and the city itself was renamed "Sultanpur," which for the next eight years minted silver, copper, and gold coins in the name of Tughluq sultans. In this way Pratapa Rudra's former kingdom was extinguished, its lands absorbed into the vast Tughluq empire (see Map 2).

There still remained, though, the tricky question of what to do with the former king himself. Leaving Pratapa Rudra in possession of his territories in a tributary relationship had already been tried and failed, whereas executing him then and there seemed dangerous, given his political importance among Andhra's large and potentially turbulent population. In these circumstances, it was decided to remove the king from the Deccan altogether and to dispatch him to Delhi, to the court of Ulugh Khan's father, Sultan Ghiyath al-Din Tughluq. Accordingly, a picked contingent of Turkish cavalry escorted the former king and his family through the gates of Warangal's concentric walls and onto the road leading north to the Tughluqs' imperial capital.[15]

But he never reached Delhi. A contemporary historian writes that the former king died on the road.[16] A Telugu inscription dated seven years after the event states that he died on the banks of the Narmada River. A still later Telugu inscription, dated 1423, states that he died by his own wish.[17] Combining the testimony found in these sources, it seems that the vanquished "lion king" of Warangal, the last of the Kakatiya line of sovereigns, committed suicide on the banks of the Narmada while being led north to Delhi. Pride and honor evidently having taken hold, Pratapa Rudra refused to meet the architect of his kingdom's demise. But as we shall see, local memory would preserve a very different fate for him, weaving an elaborate tale of his encounter with Tughluq

---

[14] Phillip B. Wagoner and John Henry Rice, "From Delhi to the Deccan: Newly Discovered Tughluq Monuments at Warangal–Sultanpur and the Beginnings of Indo-Islamic Architecture in Southern India," *Artibus Asiae* 61, no. 1 (2001): 77–117. See also Phillip B. Wagoner, "The Place of Warangal's *Kirti-Toranas* in the History of Indian Islamic Architecture," *Religion and the Arts, a Journal from Boston College* 8, no. 1 (2004): 6–36. Writes Wagoner, "The southern end of the hall [of audience] is occupied by a slightly narrower chamber with an elevated platform that would have held the throne of the ruler; the main entrance is opposite this on the north through a nesting series of diminishing vaults. Once inside this entrance, the visitor's eye is pulled forcefully toward the throne platform opposite, thanks to the focusing effect of the six transverse arches that articulate the main space of the hall. It is here that Ulugh Khan would have sat to grant formal audience to his assembled subordinates, and we can well imagine how his image of might and glory would have been augmented by the strength and power of the hall's design. Wagoner, "The Place," 19–21.

[15] 'Isami, *Futuhu's Salatin*, trans., ii:607–09.

[16] Shams-i Siraj 'Afif, *Tarikh-i Firuz Shahi*, in *History of India as Told by its Own Historians*, ed. and trans. H. M. Elliot and John Dowson (Allahabad, 1964), iii:367.

[17] P. V. Parabrahma Sastry, *The Kakatiyas of Warangal* (Hyderabad, 1978), 140.

authority that diverged dramatically from the tragic – if noble – story of his suicide by the banks of the Narmada River.

REGIONAL KINGDOMS AND SULTANATES

Pratapa Rudra, then, did not live to see the Deccan's full integration into the Delhi Sultanate. However, his acceptance of the title "refuge of sultans" that had been bestowed on him, and his receipt of ceremonial robes from both Khalji and Tughluq sultans of Delhi, together with a mace, a parasol, and another imperial insignia, formed the earliest signs of the radical redefinition of political space in the Deccan that occurred during the first half of the fourteenth century.

Similarly, the collapse of Pratapa Rudra's kingdom was only one in a series of upheavals that shook the Deccan at that time. Whereas the century had opened with a collection of stable regional kingdoms whose boundaries roughly coincided with vernacular linguistic regions, by mid-century the Deccan's geo-political situation had resolved into just two large successor-states to the Tugh-luqs' imperial presence in the Deccan. Both were large, multi-ethnic, trans-regional polities ruled by self-described sultans. One of these, the Bahmani kingdom, established its capital at the former Yadava fort of Gulbarga. The other, the Sangama kingdom, arose on the site of an ancient pilgrim-age center on the shores of the Tungabhadra River; it would become famous as Vijayanagara. In point of royal titles, public architecture, courtly dress, political economy, urban design, and styles of military recruitment, these two new states established a cultural system that had earlier evolved on the Iranian plateau and was manifested in thirteenth-century north India as the Delhi Sultanate.

The process unfolded in stages. In the first quarter of the fourteenth cen-tury, as we have seen, great kings of the northern Deccan like Pratapa Rudra were brought into tributary relations with the Delhi Sultanate, and in the process assimilated symbolic or ceremonial aspects of the sultanate's political order. In the second quarter of the century, the more properly institutional dimensions of the sultanate began to take root, as peoples of the plateau were brought under Delhi's direct or indirect suzerainty. A third stage began after a series of mid-century anti-Tughluq rebellions freed the Deccan from Delhi's imperial authority. In spite of this political severance, however, the institu-tional and ideological structures associated with the Delhi Sultanate persisted, and in fact deepened, in the several Deccani sultanates that succeeded the Tughluqs.

Here it would be useful to consider what it might have meant to declare oneself "sultan" in fourteenth-century India. The Arabic term *sultan*, meaning literally "dominion," "might," or "strength," referred to one who wields worldly power, as opposed to one who possesses religious authority. In reality, the sultanate form of polity anticipated by many centuries the ideal of secular government as theorized in early modern Europe, since in principle it separated religion from statecraft. Indeed, this heritage permitted Indian sultans – whatever their personal religion might have been – to claim the role of universal sovereign over, and supreme protector of, ethnically diverse subject peoples in the manner that a shepherd protected his flock, a stock figure of speech in contemporary political discourse. In the eastern Islamic world, where the sultanate system took shape from the tenth century on, the term *sultan* also became a vessel that contained and preserved memories of the courtly culture of pre-Islamic Iran. By the thirteenth century, sultanates throughout the Islamic world had become associated with mobile wealth, long-distance trade, military slavery, a ranked and salaried hierarchy of subordinate officers, and the ideology and court ceremony of pre-Islamic Persian kingship. Above all, Central Asia's extensive pasture lands proved ideal for horse-breeding, which in turn created an environment favoring professional armies built around a core of highly skilled mounted archers.[18]

After the establishment of the Delhi Sultanate in 1206, military and administrative manpower continued to be recruited from beyond India in the form of slaves purchased from Central Asia. This kind of recruitment created a radically open society in which social status was completely detached from descent, and where claims to a noble or proud ancestry counted for nothing. Any slave, purchased in Central Asia with ready cash and taken to a distant sultanate, could in principle rise to the highest command by sheer ability alone, an ethos that seriously undermined a much older Persian ideal that celebrated hereditary rank.

Just as they detached religion from statecraft, sultanates also detached culture from sovereign territory; that is, political frontiers knew no boundaries based on kinship, language, religion, or any other cultural marker. In fact, the sultanate knew no natural boundaries at all, save that point in space beyond which revenue could not feasibly be collected. This principle, combined with their use of highly mobile units of mounted archers, gave sultanates an

---

[18] All this is well brought out in André Wink, *al-Hind: the Making of the Indo-Islamic World.* Vol. 2: *The Slave Kings and the Islamic Conquest, 11th–13th Centuries* (Leiden, 1997).

enormously elastic and transregional character, in contrast to the more compact and territorially constricted regional kingdoms of the thirteenth-century Deccan, such as Pratapa Rudra's Kakatiya state in Telugu-speaking Andhra.[19]

Propelling sultanate systems forward was the constant infusion and flow of mobile wealth. In thirteenth-century north India, this wealth derived in part from long-distance trading networks, in which cash was received in exchange for manufactured exports. It also derived from the plunder of fixed assets beyond a sultanate's frontiers, as occurred in the late tenth and early eleventh centuries when Ghaznavid sultans plundered north Indian cities from bases in Afghanistan, or in the late thirteenth and early fourteenth centuries when the Khalji sultans of Delhi plundered Indian states beyond the Vindhyas. This pattern created a self-perpetuating cycle: cash minted from raided temple wealth could be used to recruit yet more slaves from beyond India, who could in turn be used for mounting further military expeditions undertaken for still more plunder.

Although initial encounters between sultanates and adjacent states could be extremely disruptive, especially for former ruling élites and their public monuments, once territories were annexed and authority consolidated, rulers moved swiftly to stabilize the new order by patronizing indigenous institutions.[20] Integration into sultanates also opened up local societies to the wider world. Just as the initial establishment of the Delhi Sultanate had created a migration corridor between Central Asia and the Gangetic Plain, so also the conquest of the Deccan in the fourteenth century forged a similar corridor between Delhi and the south. Fully one-tenth of Delhi's Muslim population migrated south when Devagiri, the former Yadava capital, was renamed Daulatabad and made the empire's co-capital in 1327.[21] This migration inaugurated the

---

[19] The contrast between regional kingdoms and sultanates should not be reduced to, or conflated with, an ecological difference between sedentary agriculture and pastoral nomadism. Such a reduction, though conceptually elegant, ignores the great extent of pastoral nomadism within India, especially in the Deccan's dry interior zones. On the polarity of agriculture and nomadism, see J. C. Heesterman, "Warrior, Peasant and Brahmin," *Modern Asian Studies*, 29, no. 3 (1995): 644–47, and André Wink, *al-Hind*, vol. 2. On the persistence of pastoral nomadism in the Deccan, and the religious implications of its relations with agrarian society, see M. L. K. Murty and Günther-Dietz Sontheimer, "Prehistoric Background to Pastoralism in the Southern Deccan in the Light of Oral Traditions and Cults of Some Pastoral Communities," *Anthropos* 75 (1980): 163–84.

[20] A Sanskrit inscription dated 1326 reveals that, thirteen years after the northwestern Deccan was annexed to the Tughluq empire, Sultan Muhammad bin Tughluq appointed Muslim officials to repair a Śiva temple in Kalyana (in Bidar district), thereby facilitating the resumption of normal worship that had been disrupted by local disturbances. P. B. Desai, "Kalyana Inscription of Sultan Muhammad, Saka 1248," *Epigraphia Indica* 32 (1957–58): 165–68.

[21] In 1350, 'Isami recorded: "Although only a tenth of the [Muslim] population of Delhi reached Deogir [i.e., Daulatabad] yet they were able to turn the city into a fertile and prosperous land.

second phase in the diffusion of the sultanate type of polity in the Deccan – the formation of a true "colony" in the northwestern Deccan, composed of a community of settlers or their descendants tied politically and culturally to a distant metropolis.

Deepening the sultanate system in the Deccan was the institution of the *iqta'*, a unit of land over which a military officer was given temporary rights of revenue collection. The holder of such an assignment, the *iqta'dar*, would convert this revenue to cash, remitting part of it to the central treasury and using the balance to train, equip, and pay cavalrymen at levels specified by the sultan, and available to the sultan on demand. This institution was central to the sultanate system in three respects. First, it provided the sultan with a reliable, professional army. Second, since *iqta'dars* were usually posted in garrisoned rural centers where grain was converted to the cash that was needed to pay the *iqta'dar's* troops, the *iqta'* system promoted the free flow of movable wealth within a sultanate's frontiers.[22] And third, the *iqta'* served to deepen the sultanate's political authority. By recognizing as *iqta'* those lands already held by entrenched and potentially hostile chiefs, and by designating such chiefs *iqta'dars*, the state endeavored to transform potential enemies into state servants.

As long as Deccan states like the Kakatiyas had only a tributary status with Delhi, as was the case in Andhra between 1309 and Pratapa Rudra's final defeat in 1323, such institutional fusions between the sultanate and local societies could not and did not occur. But whenever parts of the plateau were annexed and brought under Delhi's direct administration, the *iqta'* played a key role in integrating that region into the sultanate both economically and politically. In 1339, for example, Bhiran, a Hindu chieftain of the former Yadava hill-fort of Gulbarga, was confirmed as the *iqta'dar* of that place. Noting that the Tughluq government had under-assessed a neighboring *iqta'*, Bhiran then offered to raise and remit 50 percent more revenue if the government would assign that *iqta'* to him, which it did.[23] While such activities are classic instances of tax-farming, they also suggest how Tughluq authorities in the Deccan managed to draw local chieftains to their side politically, in this case by indulging the acquisitive appetites of such chieftains. By mid-century, the *iqta'* as an institution had so

Those who were ejected from Delhi formed a rich colony in Deogir where uneven places were leveled and made even." 'Isami, *Futuhu's Salatin*, trans., III:690.

[22] "The whole purpose of the *iqta'* system and [the sultanate's] garrison towns," notes Wink, "was to safeguard the flow of traffic, revenue and precious metals throughout the conquered realm." Wink, *al-Hind*, II:216.

[23] 'Isami, *Futuhu's Salatin*, trans., III:726–27.

thoroughly taken root in areas directly administered by imperial authorities that, immediately after the overthrow of Tughluq authority in the Deccan, local chiefs came forward to officials of the Tughluqs' successor-states seeking written confirmation in their respective *iqta's*.[24]

In sum, Delhi's rulers annexed the northern Deccan – the area from the Vindhyas to the Krishna River – in two stages. First, they redefined existing regional monarchs as subordinate kings, incorporating them into the rituals and ceremonial trappings of Indo-Persian kingship. In this stage, the Deccan's "regional kingdoms" were simply tucked within the imperial framework of the Delhi Sultanate as tributary states. In the second stage, Delhi's rulers extinguished all vestiges of the former kingdoms' independence and annexed their territories. New institutions were established, such as imperial coinage, governorships, and monuments. From 1314 to 1345 imperial coins were minted in Daulatabad, the former Yadava capital of Devagiri, and from 1324 to 1332 in Sultanpur, the former Kakatiya capital of Warangal.[25] Governors were appointed to both provincial cities, in the center of which were constructed imposing congregational mosques where the name of the Delhi sultan was read on Fridays. The new rulers also penetrated the grass roots of local politics by co-opting and redefining local revenue systems and personnel, transforming chieftains formerly under Yadava or Kakatiya suzerainty into Tughluq *iqta'*-holders.

PRATAPA RUDRA REMEMBERED

The story of Pratapa Rudra did not end with the Kakatiya monarch's suicide by the banks of the Narmada River. Indeed, his demise served as the starting point for a series of new and different lives as construed by subsequent generations. The earliest post-1323 notice of the king, which appeared just seven years after the Kakatiyas' collapse, testifies to the survival of the *idea*, if not the reality, of the regional kingdom, and to the notion that a righteous maharaja was necessary for the sustenance of such a kingdom. Although the Tughluqs managed to hold Sultanpur (the former Warangal) until 1335, they had been unable to consolidate their authority along the Andhra coast or in the contested borderlands between these regions. Their hold was tenuous even in Sultanpur's immediate hinterland, where a number of upstart chieftains seized effective power and strove to legitimate their new-found ruling status. From a stone inscription dated 1330, we hear of one Prolaya Nayaka, an otherwise

---

[24] *Ibid.*, III:880–81.
[25] H. Nelson Wright, *The Coinage and Metrology of the Sultans of Delhi* (Delhi, 1936), 89–147.

obscure chieftain with no record of service in the former Kakatiya state. After condemning the Turks for the devastation they had brought to Andhra, the inscription proclaims Prolaya Nayaka as the restorer of an orderly status quo ante, a time still very fresh in people's minds, when Pratapa Rudra reigned and ruled.

Unable to claim a political connection with the former king, the parvenu chieftain endeavored to legitimize his newly won status by performing deeds appropriate for a righteous monarch – i.e., re-establishing Brahmin villages and reviving Vedic sacrifices.[26] Prolaya Nayaka also portrayed himself as the legitimate successor to Pratapa Rudra, which of course he was not. And for this purpose he construed both himself *and* the last Kakatiya monarch as righteous monarchs, which Pratapa Rudra was not. In other words, Prolaya Nayaka's political project required a certain reworking of the former king's actual career, since the historical Pratapa Rudra, secure in his inheritance as the Kakatiya monarch, never needed to make strenuous claims to righteousness. Nor did he adopt imperial titles, claim *kshatriya* origins, found royal temples, or even patronize Brahmins.[27] Nonetheless, within just seven years of his ignominious departure from Sultanpur/Warangal, the former king had been recast as a paragon of righteousness; in another fifteen years, he would be recalled as "the jewel in the crown of the Kakatiya clan."[28]

Given the complete destruction of the Kakatiya state in 1323, one can understand why survivors portrayed the conflict between Turks and Telugus in stark, Manichean terms – of unrighteous barbarians vs. righteous restorers of *dharma*. But in time, perceptions changed. By about 1420, as Cynthia Talbot has argued, Muslim rulers in Andhra had become so thoroughly accommodated to Deccani society and culture that it was simply impossible for non-Muslims to conceive of the region without a Muslim presence. And this contextual shift, too, prompted another turn of the kaleidoscope through which Pratapa Rudra was viewed. An inscription dated 1423 divides "the world" (i.e., peninsular India) into the domains of three lords – a Lord of Elephants, a Lord of Men,

---

[26] Cynthia Talbot, "Inscribing the Other, Inscribing the Self: Hindu-Muslim Identities in Pre-Colonial India," *Comparative Studies in Society and History* 37, no. 4 (October 1995): 703.

[27] He did, however, patronize the Sanskrit poet Vidyanatha, whose *Prataparudra-sobhusama* employed the *alamkara* tradition, argues Narayana Rao, "as a mode of creating a hero out of the biographical material about his royal deity Prataparudra." We cannot know whether Pratapa Rudra considered himself divine, but if he did, such a claim would appear to be at odds with his public persona, which projected an image more of humility than of divinity. See V. Narayana Rao, "Kings, Gods and Poets: Ideologies of Patronage in Medieval Andhra," in *Powers of Art*, ed. Barbara S. Miller (Delhi, 1992), 151. For a translation of Vidyanatha's work, see Pierre-Sylvan Filliozat, trans., *Le Prataparudriya de Vidyanatha* (Pondicherry, 1963).

[28] Talbot, "Inscribing the Other," 703.

and a Lord of Horses. The first lord was identified as the king of Orissa, the second as Pratapa Rudra, and the third, as the Muslim sultan of the Bahmani kingdom, one of the two Tughluq successor-states in the Deccan.[29] By the second quarter of the fifteenth century, then, Pratapa Rudra and a Muslim sultan in the Deccan were no longer juxtaposed in terms of a paragon of righteousness vs. a demonic barbarian. Rather, both could find an equal footing as mighty lords.

Much the same sentiment is found in the *Prataparudra Caritramu*, an elaborate self-styled biography of Pratapa Rudra that reflects the perspective of Telugu warriors who had become dominant in Vijayanagara by the early sixteenth century, when the text was composed.[30] By tracing the origins of these warriors to a Golden Age in early fourteenth-century Andhra, this text provided Vijayanagara's ruling élite with a foundational myth, or what Talbot calls a "charter of legitimacy." As this text would have it, Pratapa Rudra's great accomplishment was to create and to authorize a class of Telugu warriors – the so-called *padmanayaka*s – who would go on to achieve fame and glory in a post-Kakatiya Deccan. Far, then, from finding an historical rupture between the Kakatiya and Tughluq eras in the Deccan's history, this text affirms an orderly continuity between the two.

According to this account, in fact, not only did Andhra's Telugu warrior tradition survive the Tughluq conquest. So did Pratapa Rudra. The text records that one of the king's predecessors on the "lion throne," Ganapati (1199–1263), had unwisely conferred chieftain (*nayaka*) status on peoples of diverse castes, with the result that by the time Pratapa Rudra ascended the throne, wicked and corrupt *nayaka*s were committing outrageous acts such as attacking Warangal's royal temple or robbing Brahmins. To correct this situation, Pratapa Rudra summoned a group of seventy-seven *padmanayaka*s "rich in honor, exceedingly trustworthy, imbued with discernment, like an ocean in profundity, very judicious, afraid of sin, acting in the lord's best interests, respectable *sudra*s." Giving these men emblems of royalty, the king then appointed them to each of the seventy-seven bastions built into Warangal's inner, stone

---

[29] *Ibid.*, 708. Of course, one can find a material basis to this tripartite mapping of space: the jungles of Orissa are a natural domain of elephants; the power of the Kakatiyas had been based on the Telugu warrior tradition, and the Bahmani sultans, through their commercial links with Arabia and the Persian Gulf, had access to heavy warhorses.

[30] An annotated translation and study of this text is under preparation by Cynthia Talbot and Phillip B. Wagoner. See also Cynthia Talbot, "The Story of Prataparudra: Hindu Historiography on the Deccan Frontier," in *Beyond Turk and Hindu: Rethinking Religious Identities in Islamicate South Asia*, ed. David Gilmartin and Bruce Lawrence (Gainesville FL, 2000), 282–99.

wall.[31] He also apportioned the governing of most of his kingdom to these men.

The *Prataparudra Caritramu* now deployed the following plot-line to account for the kingdom's defeat at the hands of the imperial Tughluqs. In the course of apportioning his kingdom amongst the virtuous *padmanayakas*, Pratapa Rudra had also dismissed and disenfranchised his unworthy nobles. Consequently, when the kingdom was invaded by a Tughluq army, these disgruntled men accepted bribes from Ulugh Khan and quietly withdrew their services, allowing a Tughluq victory despite the *padmanayakas*' valiant efforts to defend the kingdom. The king was now led off to Delhi. But instead of dying on the banks of the Narmada, as we know actually happened, the ex-king reached Delhi and was greeted by the sultan. When the sultan's mother realized that the captured king was a manifestation of Śiva – and her son a manifestation of Vishnu – she advised her son to resolve their differences, whereupon the sultan, now recognizing Pratapa Rudra's truly superlative qualities, set the captive ex-king free. Returning to Warangal, the king summoned his brave and loyal *padmanayakas* and, commending them for their loyal service, released them from his service and authorized them to become independent kings in their respective lands. His great political project now accomplished, Pratapa Rudra died.[32]

What does this text tell us about social history? For one thing, its characterization of the *padmanayakas* as "respectable *sudras*" is significant, since it corroborates contemporary inscriptional evidence showing that the last Kakatiya maharaja actually *did* recruit such non-aristocratic elements into his military system. Second, the text provides a post facto justification for the rise of Telugu warriors in the Vijayanagara state. Of course its mention of the *padmanayakas* appearing as subordinates of Vijayanagara is clearly anachronistic, since that state did not come into existence until several decades after the fall of Warangal. In fact, the text even portrays Vijayanagara as an *ally* of the Kakatiyas during Pratapa Rudra's struggle with Delhi. But such problems disappear when the work is placed in the context of its composition – the early sixteenth century, by which time Vijayanagara had already annexed Andhra south of the Krishna River, in the process assimilating Telugu warriors of that region as subordinate rulers. Even Vijayanagara's central court had by that time taken on a distinctly Telugu character. For its contemporary audience, then, the *Prataparudra*

---

[31] The wall today has only forty-five bastions, and it does not appear that it ever had any more, suggesting that the figure seventy-seven had itself become a standard literary trope.

[32] Talbot, *Precolonial India*, 183–89.

Caritramu provided a coherent explanation for the arrival of diverse groups of Telugu warriors – grouped collectively under the neologism "padmanayaka" – into the mainstream of Vijayanagara's cultural and political life.

Finally, the *Prataparudra Caritramu*, like other texts produced in sixteenth-century Vijayanagara, identifies the sultan of Delhi as the overlord whose actions served to sanction the authority of Vijayanagara's ruling class – in this instance, the Telugu warriors who by that time had come to hold a dominant position within that class. Pratapa Rudra could not launch the careers of his loyal *padmanayakas* until after the sultan of Delhi had first launched his own career. It was because the sultan recognized Pratapa Rudra's superlative – even divine – qualities that he released the ex-king from captivity and allowed him to return to the Deccan. All of this points to the self-perception of Vijayanagara's ruling establishment of their kingdom as being a worthy successor-state to the imperial Tughluqs.[33]

Different contexts, however, produce different memories. Around 1600, the Deccan historian Rafi'al-Din Shirazi related how the other Tughluq successor-state of the Deccan, the Bahmani kingdom, had come into being in 1347. Instrumental in this process, he writes, was Shaikh Siraj al-Din Junaidi, a Muslim holyman who, born in Peshawar in northwest India, had migrated to Daulatabad in 1328 just after that city, as the Tughluq empire's new co-capital, was swelling with throngs of other transplanted northerners. This shaikh was said not only to have been the spiritual guide for the first Bahmani sultan; he even symbolically "crowned" that sultan with his own turban before the monarch's actual coronation.[34] Later hagiographies of Siraj al-Din went further still, associating this shaikh with the collapse of Kakatiya rule in the Deccan. One of these traditions reported that Siraj al-Din Junaidi had been on hand during the 1309 invasion of Warangal by armies of the Delhi Sultanate, and that it was the shaikh who had led Pratapa Rudra from Warangal to the imperial camp outside the city. There, the Kakatiya king indicated to the shaikh that he preferred conversion to Islam to being taken in chains to Delhi as a captive of the Sultan. After consulting with Delhi's field commanders on the matter,

---

[33] For a discussion of various texts produced in Vijayanagara, and of the different ways they situate the sultan of Delhi in that kingdom's remembered past, see Phillip B. Wagoner, "Harihara, Bukka, and the Sultan: the Delhi Sultanate in the Political Imagination of Vijayanagara," in *Beyond Turk and Hindu*, ed. Gilmartin and Lawrence, 300–26. See also Wagoner, "Delhi, Warangal, and Kakatiya Historical Memory," *Deccan Studies* [Journal of the Centre for Deccan Studies, Hyderabad], 1, no. 1 (2002): 17–38.

[34] Rafi'al-Din Shirazi, *Tazkirat al-muluk*, extracts trans. J. S. King, "History of the Bahmani Dynasty," *Indian Antiquary* 28 (June 1899): 154–55.

Siraj al-Din performed a simple conversion ceremony for the Kakatiya king, who was accordingly allowed to remain in Warangal as a tributary king.[35]

It is true that for several decades after 1309, Pratapa Rudra was a tributary king in the Tughluq imperial system. But by conflating conquest with conversion, this later hagiographer, writing centuries after Pratapa Rudra's life, was constructing his own idealized, imagined history. The conversion of the Kakatiya king to Islam had confirmed, consummated, even justified Delhi's conquest of this non-Muslim territory. Different generations, then, would remember the famous king's career in very different ways, using his refashioned life as a screen onto which they could project justifications for social arrangements of their own day.

SUMMARY

Both in his own day and for subsequent generations of Deccanis, Pratapa Rudra was understood as a bridge between two eras, and between two distinctly different kinds of socio-political order. The earlier order was the regional kingdom, manifested in Andhra by the Telugu-speaking Kakatiya state, in Maharashtra by the Marathi-speaking Yadava state, and in Karnataka by the Kannada-speaking Hoysala state. The state about which we have the most information, the Kakatiya, was very much on the move during the final decades of its existence, incorporating a largely pastoral society in the eastern Deccan's dry interior into its expanding agrarian order. In this society men of humble origins rose to political prominence; even monarchs professed *sudra* status. Above all, it was a predominantly Telugu kingdom, by 1323 well on its way to aligning its political frontiers with those of the Deccan's Telugu-speaking region.

In the early fourteenth century, however, a rival form of polity bearing a radically different socio-political vision, the transregional sultanate, challenged and finally overwhelmed the idea of the regional kingdom. This newer model prevailed in the Deccan not solely because its introduction was accompanied by the physical destruction of the earlier, regional kingdoms. More importantly, it presented itself, and was locally understood, as a larger, more powerful, and more cosmopolitan socio-political system. These qualities conferred upon the sultanate, or rather the idea of the sultanate, transregional prestige and

---

[35] Sultan Muhammad, *Armughan-i sultani* (Agra, 1902), cited in Muhammad Suleman Siddiqi, *The Bahmani Sufis* (Delhi, 1989), 122, n 5. Sultan Muhammad refers to this shaikh as Rukn al-Din Junaidi.

authority, which in turn explains why the *Prataparudra Caritramu* did not demonize the Tughluq sultan of Delhi. Rather, by allowing Pratapa Rudra to return to Warangal, there to perform his final political acts, the text effectively has the sultan of Delhi incorporating the Deccan monarch as a subordinate king in the Tughluqs' imperial system. Helping to facilitate the transmission of the sultanate idea from Indo-Turkish Muslims to Deccani Hindus was that idea's profoundly secular basis: being or becoming a sultan, or being subordinate to one, said nothing with respect to one's religious identity.

That said, one might ask how the religious component of the conquerors' cultural identity, Islam, diffused into the Deccan, and with what consequences. We now turn to this matter.

CHAPTER 2

MUHAMMAD GISU DARAZ (1321–1422): MUSLIM PIETY AND STATE AUTHORITY

A Deccani, on being once asked whom he considered the greater personage, the Prophet Muhammad or the Saiyid, replied, with some surprise at the question, that although the Prophet was undoubtedly a great man, yet Saiyid Muhammad Gisu-daraz was a far superior order of being.[1]

Muhammad Qasim Firishta (d. 1611)

In July 1321, about the time Ulugh Khan's army was sent to Warangal to recover the unpaid tribute owed by Pratapa Rudra, an infant son was born in Delhi to a distinguished family of Saiyids – that is, men who claimed descent from the Prophet. Although he lived most of his life in Delhi, Saiyid Muhammad Husaini Gisu Daraz would become known mainly for his work in the Deccan, where he died in 1422 at the ripe age of just over a hundred years.

As seen in the extract from Firishta's history quoted above, this figure occupies a very special place in Deccani popular religion: soon after his death his tomb-shrine in Gulbarga became the most important object of Muslim devotion in the Deccan. It remains so today. He also stands out in the Muslim mystical tradition, as he was the first Indian shaikh to put his thoughts directly to writing, as opposed to having disciples record his conversations. But most importantly, Gisu Daraz contributed to the stabilization and indigenization of Indo-Muslim society and polity in the Deccan, as earlier generations of Sufi shaikhs had already done in Tughluq north India. In the broader context of Indo-Muslim thought and practice, his career helped transform the Deccan from what had been an infidel land available for plunder by north Indian dynasts, to a legally inviolable abode of peace.

FROM DELHI TO DAULATABAD

In 1325 Ulugh Khan was crowned Sultan Muhammad bin Tughluq, ruler of a vast empire that under his reign would become India's largest until the British Raj. Two years later, in a bold move that brought about a major shift in the

---

[1] Muhammad Qasim Firishta, *Tarikh-i Firishta* (Lucknow, 1864–65), I:320; trans. John Briggs, *History of the Rise of the Mahomedan Power in India* (London, 1829: repr. Calcutta, 1966), II:245–46.

Delhi Sultanate's geo-political center, the new sovereign declared Daulatabad, though located some 600 miles south of Delhi, the co-capital of his sprawling domain. In doing so the sultan implemented a strategic vision for the imperial domination of the entire subcontinent. He also determined to populate the city with northern colonists, and in the end a tenth of Delhi's Muslim population made the long trek south to settle in the new colonial city. In order to induce northerners to shift south – a disruptive move bitterly resented by many who considered their sovereign tyrannical or even mad – the sultan ordered the construction of a pukka road from Delhi to Daulatabad, which continued on to Sultanpur and the Coromandel coast. Recalling a trip made in 1342, the famous Moroccan world-traveler Ibn Battuta later wrote, "The road between Delhi and Daulatabad is bordered with willow trees and others in such a manner that a man going along it imagines he is walking through a garden; and at every mile there are three postal stations . . . At every station (*dawa*) is to be found all that a traveler needs."[2]

Among the residents of Delhi who joined the throngs moving south was the seven-year-old boy Muhammad Husaini who, traveling with his parents, reached the new Tughluq colony of Daulatabad in November 1328. Seven years later he returned to Delhi with his mother and older brother, his father having died while the family was still in Daulatabad. He would remain in Delhi for the next sixty-three years, growing into maturity in the principal capital of the most expansive empire in India's history, and affiliated to the Sufi order – the Chishti – that was most closely identified with the fortunes of that empire.

At the time of the boy's birth, the leading Chishti shaikh in Delhi, indeed in India, was Nizam al-Din Auliya, whose hospice (*khanaqah*) in Delhi attracted full-time spiritual seekers as well as lay devotees who sought the shaikh's bless-ings in the pursuit of more mundane goals. Some of the most widely read publicists for Tughluq imperialism, such as the poet Amir Khusrau and the historian Zia al-Din Barani, were also devoted disciples (*murids*) of Nizam al-Din, meaning that in the popular mind the legitimacy of the Tughluq state and the expansion of its frontiers became subtly associated with Chishti piety. Moreover, many of the great shaikh's disciples moved from Delhi out to the Tughluq empire's far-flung provinces, where they enjoyed public patronage by local power-holders seeking to deepen the roots of their own legitimacy. In this way, Sufis of the Chishti order – despite their well-known self-perception

---

[2] Ibn Battuta, *The Rehla of Ibn Battuta*, trans. Mahdi Husain (Baroda, 1953), 44. Coming from a veteran traveler of north Africa, Egypt, Syria, Anatolia, Iran, Central Asia, and Afghanistan, this is an impressive testimonial.

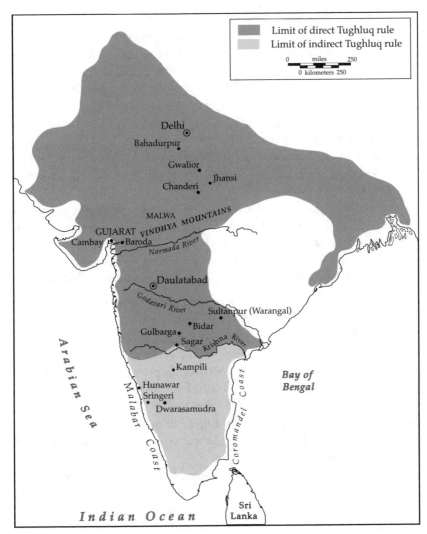

Map 2. Direct and indirect Tughluq rule, 1327–47.

of avoiding association with political power – became deeply implicated in the Tughluq project of planting Indo-Muslim political authority throughout South Asia.

When Nizam al-Din died in 1325, the great shaikh's leading disciple, Nasir al-Din Mahmud, took his place as the premier Chishti shaikh in the Tughluq metropolis. Nasir al-Din was still in this position ten years later, when the youthful Muhammad Husaini and his family returned to Delhi from Daulatabad. Whereas his older brother Saiyid Chandan took up a worldly occupation, Muhammad soon joined the circle of Sufi adepts that had formed around Shaikh Nasir al-Din's hospice, and because his hair at this time reached his knees he was called "that Saiyid with the long locks (*gisu-daraz*)."[3] The sobriquet stuck, and he has been known by the name ever since.

By the 1350s, when in his thirties, Gisu Daraz began spending much of his time in isolated retreat, studying and meditating, though still under the spiritual direction of Shaikh Nasir al-Din. In 1356, a cholera epidemic swept through Delhi, and Gisu Daraz fell so ill that he coughed up blood. He recovered, however, after Shaikh Nasir al-Din arranged to have medicinal oil brought all the way from the cradle of Chishti piety, the town of Chisht in western Afghanistan, and administered to his ailing disciple. But the senior shaikh, aware of his own mortality, saw more at work in Gisu Daraz's recovery than the effects of exotic medicines. One day, summoning his disciple to his house, Nasir al-Din listened as Gisu Daraz narrated a cryptic dream he had just had:

In my illness, I saw people coming and instructing me to put on and then take off, successively, the robe (*jama*) of Dominion, the robe of Prophethood, the robe of Unity, and the robe of Divine Essence.[4]

Glowing with delight on hearing these words, whose inner meaning he immediately grasped, Nasir al-Din handed his personal prayer carpet to Gisu Daraz, symbolizing the transmission of his spiritual authority to the younger adept.[5] Soon thereafter, in September 1356, Shaikh Nasir al-Din died, and for the next forty years Gisu Daraz became a public figure in the imperial capital, catering to the spiritual needs of Delhi's learned men, nobles, women, merchants, and the general population.

Toward the end of the fourteenth century, however, his career took a dramatic turn when Delhi was invaded and sacked by the renowned Central Asian conqueror Timur, known to Europeans as Tamerlane. In December 1398, as Timur's vast army was approaching the capital, having smashed through Tughluq defensive lines in the Punjab, Gisu Daraz – sensing the devastation

---

[3] Muhammad 'Ali Samani, *Siyar al-Muhammadi* [composed 1427], ed. S. N. Ahmad Qadri (Hyderabad, 1969), 15.

[4] *Ibid.*, 22–23. Recalling Pratapa Rudra's donning of Tughluq robes while submitting to Delhi, we again note the symbolic role played by robes – whether physical as in the case of the Kakatiya raja, or seen in a vision, as in the case of Gisu Daraz – in effecting the transfer of political or spiritual authority.

[5] *Ibid.*, 23. The text relates that Nasir al-Din had actually bestowed his spiritual authority on three others in addition to Gisu Daraz, but since those three died, all of the shaikh's blessings fell to Gisu Daraz, who then became the spiritual heir (*sajjada-nishin*) to Nasir al-Din's hospice.

that would soon visit the Tughluq capital – decided to abandon Delhi for good. Gathering a considerable entourage of disciples, family, and companions, he left Delhi on December 17, the day after Timur's army routed Tughluq forces just outside the capital, and a day before his forces would begin sacking the city.

Once again Gisu Daraz, now a grizzled shaikh of seventy-seven years, struck out on the road to the Deccan. His party's leisurely journey south provides ample evidence of the dispersion of Delhi-trained Chishti shaikhs that had taken place over the course of the fourteenth century, for everywhere they stopped, they were greeted and entertained by followers and devotees who had trained in Delhi. In Bahadurpur, southwest of Delhi (in present-day Alwar district), Gisu Daraz was hosted by former disciples. From there he notified others in Gwalior that he had managed to escape Delhi "before the disaster" – referring to Timur's sacking of the city – and instructed them to prepare for his arrival. On January 1, 1399, the shaikh reached that city, having survived attacks by brigands along the road. In late February, after giving a cloak of spiritual legitimacy to his host in Gwalior, he and his party continued on to Jhansi. From there the party proceeded to Chanderi, in modern Guna District, finally reaching Baroda on June 6, and Cambay a month later.[6]

In 1400, while still in Gujarat, Gisu Daraz resolved to return to his childhood home of Daulatabad and pay respects at the tomb of his father, Saiyid Yusuf. It was a fateful decision. Sixty-four years had elapsed since he left the Deccan as a boy of fourteen. In the meantime the shaikh, having succeeded to the spiritual authority of the powerful Chishti shaikhs Nizam al-Din Auliya and Nasir al-Din, had himself ripened into a venerable Sufi master. Nor was the Deccan in 1400 the same as in the days of the shaikh's boyhood. In those earlier days, Daulatabad had been a colonial outpost of the Tughluq empire, populated mainly by northern immigrants. But in the 1330s and 1340s, while Gisu Daraz was still in Delhi studying under Nasir al-Din's tutelage, tumultuous anti-Tughluq revolutions had totally transformed the region's socio-political fabric.

A TALE OF TWO FAMILIES:
THE SANGAMAS AND BAHMANIS

During Gisu Daraz's earlier stay in the Deccan from 1328 to 1335, the properly "colonial" area of Tughluq influence in the Deccan had been confined to

---

[6] *Ibid.*, 26–32.

the northern half of the peninsula, from the Vindhya Mountains down to the Krishna River. Here, especially in the imperial co-capital of Daulatabad, the bulk of northern immigrants had settled, including Gisu Daraz's own family. Here, too, imperial coins minted in Daulatabad or Sultanpur (formerly Warangal) freely circulated, while chieftains formally in Yadava or Kakatiya service were assimilated into Tughluq service as *iqta'dars*.

South of the Krishna River, however, the Tughluqs exercised a much looser sort of authority (see Map 2). Here, kings of the Hoysala dynasty, though tributaries of the Tughluqs since 1311, still reigned for several decades as sovereign monarchs, their capital of Dwarasamudra located some 400 miles south of Daulatabad, and hence beyond the Tughluqs' effective reach. But the authority of the declining Hoysalas was as weak in this region as that of the distant Tughluqs. Malik Kafur's looting of the Hoysala capital in 1311 had severely damaged the dynasty's credibility among subordinate officers, many of whom quietly withdrew their allegiance to the dynasty and began commanding roving armies, setting themselves up as de facto lords all over the South.[7]

Among these strongmen were the five sons of Sangama, an obscure chieftain who at the opening of the fourteenth century appears to have been in Hoysala service in southeastern Karnataka.[8] As early as 1313, one of Sangama's older sons, Kampamna, emerged as a politically active chieftain in the present Kolar district. In 1327, just when Muhammad bin Tughluq began tightening Delhi's control over the northern Deccan by declaring Daulatabad his imperial co-capital, another of Sangama's sons, Muddamna, asserted his authority in the present Mysore district.[9] By this time, both the Sangama brothers and the Delhi sultan were busy picking up the pieces of the disintegrating Hoysala state. The sultan did this by co-opting independent chieftains or those formerly

[7] In 1254 the Hoysala king Somesvara had divided his kingdom between two sons by different queens. After these two had died, Ballala III (1292–1342) united the kingdom in 1301, but from 1303 to 1309 the dynasty was intermittently at war with the Yadavas. As Duncan Derrett writes, "The effect of the long and complex struggle against the Sevunas [Yadavas], against rebels, adherents of Ramanatha's family, and enemies below the Ghats, was evidently to weaken the class who had, until the second half of the previous century, been in unchallenged control of the social and political life of the country. Now acts of terrorism were frequent, patronage had suffered a severe blow, and the land-holders were obliged to oppress the cultivators." J. Duncan M. Derrett, *The Hoysalas, a Medieval Indian Royal Family* (Madras, 1957), 148.

[8] For a discussion of the complicated historiography of the early Sangamas, and of the family's origins, see Vasundhara Filliozat, *l'Épigraphie de Vijayanagara du début à 1377* (Paris, 1973), especially p. xviii. Another review of the evidence and the debate over the origins of the Sangamas is found in Hermann Kulke, "Maharajas, Mahants and Historians: Reflections on the Historiography of Early Vijayanagara and Sringeri," in *Vijayanagara – City and Empire: New Currents of Research*, ed. Anna L. Dallapiccola (Stuttgart, 1985), 1:120–43.

[9] Filliozat, *l'Épigraphie*, 1.

subordinate to Hoysala authority and by installing them over their former territories as Tughluq *amirs* ("commanders"). Such is what happened in Kampili, a small kingdom in modern Bellary district that sat astride the former Yadava–Hoysala frontier. In 1327 the raja of this kingdom had died a heroic death in an unsuccessful rebellion against Tughluq authority. But the king's eleven sons had no such taste for martyrdom. The Arab traveler Ibn Battuta, who met three of these sons sometime between 1337 and 1342, records that the sultan of Delhi had made them all imperial *amirs* "in consideration of their good descent and [the] noble conduct of their father."[10]

Some time in the 1320s or 1330s another Sangama brother, Harihara, also became one of these *amirs*, at least nominally enlisting himself in Tughluq imperial service.[11] This much is confirmed by the local observer 'Isami, who in 1350 described Harihara as a *murtadd*, the Arabic for "turncoat," "renegade," or "apostate" – literally, "one who turns away."[12] The reference is to Harihara's subsequent renunciation of his former association with Tughluq authority. Yet his service to the Delhi Sultanate seems to have persisted in folk memory, for we read in the *Vidyaranya Kalajñana*, a Sanskrit chronicle composed soon after 1580, that the Delhi sultan had "bestowed" the entire Karnataka country on Harihara and his brother Bukka because the sultan, in his wisdom, had recognized the two men as eminently trustworthy and hence deserving of imperial service.[13]

In the second quarter of the fourteenth century, then, two forms of Tughluq rule had emerged in the Deccan plateau. In the annexed regions of the north, as we have seen in chapter 1, the Tughluqs imposed a *colonial* idea, and a system of "direct rule." Here they planted colonies of northern immigrants, established mints and coined money on the same standard as that of Delhi, and wherever possible redefined local landholders as *iqta'dars*. Over the turbulent

---

[10] Ibn Battuta, *Rehla*, 96.

[11] Both Ibn Battuta and the historian Zia al-Din Barani record that in the wake of the uprising at Kampili, the sultan placed native chieftains in charge of governing the southern Deccan. Barani further identified the leader of a 1336 anti-Tughluq uprising in the Kampili region as a chieftain who had been appointed nine years earlier by Muhammad bin Tughluq to administer that reconquered region. While it is not certain that figure was Harihara Sangama, there is no doubt that Harihara had, at some point in his early career, been employed in Tughluq service. Zia al-Din Barani, *Tarikh-i Firuz Shahi*, in *The History of India as Told by its Own Historians*, ed. and trans. H. M. Elliot and John Dowson (Allahabad, 1964), III:245.

[12] 'Isami, *Futuhu's Salatin*, trans., III:902.

[13] Phillip B. Wagoner, "Harihara, Bukka, and the Sultan: the Delhi Sultanate in the Political Imagination of Vijayanagara," in *Beyond Turk and Hindu: Rethinking Religious Identities in Islamicate South Asia*, ed. David Gilmartin and Bruce B. Lawrence (Gainesville FL, 2000), 312–20. This source makes no mention of Harihara's and Bukka's religious conversion or reconversion – only of their political loyalty and trustworthiness.

and distant southern Deccan, on the other hand, they imposed an *imperial* idea, and a system of "indirect rule." Here they planted no colonies, appointed no governors, established no mints, and made no effort to reach the grass roots of agrarian society, remaining content only to redefine powerful and effectively autonomous chieftains like Harihara Sangama as tribute-paying *amirs*.

But the whole system began to unravel in 1336, when a Telugu chieftain of obscure origins led a successful uprising in Warangal that forced the Tughluq governor there to flee to Delhi, permanently ending imperial authority in Andhra.[14] Rebellious forces throughout the Deccan now gathered momentum. Up to this point the younger two Sangama brothers, Bukka and Harihara, had not appeared in the inscriptional record. But in 1336, we find Bukka described as a subordinate chief (*odeya*) – technically still in the Hoysala system – in the Sangama stronghold in Kolar district. Three years later, his brother Harihara emerged rather suddenly as the ruling lord over several widely dispersed regions, including the modern Bijapur and Shimoga districts in Karnataka, and Chingleput district in Tamil Nadu – an area stretching from the Malabar to the Coromandel coasts. At the same time, he adopted the grandiose title "Lord of the Oceans of East and West,"[15] a claim partially confirmed by Ibn Battuta, who in 1342 identified Harihara as the suzerain over the Muslim ruler of the port of Honavar in northern Malabar.[16] Since Ibn Battuta made no mention of Harihara's service to the Tughluqs at that time, it seems likely that his inscriptions of 1339 reflect his and his brothers' de facto declaration of independence from both Delhi and Dwarasamudra. In 1342 he appears as the master of modern Bangalore district, and the next year, both Harihara and Bukka appear as ruling chiefs in the family power-base in Kolar district, while Harihara emerged as the dominant lord in Mysore district, as did Bukka in the Tamil district of Pudukottah.[17]

The consolidation of power by the Sangama brothers in the sub-Krishna Deccan, which ultimately led to the founding of the Vijayanagara state, precisely coincides in time with the political activities of another family of brothers operating north of the Krishna River. Although the Tughluq revolution of 1320 had overthrown the Khalji dynasty in Delhi, that movement never ran its course in the Deccan, where many former Khaljis, together with Afghans sympathetic to that house, remained entrenched as local administrators and harbored an abiding resentment toward the Tughluqs and their revolution in north India.

---

[14] The dating of the uprising at Warangal can be deduced by piecing together contemporary evidence from Barani, Ibn Battuta, and 'Isami. See Mahdi Husain, *Tughluq Empire* (New Delhi, 1976), 245–50.

[15] Filliozat, *l'Épigraphie*, 2–4.   [16] Ibn Battuta, *Rehla*, 180.   [17] Filliozat, *l'Épigraphie*, 5–7.

Among these was one Zafar Khan and his three brothers, all of them junior officers serving in the Deccan and nephews of a former high official in the deposed Khalji court. For his participation in the Tughluq siege of Kampili in 1327, Zafar Khan had been rewarded with *iqta*'s in present-day Sangli and Belgaum districts.[18] But in 1339, the same year that Harihara emerged as the dominant player amidst the chaos of the crumbling Hoysala dynasty further to the south, Zafar Khan joined his three brothers in an anti-Tughluq uprising in which the forts of Gulbarga, Bidar (or Badrkot), and Sagar were all briefly seized.

Although imperial authorities suppressed this revolt, capturing and exiling to Afghanistan all four brothers and their supporters, anti-Delhi sentiment continued to build, and not just among those harboring pro-Khalji sympathies. Many among Daulatabad's settler-community who had migrated from north India felt increasingly alienated by Muhammad bin Tughluq's high-handed methods of running his Deccan colony. In 1344 Qutlugh Khan, a popular Tughluq governor of Daulatabad, and a man to whom Deccanis had looked as their defense against Muhammad bin Tughluq's arbitrary and erratic actions, was dismissed by the sultan on grounds of fiscal irresponsibility.[19] The sultan also sent investigators to look into the causes of disaffections at Daulatabad, after which he ordered his new governor there to transfer 1,500 cavalrymen, together with the most noted "commanders of a hundred" (*amir-i sadagan*), from Daulatabad to Gujarat.

By the time this order was received, however, the sultan had already ordered the Tughluq governor of the neighboring province of Malwa to track down and execute Malwa's own "commanders of a hundred," whom the court had blamed for fomenting rebellion there. Consequently officers of the same rank in Daulatabad, aware of the bloody events in nearby Malwa, concluded while already on the road to Gujarat that they, too, would in all likelihood be similarly charged and, if they continued to Gujarat, would face certain execution. So they returned to Daulatabad, seized and confined the new Tughluq governor, and executed the officials who had been sent south by the sultan to investigate matters. Other "commanders of a hundred" in Gujarat joined their comrades in Daulatabad in what had now become a general uprising against Tughluq authority, in which both Hindus and Muslims took part.[20] These events occurred in 1345, the last year imperial coins would be minted anywhere in the Deccan.

[18] Husain, *Tughluq Empire*, 300.   [19] Barani, *Tarikh*, in Elliot and Dowson, *History*, III:251.
[20] Barani notes, "the people of the country joined them." *Ibid.*, III:257–58.

In Karnataka, meanwhile, the Sangama brothers continued to consolidate their own authority, picking up the pieces of the rapidly crumbling Hoysala state while at the same time throwing off any former allegiance to Delhi. By early 1344, most of Karnataka had accepted rule by the Sangama brothers, a transfer of allegiance that seems to have been both gradual and bloodless, as ex-Hoysala officers simply melted away from the enfeebled Hoysala king, Ballala IV, and to the Sangama cause.[21] On February 23, 1346, all five Sangama brothers gathered at the Śaiva center of Sringeri, in modern Chikmaglur district, to celebrate Harihara's coast-to-coast conquests of the southern peninsula. The occasion anticipated the formation of a new sub-Krishna state, as well as the collapse of the Hoysala dynasty, whose last known inscription appeared just two months later.[22] Meanwhile to the north, Zafar Khan, banished to Afghanistan since 1339, managed to return to the Deccan from exile. In April 1346, two months after the Sangamas' celebrations at Sringeri, he joined an anti-Tughluq siege of Gulbarga, and in August that strategic fort-city also slipped from imperial to rebel control.[23]

On either side of the Krishna River, then, two movements were unfolding on nearly parallel tracks. To the south, another Sangama brother, Marappa, in February 1347 declared Virupaksha, the principal deity at the site later known as Vijayanagara, to be the Sangama family deity. On the same occasion he publicly proclaimed himself, among other titles, "sultan," or in its Kannada formulation, "Sultan among Indian kings" (*hindu-raya-suratalah*).[24] To the north of the Krishna, meanwhile, Tughluq forces, which had briefly retaken Daulatabad,[25] were driven out of that city for good. On August 3, 1347, six months after one sultan had appeared among the Sangamas, another one appeared in Daulatabad's great mosque, where Zafar Khan was crowned as Sultan 'Ala al-Din Hasan Bahman Shah.[26] This new sultan's dominion, known after its founder as the Bahmani kingdom, claimed sway over the northern Deccan, where the Tughluqs had exercised a direct, colonial rule. Meanwhile the Sangama sultans, operating from their base on the banks of the Tungabhadra River, would fill the political vacuum that had emerged between the collapsing Hoysala power to the south of the Krishna, and the newly emerging Bahmani power north of that river.

With rebellions on either side of the Krishna now consummated, the leaders of both movements had assumed the most powerful political title available in

---

[21] Derrett, *Hoysalas*, 173; Filliozat, *l'Épigraphie*, xxiv–xxv.
[22] Filliozat, *l'Épigraphie*, 8–10.   [23] 'Isami, *Futuhu's Salatin*, trans., III:784.
[24] Filliozat, *l'Épigraphie*, 134–36. *Mysore Archaeological Reports*, No. 90 (1929), pp. 159ff.
[25] 'Isami, *Futuhu's Salatin*, trans., III:726, 737, 745.   [26] *Ibid.*, III:827.

their day. In 1352 Bukka, following the lead of his brother Marappa, styled himself "Sultan among Indian kings," and two years later, during a period of apparent joint-rule, both he and his brother Harihara adopted this, among other titles. In 1354, Bukka also reaffirmed the god Virupaksha as the Sangama family deity, who by now had effectively become the state deity of the fledgling new polity headed up by the Sangama brothers.[27] And in 1355 Bukka for the first time described himself generically as the "sultan," and not just "Sultan among Indian kings."[28] When Harihara died in 1357, Bukka, apparently the only surviving Sangama brother at this time, became sole ruler of the new state. In October of that year, we find Bukka reigning from the city that he was now calling Vijayanagara, "City of Victory." In early 1358 he began styling himself with grandiose Sanskrit imperial titles in addition to "Sultan among Indian kings." By 1374, aspiring for truly pan-Asian recognition, he even sent an ambassador from Vijayanagara to Ming China.[29]

Clearly, a new political age had dawned in the Deccan. Between 1339 and 1347, two families of obscure or humble origins, operating on opposite sides of the Krishna River, led movements that radically redrew the Deccan's political, and more importantly, conceptual map. Even while expelling Tughluq imperial might from the region, leaders of these two families defiantly and successfully appropriated the conceptual basis of Delhi's authority – the title "sultan," charged as it was with allusions to supreme, transregional power. To be sure, at mid-century memories of regional kingdoms like the Yadavas and Hoysalas still lingered in people's minds. But on the ground, such kingdoms had been replaced by two new, transregional sultanates, with rulers of both states asserting de facto claims to being regional successors to the imperial Tughluqs (see Map 3).

EARLY SHAIKHS IN THE BAHMANI KINGDOM

In the northern Deccan, Sultan 'Ala al-Din Hasan Bahman Shah, soon after throwing off Tughluq authority in 1347, shifted the Bahmani capital from Daulatabad to the ancient fort-city of Gulbarga. As the new capital lay in

---

[27] Anila Verghese, *Religious Traditions at Vijayanagara, as Revealed through its Monuments* (New Delhi, 1995), 141.

[28] He also identified the most powerful armies of the Deccan as, besides his own, the Turkish army, the Hoysala army, the Yadava army, and the Pandya army. Inasmuch as the last three dynastic houses had ceased to exist by 1355, the only effective armies then operating in the Deccan were Bukka's own and that of the "Turks," represented by the Bahmani kingdom recently established by Sultan 'Ala al-Din Hasan Bahman Shah. See Filliozat, *l'Épigraphie*, 25–28.

[29] *Ibid.*, xxxii, 39–42.

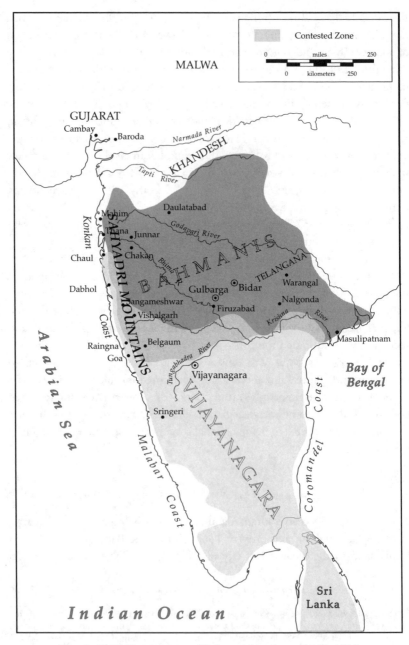

Map 3. The Vijayanagara and Bahmani kingdoms, 1347–1518.

the heart of the Deccan plateau and at a safe distance from north India, the move south doubtless served as a precaution against the possibility of renewed invasions from Delhi. Launching the new state required more than just physical security, however. Also needed was a legal basis for rebelling against Tughluq rule and establishing the new sultanate. In this respect the Vijayanagara and Bahmani states would take very different paths.

It is not unusual for colonial offshoots to appeal to the same pool of symbols that were associated with the parent state against which they had rebelled. Gulbarga's earliest architecture thus slavishly replicated contemporary northern styles – i.e., the thick, sloping walls, flat domes, and plain exteriors characteristic of the imperial Tughluqs. The Bahmanis also sought the blessings of charismatic and spiritually powerful Sufi shaikhs who had been associated with the parent Tughluq house. Publicists connected the founder of the new dynasty with the foremost representative of Chishti piety during the height of Tughluq prosperity and political expansion, Nizam al-Din Auliya (d. 1325). According to a local tradition recorded in the late 1500s, Nizam al-Din had just finished meeting with Sultan Muhammad bin Tughluq at his hospice when he found Zafar Khan, the future Sultan 'Ala al-Din Hasan Bahman Shah, waiting outside. The shaikh remarked, "One sultan has left my door; another is waiting there."[30] The anecdote illustrates the theme, very common in those days, of a Sufi shaikh *predicting* future kingship for some civilian, with that "prediction" actually serving as a veiled form of royal appointment. For in the Perso-Islamic literary and cultural world of the day, spiritually powerful Sufi shaikhs, not sultans, were understood as the truly valid sovereigns over the world. It was they who leased out political sovereignty to kings, charging them with the worldly business of administration, warfare, taxation, and so forth.[31]

Writing in 1350 'Abd al-Malik 'Isami, the earliest panegyrist at the Bahmani court, clearly states that certain Sufi shaikhs could "entrust" royal sovereignty (*hukumat*) to future kings, whose rule was understood as dependent on such shaikhs. In fact, history itself was but the working out of divine will as mediated by spiritually powerful shaikhs, especially those of the Chishti order. "Although there might be a monarch in every country," wrote 'Isami, "yet it is actually under the protection of a fakir [i.e., a Sufi shaikh]."[32] The poet then noted that with the death in 1325 of Delhi's greatest Chishti master,

---

[30] 'Ali Tabataba, *Burhan-i ma'athir* (Delhi, 1936), 12; Firishta, *Tarikh*, 1:274.

[31] For a discussion of the intricate relations between Chishti shaikhs and sovereigns of the Delhi Sultanate, see Simon Digby, "The Sufi *Shaykh* and the Sultan: a Conflict of Claims to Authority in Medieval India," *Iran* 28 (1990): 71–81.

[32] 'Isami, *Futuhu's Salatin*, trans., III:687.

Shaikh Nizam al-Din Auliya, the city and empire of Delhi had sunk to deso-
lation, tyranny, and turmoil. But the Deccan, he continued, suffered no such
fate. To the contrary, just four years after Nizam al-Din's death, and only two
years after Sultan Muhammad bin Tughluq had made Daulatabad his imperial
co-capital, one of Nizam al-Din's leading disciples, Burhan al-Din Gharib,
joined the throngs of northerners who migrated to Daulatabad. For 'Isami, it
was Burhan al-Din Gharib's benevolent presence that had caused that city to
prosper.[33]

When Burhan al-Din died in 1337, that protective presence passed to his
own leading disciple, Shaikh Zain al-Din Shirazi (d. 1369). And it was through
this shaikh's indirect agency that the Bahmani state was transformed from a
rebel movement into a legitimate Indo-Islamic kingdom. 'Isami writes that
the very robe worn by the Prophet Muhammad on the night he ascended to
Paradise – a robe subsequently passed on through twenty-three generations
of holymen until finally received by Zain al-Din – was bestowed upon the
founder of the Bahmani state at his coronation in 1347.[34] Once in power, the
new sultan wasted no time expressing his gratitude to Chishti shaikhs of both
the Deccan and Delhi, living and deceased. He ordered a gift of 200 lbs of
gold and 400 lbs of silver to be given to the shrine of Burhan al-Din Gharib,
near Daulatabad.[35] This gift acknowledged the memory not only of Burhan
al-Din Gharib, but also of that shaikh's own master, Nizam al-Din Auliya, who
was the spiritual patriarch of the entire Tughluq dynasty and the shaikh said
to have predicted the new sultan's temporal sovereignty.

Thereafter, Sultan 'Ala al-Din's earliest successors to the Bahmani throne
actively sought the support of Sufi shaikhs. 'Ala al-Din's son and successor,
Sultan Muhammad I (1358–75), even demanded an oath of allegiance from
all Sufi shaikhs in his domain.[36] One shaikh in particular, Shaikh Siraj al-Din
Junaidi (d. 1379–80), was more than obliging in this respect. He not only
shifted his own residence from Daulatabad to Gulbarga when the Bahmani
capital moved to the latter city; he is also said to have presented a robe (*pirahan*)
and a turban to all three of the first Bahmani sultans on the occasion of their

---

[33] *Ibid.*, III:691–92, 696. Majd al-Din Kashani, *Ghara'ib al-karamat*, 11. Cited in Carl W. Ernst,
Eternal Garden: Mysticism, History, and Politics at a South Asian Sufi Center (Albany, 1992), 119.
Kashani, the author of this unpublished narrative, was a disciple of Shaikh Burhan al-Din and
compiled the work in 1340, just three years after his master's death.

[34] 'Isami, *Futuhu's Salatin*, trans., I:13;. The robe is kept in a glass trunk at Zain al-Din Shirazi's shrine
in Khuldabad. Once a year, on the occasion of the Prophet Muhammad's birthday ('Id-i Milad-i
Nabi), it is brought out for public viewing. For the activities of Zain al-Din during this time, see
Ernst, *Eternal Garden*, 134–38.

[35] Firishta, *Tarikh*, I:277.   [36] Briggs, *Rise*, II:200.

coronations in 1347, 1358, and 1375 respectively.[37] Such attention did not go unrewarded. In 1362, on returning to Gulbarga after a successful campaign against Vijayanagara, Sultan Muhammad I visited Shaikh Siraj al-Din Junaidi's residence and gave thanks to the shaikh, believing that the latter's prayers had assisted his military efforts. On concluding a campaign in Telangana, he went further and gave this shaikh a fifth of the war booty – "to be distributed among Syuds and holy men" – again attributing his success to the shaikh's prayers.[38]

Not all Sufis of the kingdom, however, were so accommodating. Despite the association of Chishti shaikhs with political power – first in Tughluq Delhi, and then with the rise of the Bahmani state – Zain al-Din Shirazi, the only major Chishti shaikh in the Deccan after the death of Burhan al-Din Gharib, avoided association with *all* Bahmani sultans down to his death in 1369. He alone refused Sultan Muhammad I's demand that all shaikhs of the realm swear allegiance to him. On one occasion he even gave succor to anti-Bahmani rebels in Daulatabad, for which the sultan angrily expelled him from the city. Although the two men were later reconciled, such incidents draw attention to the tense relationship that could exist between the kingdom's court and its saintly élite.[39]

FROM DAULATABAD TO GULBARGA

It is against the backdrop of this complex relationship between Bahmani sultans and shaikhs, exhibiting both mutual attraction and mutual repulsion, that we return to our narrative of Gisu Daraz. Having spent sixty-three years in Delhi until the very week Timur sacked that city, the venerable Chishti shaikh reached Gujarat in June 1399. Now he was preparing to travel to Daulatabad, the city of his boyhood, with the intent of visiting his father's grave-site. When he and his entourage reached the former Tughluq colonial capital,[40] news of the shaikh's arrival spread swiftly to the palace of the reigning Bahmani monarch, Sultan Firuz (1397–1422), in Gulbarga. The sultan promptly instructed his

---

[37] Rafi' al-Din Shirazi, *Tadhkirat al-muluk* (completed 1608), extracts trans. J. S. King, "History of the Bahmani Dynasty," *Indian Antiquary* 28 (July 1899): 182.

[38] Briggs, *Rise*, ii:186, 191, 197.

[39] *Ibid.*, ii:200. This version of the story of Zain al-Din Shirazi may be compared with the slightly different one found in the shaikh's own discourses, whose moral, writes Ernst, seems to be "that God loves the saints, not . . . that the saints love the kings." See Ernst, *Eternal Garden*, 212–14.

[40] We do not have an exact date for his arrival in Daulatabad or Gulbarga. The *Siyar al-Muhammadi*, the earliest hagiography of Gisu Daraz, states only that he had reached Cambay between early July and early August, 1399, and stayed for some time before returning to Baroda, from where he started toward Daulatabad. Samani, *Siyar*, 32. The earliest history of the Bahmani dynasty, the *Burhan al-ma'athir*, states that he reached Gulbarga in the year 802 AH, which began on September 3, 1399. Tabataba, *Burhan*, 43.

governor in Daulatabad to convey his warmest greetings to the honored guest. And to prove his sincerity in the matter, the sultan even rode with an armed detachment up to Daulatabad and personally invited Gisu Daraz to come and settle in the Bahmani royal capital. "I would be inclined to accept your offer," replied the shaikh, "but in view of the fact that you are not destined to live much longer, how could I find contentment if I were to settle there without you present?"

Unshaken by this disarming question, the sultan shrewdly replied, "Very well. If my life is destined to end soon, could you not beseech God to lengthen it?" The shaikh answered that he would that very evening busy himself in prayer and report on the matter the following day. When the two met the next morning, Gisu Daraz quoted God as having told him, "We have lengthened the sultan's life-span so that you [Gisu Daraz] can live longer [in contentment]."[41] This exchange, recorded by a disciple who had accompanied the shaikh from Delhi to Daulatabad, explains – within the logic of hagiographic writing – why Gisu Daraz accepted Firuz's invitation, and why he lived to the extraordinary age of 101 years. It also accounts for the apparent coincidence that Gisu Daraz and Sultan Firuz Bahmani both died twenty-three years later, within a month of one other. In death, as in life, the careers of the two men would be closely intertwined.

Who was this king who had thrown in his lot with Gisu Daraz? Crowned just three years before the shaikh's arrival in the Bahmani capital, Sultan Firuz Bahmani possessed remarkable intellect, ambition, and ability. He could converse in many languages, had a prodigious memory, would read the Jewish and Christian scriptures, respected the tenets of all faiths, wrote good poetry, and was said to have exceeded even Muhammad bin Tughluq in literary attainments. On Saturdays, Mondays, and Thursdays, he would give lectures on mathematics, Euclidian geometry, and rhetoric, and if business did not interfere, these would continue into the evenings.[42] On the political side, the sultan gave high office to Brahmins, transformed Hindu chieftains into Bahmani commanders, and formed alliances with Telugu warrior lineages.

He was also the first Muslim king of the Deccan to marry the daughter of a neighboring non-Muslim monarch, in this respect anticipating by more than a century-and-a-half Akbar's policy of forming strategic marital alliances with Rajput houses. What was exceptional about Firuz's alliance, however, was the manner in which he celebrated his marriage, in 1407, to the daughter of his powerful neighbor to the south, Deva Raya I of Vijayanagara. Rather than

41 Samani, *Siyar*, 33–35.   42 Briggs, *Rise*, II:227; Firishta, *Tarikh*, I:308.

Chart 1 Bahmani dynasty

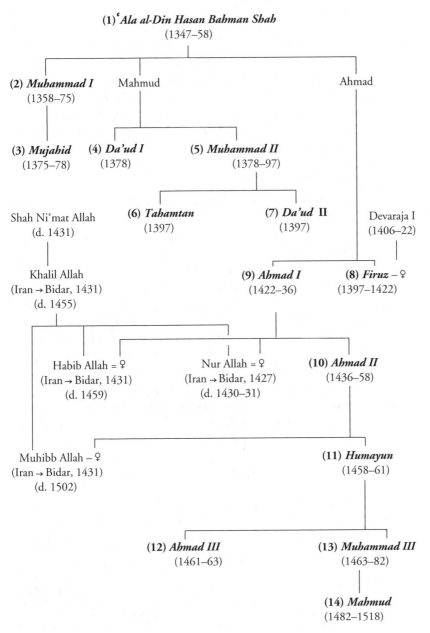

(1) *'Ala al-Din Hasan Bahman Shah*
(1347–58)

(2) *Muhammad I*   Mahmud   Ahmad
(1358–75)

(3) *Mujahid*   **(4)** *Da'ud I*   **(5)** *Muhammad II*
(1375–78)   (1378)   (1378–97)

Shah Ni'mat Allah   **(6)** *Tahamtan*   **(7)** *Da'ud II*   Devaraja I
(d. 1431)   (1397)   (1397)   (1406–22)

Khalil Allah   **(9)** *Ahmad I*   **(8)** *Firuz* – ♀
(Iran → Bidar, 1431)   (1422–36)   (1397–1422)
(d. 1455)

Habib Allah = ♀   Nur Allah = ♀   **(10)** *Ahmad II*
(Iran → Bidar, 1431)   (Iran → Bidar, 1427)   (1436–58)
(d. 1459)   (d. 1430–31)

Muhibb Allah – ♀   **(11)** *Humayun*
(Iran → Bidar, 1431)   (1458–61)
(d. 1502)

(12) *Ahmad III*   **(13)** *Muhammad III*
(1461–63)   (1463–82)

(14) *Mahmud*
(1482–1518)

demand delivery of a bride to his court at Gulbarga in the manner that Akbar would build up his harem in the Mughal court, Firuz indulged in a leisurely wedding celebration at Deva Raya I's own capital, where the Vijayanagara king presided over ceremonies. For forty days a great processional market stretched along the road between Vijayanagara and Firuz's camp, some twenty-one miles outside the great city. The bride having been brought to the sultan's camp, she and Firuz proceeded to the city gate, where Deva Raya I greeted his daughter and royal son-in-law. From there the two kings rode together in great pomp to the royal palace, along a six-mile road lined with velvet and satin fabrics, and strewn with flowers. For three days Firuz stayed as a guest at Deva Raya I's palace, amidst much feasting and exchanging of gifts.[43]

Firuz's lavish wedding ceremony epitomized an era of considerable cultural exchange across the Deccan plateau. When he returned to his capital from Vijayanagara, the sultan brought with him 2,000 male and female slaves, singers, dancers, and musicians.[44] Their arts would certainly have been indigenous to Karnataka, the area from which the Sangama house had sprung. Complementing that south-to-north flow of Deccani culture into the Bahmani court, Persian culture flowed in the reverse direction into indigenous courts. A case in point is the Telugu chieftain Kapaya Nayaka, who led the rebellion that drove the Tughluqs out of Sultanpur/Warangal in 1336 and who then ruled over Telangana for the next thirty years. One contemporary inscription compared him in majesty with the last Kakatiya ruler, Pratapa Rudra.[45] But he also adopted the Persianized title "Sultan of the Andhra country." And he took care to preserve from destruction, and probably himself used, the only Tughluq monument that survived the overthrow of Delhi's rule in Sultanpur/Warangal – the Tughluqs' stunning audience hall, known today as the "Khush Mahal" (see Plate 3).[46] Finally, the Telugu chieftain patronized the construction of one of the most potent symbols of Bahmani royal power, the famous Turquoise Throne, which he gave to Sultan Muhammad I in 1361.[47]

---

[43] Briggs, *Rise*, II:238–39.   [44] *Ibid.*, II:238.

[45] Cynthia Talbot, *Precolonial India in Practice: Society, Region, and Identity in Medieval Andhra* (New York, 2001), 178.

[46] See Phillip B. Wagoner, "Delhi, Warangal, and Kakatiya Historical Memory," in *Deccan Studies* 1, no. 1 (January–June 2002): 24–27.

[47] Briggs, *History*, II:189–90; Firishta, *Tarikh*, I:288. Crafted by Telugu artisans, the throne was framed in ebony, covered with plates of pure gold, studded with precious gems, and enameled with a turquoise hue. It had originally been built for Sultan Muhammad bin Tughluq, probably intended as tribute during the period that the Tughluqs ruled Sultanpur/Warangal (1323–36). But the Tughluqs were driven out of Warangal before the throne could be delivered to Delhi. Ultimately, Kapaya Nayaka transferred it to Sultan Muhammad I (1358–75) as part of a treaty agreement in which the two rulers fixed their common border. It was then used by every Bahmani ruler until the last, Sultan Mahmud (1482–1518), who dismantled it for its valuable gems.

But the flow of Persian cultural influence into the Deccan quickened dramatically during Firuz's reign (1397–1422). When he rose to power, the most lavish patron of the Persian arts and arguably the mightiest ruler on earth was the Central Asian conqueror Timur (r. 1370–1405). Throughout the Persian-speaking world, Timur's dazzling court at Samarqand had set the international standard in matters of architecture, aesthetic sensibility, and imperial ambition. Like other aspiring rulers of the day, Firuz held the Turkish prince in awe. Soon after Timur's destructive invasion of north India and his sacking of Delhi in 1398–99, the Bahmani sultan prudently sent ambassadors and gifts to Timur's court, begging to be counted among the Central Asian's dependents. In return, Timur graciously offered Firuz sovereignty over Malwa and Gujarat – even though neither sovereign had ever conquered these regions – and, addressing him as his son (*farzand*), sent the Bahmani king a belt, a gilded sword, four royal robes (*qaba*), a Turkish slave, and four splendid horses.[48]

Timur's destruction of Delhi stimulated Firuz's ambitions in still other ways. With that ruined city only a shadow of its former self, the capitals of India's provincial sultanates now vied for Delhi's legacy of power and splendor. For his part, Firuz was determined to make Gulbarga the most splendid of these provincial capitals, a true successor to Delhi's former glory. Each year he sent ships from his kingdom's two principal western seaports, Goa and Chaul, to the Persian Gulf to recruit talented men of letters, administrators, soldiers, and artisans.[49] In 1399, on the heels of Timur's destruction of Delhi, the sultan embarked on a building project that, like Akbar's Fatehpur Sikri, gave outlet to his architectural sensibilities and creative energies – the palace-city of Firuzabad. Located seventeen miles south of Gulbarga, the city was adorned with shops, wide streets, a citadel that opened out onto the Bhima River, sumptuous apartments for the king's harem and servants, and a mosque double the size of Gulbarga's royal mosque.[50]

This was the context in which the ambitious and learned Sultan Firuz seized the opportunity of having Gisu Daraz, the spiritual successor to India's most distinguished Sufi order and a scholar of formidable repute, come and adorn his court at Gulbarga. Firuz's capital would now become the true heir to the legacy of the recently ruined Delhi. News that Gisu Daraz had accepted the invitation delighted the sultan. When the shaikh reached Gulbarga in late 1399 or early 1400, Firuz rode up to the capital from his palace in Firuzabad to give

---

[48] Firishta, *Tarikh*, i:312; Briggs, *Rise*, ii:234. [49] Briggs, *Rise*, ii:227.
[50] See George Michell and Richard Eaton, *Firuzabad: Palace City of the Deccan* (Oxford, 1992).

a warm welcome to the saintly newcomer. He also encouraged his nobles to visit him. Everything seemed promising; it was a happy beginning.

Although there is some controversy over the site of the shaikh's original hospice in Gulbarga, local residents identify it with a low-lying rectangular building located behind a shaded garden just outside the moat and massive walls of the fort's western gate. If that was indeed the site of his original *khanaqah*, it was not his permanent dwelling. A major event in the careers of both the sultan and the shaikh occurred some time before 1409, when Gisu Daraz shifted his residence – or more accurately, was obliged to shift his residence – to another site at considerable distance to the east of the fort.[51] Our sources differ as to why this shift took place, but they all agree that it resulted from a bitter falling out that had occurred between the two men. On the basis of contemporary chronicles now lost to us, Firishta reported that the sultan found Gisu Daraz "deficient in the external sciences ['*ilm-i zahiri*]" – that is, in the very branches of knowledge, such as rhetoric or geometry, in which the sultan himself had excelled, and even lectured on. As a result, the sultan withdrew his support for the shaikh. What is more, Firuz's younger brother Ahmad, who had loyally supported his older brother throughout their lives, publicly displayed great personal veneration for the shaikh, attending his lectures, distributing money to those attending the *khanaqah*'s musical sessions, and even building a residence for him – by tradition, the above-mentioned dwelling just beyond the fort's western gate.

The rift between Firuz and Gisu Daraz widened further when Firuz failed to secure the shaikh's support for his plan to be succeeded by his son Hasan, described by Firishta as a "weak and dissipated" prince. "To one chosen by the king," the shaikh humbly responded to Firuz's request, "the prayers of a poor beggar could be of no avail." Disappointed, the king repeated his request. This time, the shaikh bluntly replied that the crown was destined for his brother Ahmad. Angered at the response, Firuz ordered Gisu Daraz to leave the city, on the trumped up grounds that the shaikh's *khanaqah* was situated so close to the fort that the huge crowds attending his sessions posed a security threat to the capital. The old shaikh obediently moved his residence to a site several miles east of the fort, where his tomb-shrine is presently located.[52]

---

[51] Although the precise date of the move is not known, it is known that Gisu Daraz's elder son Saiyid Akbar died in 1409 and was buried next to Gisu Daraz's present shrine. Since Chishti saints were customarily buried at the site of their *khanaqah*s, Akbar and his father must have been living there at the time of the former's death. See Muhammad Suleman Siddiqi, *The Bahmani Sufis* (Delhi, 1989), 144–45.

[52] Firishta, *Tarikh*, 1:316; Briggs, *Rise*, 11:240.

But more was involved here than politics. One of Gisu Daraz's followers and earliest biographers writes of the shaikh's theological conflicts with the Bahmani court. Even while in Delhi, records Muhammad ʿAli Samani, Gisu Daraz had a history of such conflicts with the Tughluq court.[53] In the Deccan, religious tensions surfaced shortly after 1403, when Maulana ʿAla al-Din Gwaliori, the shaikh at whose home in Gwalior Gisu Daraz had stayed while fleeing Delhi several years earlier, came down to Gulbarga to study some classic mystical texts with Gisu Daraz. These included the *Tamhidat* by ʿAyn al-Qudah al-Hamadhani (d. 1121), the *Savanih* by Ahmad Ghazali (d. 1126), and the *Fusus al-hikam* by Ibn al-ʿArabi (d. 1240).

It was the last book – an exposition on how the careers of twenty-seven Islamic prophets corresponded to divine attributes – that incited suspicion in official circles, not just in Gulbarga, but throughout the medieval Islamic world. Claiming that the *Fusus* was not written by himself, but by divine dictations received from visionary encounters with the Prophet Muhammad, Ibn al-ʿArabi seemed to have shed the veils that, for most Muslims, separated ordinary humans from prophets, or even from God. Not surprisingly, the great Spanish Arab mystic drew charges of being delusionary, even heretical.[54] And consequently, even though Gisu Daraz was himself critical of Ibn al-ʿArabi's thought,[55] when word reached the court that the shaikh was teaching the *Fusus*, scholars close to the sultan voiced their view that the book was theologically deviant and that the court should deputize somebody to investigate exactly what Gisu Daraz had been saying. For this purpose a secretary named Khwaja Ahmad Dabir was dispatched to the shaikh's *khanaqah*. Upon arriving at the hospice and interacting with the shaikh's circle of devotees and students, however, Ahmad Dabir got swept into the

---

[53] It seems that a Tughluq prince once asked to see one of Gisu Daraz's books, in which the shaikh had argued that God's coexisting diversity pervades nature. Having read the book, the prince complained to another shaikh that Gisu Daraz's position was contrary to Islamic law. When the other shaikh failed to support Gisu Daraz's view, the prince took the matter to the Sultan of Delhi, Firuz Tughluq, who ordered several trusted religious scholars to investigate the matter. They did, and Gisu Daraz satisfied all of them that what he had been teaching did not contradict Islamic law. Samani, *Siyar*, 70–73.

[54] See Nile Green, "The Religious and Cultural Roles of Dreams and Visions in Islam," *Journal of the Royal Asiatic Society* 13, no. 3 (November 2003), 287–313. For details, see Ibn alʿArabi, *The Bezels of Wisdom*. Trans. R. W. J. Austin (New York, 1980), esp. 16–26. For a discussion of the theological controversies that swept over the Muslim world respecting Ibn al-ʿArabi's thought, and the way that subsequent writers wrongly attributed to him a position of strict ontological monism – which they, not the Great Shaikh himself, called *wahdat al-wujud* – see William C. Chittick, "Rumi and *Wahdat al-Wujud*," in *Poetry and Mysticism in Islam: the Heritage of Rumi*, ed. Amin Banani, Richard Hovannisian, and Georges Sabagh (New York, 1994), 70–111.

[55] Syed Shah Khusro Hussaini, "Gisudaraz on *Wahdat al-wujud*," *Studies in Islam* (October 1982): 233–45.

spiritual life of the place and ultimately became himself one of Gisu Daraz's disciples.[56]

It is by no means certain that the court's theological disagreements with Gisu Daraz were in fact the cause of the shaikh's forced relocation. Both theological and political considerations probably lay behind the rift between sultan and shaikh. Given Prince Ahmad's devotion to Gisu Daraz, the court's theological differences with the shaikh would only have aggravated a political rivalry between the two brothers. In any event, despite Gisu Daraz's relocation, relations between Sultan Firuz and Gisu Daraz were never reconciled, and in fact appear to have worsened over the years, as did, too, relations between the two brothers. The final rupture occurred when Firuz, old and infirm, and still trying to secure his son's succession to the throne, plotted to have his brother blinded. Learning of this, Ahmad, together with his own son 'Ala al-Din, paid a fateful visit to Gisu Daraz's relocated *khanaqah* to obtain the shaikh's blessings and advice. The climax of the meeting came when the shaikh removed the turban from his head and, dividing it into two parts, tied one part on Ahmad's head and the other on 'Ala al-Din's. The symbolism was clear: both Ahmad and his son were destined to ascend the Turquoise Throne.[57]

Now came the final denouement. Gathering his supporters, Ahmad stole away from the fort at dawn the next morning, September 22, 1422, and when rival factions of cavalry skirmished later that day, Firuz's supporters simply melted away. Realizing the futility of his son's cause, the sultan ordered the fort's gates opened and welcomed his brother to his bedside. After a tearful reconciliation, Ahmad crowned himself – but with no shaikh present, not even Gisu Daraz – and took his seat on the Bahmani throne. Ten days later Firuz died; a month later under a full moon, Gisu Daraz, too, passed away.

Shortly after the shaikh's death, the grave-site of Gisu Daraz grew to become the most popular Muslim shrine in the Deccan, as it has remained ever since. As Firishta wrote, "the inhabitants of the Deccan chose him for their guide in religious affairs, so that his residence became a place of pilgrimage to all sects."[58] The historian went even further, making the remarkable observation that

a Deccani, on being once asked whom he considered the greater personage, the Prophet Muhammad or the Saiyid, replied, *with some surprise at the question*, that although the Prophet was undoubtedly a great man, yet Saiyid Muhammad Gisu Daraz was a far superior order of being.[59]

[56] Samani, *Siyar*, 54, 143–46.   [57] Firishta, *Tarikh*, 1:317; Briggs, *Rise*, II:242.
[58] Firishta, *Tarikh*, 1:319; Briggs, *Rise*, II:245. The text reads *mutaf-i jahanian*, or "pilgrimage center for all creatures/creation."
[59] Firishta, *Tarikh*, 1:319; Briggs, *Rise*, II:245–46. Emphasis mine.

How was it that a resident of the medieval Deccan could be surprised that one might even attempt comparing the Prophet Muhammad with Gisu Daraz?

Several factors favored Gisu Daraz's rapid rise to such an exalted status, two of them initiated by his royal disciple, Sultan Ahmad. First, the new king honored the memory of his former benefactor by constructing the magnificent mausoleum that stands on his grave-site today. Second, he conferred land grants on the descendants of the shaikh. These actions served to institutionalize the shaikh's cult by creating a physical monument and an economic base both for it and for the shaikh's descendants. A third factor was initiated by Gisu Daraz himself. By designating his younger son, Saiyid Asghar, as his spiritual successor (*sajjada-nishin*), the shaikh stabilized the transmission of his spiritual authority over time, since that authority now came to rest on the principle of hereditary succession, and not on that of appointment.[60] Perhaps most importantly, Gisu Daraz – like Delhi's Nizam al-Din Auliya at the height of Tughluq power – happened to be associated with the court of an Indo-Muslim state at the moment of its political and cultural ascendancy. Despite his troubles with Sultan Firuz, this association seems to have lent a luster to the saint that would long outlast the state itself.

For his part, however, Sultan Ahmad did not take as his own spiritual adviser any of the progeny of Gisu Daraz. Nor did he patronize the family of shaikhs that had been most closely associated with the first fifty years of Bahmani royal power, that of Siraj al-Din Junaidi. Evidently considering any of the spiritual lineages associated with his ancestors as too enmeshed in politics – a bloody legacy that had seen two of his eight royal predecessors assassinated and two others blinded – Sultan Ahmad resolved to wipe the slate clean and embark on a new policy. He would ignore all shaikhs then residing in his kingdom and instead import from abroad men of spiritual eminence who had had no prior contact with Gulbarga's murderous politics.

Having heard of a renowned shaikh then residing in Kirman, in southeastern Iran, Sultan Ahmad looked to the west. This was Shah Ni'mat Allah Wali (d. 1431), the founder of a minor branch of the Qadiri Sufi order who had already gained luster by spending some time living in the heart of the domain of the great Timur. In the hagiographic tradition, Shah Ni'mat Allah gained even more luster by defiantly rejecting Timur's patronage, around 1369, with the brave – and probably hyperbolic – words:

---

[60] See Simon Digby, "*Tabarrukat* and Succession among the Great Chishti Shaykhs of the Delhi Sultanate," in *Delhi through the Ages*, ed. R. E. Frykenberg (New York, 1986), 63–103.

Off with you, my prince!
Don't flaunt gold and silver before me! . . .
While your domain stretches
from China to Shiraz,
Mine is a realm
which has no frontier.[61]

As Sultan Ahmad was hardly in Timur's league when it came to world-conquering, to lure to his court a shaikh who had defied the most powerful sovereign of the world would have been an exceptional achievement. Accordingly, Ahmad sent a delegation to Kirman, Iran, inviting the shaikh to settle in the Deccan. When Shah Ni'mat Allah declined the invitation, Ahmad sent a second delegation that repeated his request. This time the Iranian sent in his place his grandson, Nur Allah, to whom the sultan gave a special residence and even his own daughter in marriage. Soon thereafter, most of Shah Ni'mat Allah's family would emigrate from Iran to the Bahmani court where they enjoyed state patronage for the rest of the dynasty's history.[62]

SUMMARY

The arrival of north Indian Sufis in the Deccan during the fourteenth and fifteenth centuries wrought deep changes in the region's political and religious fabric. Whereas Khalji and early Tughluq invasions of the plateau had lacked a moral basis, being undertaken simply for plunder or tribute, the extension of the Sufis' notion of spiritual sovereignty (*wilayat*) in the region lent moral legitimacy to the planting of subsequent Indo-Muslim political authority (*hukumat*). No longer available for plunder, such land – its people, its produce, and its fixed assets (including temples) – now merited state protection. In the language of classical Islam, the presence and blessings of great Sufi shaikhs could transform yesterday's Abode of War (*Dar al-Harb*) into today's Abode of Peace (*Dar al-Islam*), thereby bringing about an internally coherent basis for the transplanting of legitimate Indo-Muslim rule and civilization from region to region within South Asia.

As vessels into which God's favor was believed to have been poured, great shaikhs thus exercised a quasi-political dominion over the lands in which they resided. Muslim rulers naturally sought the blessings of such men to help secure

---

[61] Cited in Terry Graham, "Shah Ni'matullah Wali: Founder of the Ni'matullahi Sufi Order," in *The Heritage of Sufism*, ed. Leonard Lewisohn, vol. 2: *Legacy of Medieval Persian Sufism (1150–1500)* (Oxford, 1999), 183. See also Jean Aubin, *Matériaux pour la Biographie de Shah Ni'matullah Wali Kermani* (Teheran and Paris, 1956), 8–19.

[62] Graham, "Shah Ni'matullah Wali," 184–85.

their own claims to legitimate authority, especially in areas not previously ruled by Muslims. Because the rise of the Chishti order of shaikhs coincided with that of Khalji and Tughluq power in north India, Chishti shaikhs were especially well positioned to confer legitimacy on fledgling Indo-Islamic states beyond Delhi. A legitimate Indo-Islamic presence in the Deccan was thus inaugurated in 1329 with the arrival in colonial Daulatabad of Burhan al-Din Gharib, on whom Nizam al-Din Auliya had bequeathed spiritual sovereignty over the Deccan. Legitimate *independent* Indo-Muslim rule in the region, however, had to await the coronation of Sultan 'Ala al-Din Hasan Bahman Shah in 1347, when the mantle of the Prophet, passed down to Burhan al-Din's successor, Shaikh Zain al-Din Shirazi, was conferred on the new ruler. But the maintenance of that legitimacy required the continued presence and blessings of such shaikhs, and by the time Sultan Firuz rose to power in 1397, the great shaikhs who had played decisive roles in launching the Bahmani state had all died. So with the unexpected arrival in Gulbarga of Gisu Daraz, who followed in direct succession from the main trunk of north India's illustrious genealogy of Chishti shaikhs, Firuz Bahmani was presented with a golden opportunity such as his predecessors had never had.

Once settled in Gulbarga, however, Gisu Daraz experienced problems with Firuz that, while purely political on one level, and theological at another, stemmed from irreconcilable conceptions of the nature and limits of sovereign authority. Unlike small-time shaikhs or ordinary sycophants, as Simon Digby has noted, the great shaikhs were obliged by their own pretensions to reject courtly patronage. This meant that their own *khanaqah*s could become a refuge *from* sovereign authority, or even an alternative to that authority.[63] The *khanaqah* of Gisu Daraz provided precisely such a refuge, and for none other than the sultan's own brother. From Firuz's perspective, moreover, Gisu Daraz's visible independence from the court was made all the more intolerable when the shaikh flaunted musical sessions and theologically suspect lectures in a thronged residence located just outside the fort's walls, nearly under the sultan's nose. Of course, had the sultan wanted to be completely rid of the shaikh, he could have publicly suggested a pilgrimage to Mecca, a proposal few

---

[63] Writes Digby: "If a major Sufi *shaykh* laid claims to *wilayat* or spiritual rule over a territory which the Sultan held by the force of his arms and ordered through the civil administration, he could ill afford to be seen to be under the Sultan's patronage, as indicated by such gestures as accepting largesse, alms or grants, directly from the Sultan . . . From the point of view of the Sultan, the failure of the *shaykh* to perform such gestures might constitute a threat to his authority, because of the visible independence of the *shaykh* from that authority and the possibility that the *shaykh*'s *khanaqah* might provide a refuge and a rallying point for dissidents and plotters against it." Digby, "Sufi Shaykh," 71.

men of piety could refuse. In medieval India, this was indeed a common ploy for deporting undesirable Muslim subjects. Gisu Daraz's immense popularity with the masses, however, seems to have prevented Firuz from attempting this subtle form of expulsion.

Gisu Daraz and Sultan Firuz, then, seemed locked in a fatal embrace from which neither could become fully extricated, each one simultaneously needing while repelling the other. Sultan Ahmad, who initially rejected contact with *all* shaikhs, seems to have understood this. By importing from a distant land not a great shaikh but the *sons* and *grandsons* of a great shaikh, he overcame difficulties in two ways. First, coming from Iran, the Ni'mat Allahi family had no prior record of involvement in Gulbarga's deadly politics. And second, because those offspring were spiritually lesser lights than the great shaikh himself, they had no qualms about accepting the poisoned chalice of courtly patronage, or even marrying into the royal family.

Ahmad's recruitment and patronage of the Ni'mat Allahi family thus solved the problem of reconciling the courtly and Sufi claims to Islamic authority. And yet the wider policy in which he found that solution – that of systematically recruiting scholars, administrators, military men from abroad – created another, unexpected problem: a conflict between families of long-standing residence in the Deccan, and newcomers from overseas who had never detached themselves mentally or culturally from their homelands. This helped create a rift that would tear Deccani society apart, a process to which we now turn our attention.

CHAPTER 3

MAHMUD GAWAN (1411–1481): DECCANIS AND WESTERNERS

The sultan [Ahmad Bahmani II, r. 1436–58] . . . ordered that, both at court and in cavalry formation, the Westerners should appear on the right side, while the Deccanis and Ethiopians should be on the left. From that time to the present, an inveterate hostility has taken hold between the Deccanis and Westerners, and whenever they get the chance, the former have engaged in killing the latter.[1]

Muhammad Qasim Firishta (d. 1611)

BY THE DOCKS OF DABHOL, 1453

Sometime in 1453, the same year that the Ottoman conquest of Constantinople carried Persian civilization to the frontiers of Europe, a high-born Iranian merchant named Mahmud Gawan stepped onto India's western shores. Then forty-two years of age, Gawan arrived aboard a merchant ship that had sailed down the Persian Gulf and across the Arabian Sea, docking at Dabhol on the Konkan coast. The ports of Chaul and Dabhol, located respectively some twenty and eighty-five miles south of modern Mumbai, were the Bahmani sultanate's two principal windows on the wider world to the west (see Map 3). For the next several centuries, the two ports would link states of the Deccan ever more tightly with that world – a world permeated with Persian art, thought, cuisine, language, literature, dress, styles of piety, and models of comportment. Hailing from an aristocratic family of northern Iran, Gawan himself represented the most refined and cosmopolitan vision of contemporary Persian culture.

From the docks of Dabhol, Gawan oversaw the off-loading of the consignments he had brought with him from Iran to India: silken fabrics, Turkish and Ethiopian slaves, pearls, jewels, and Arabian horses. He knew that all of these goods, especially the last, would fetch fine prices along the ports of the Konkan coast. From these ports, caravans would wend their way up the narrow defiles of the Sahyadri Mountains and carry goods like his to the markets and urban centers of the Deccan plateau. Heavy warhorses were in special demand, since in the Deccan, as in India generally, state power rested ultimately on

---

[1] Muhammad Qasim Firishta, *Tarikh-i Firishta* (Lucknow, 1864–65), 1:332; my translation.

units of mounted archers. But since the kind of grains produced in South Asia were unsuitable for raising large warhorses, the latter had constantly to be imported from outside. Moreover, regular trade between the Deccan and north India had virtually ceased ever since the Bahmanis revolted against their former Tughluq overlords a century earlier. As a result, horses could no longer be brought to the Deccan overland from Central Asia and north India, but had to be shipped across the Arabian Sea. Little wonder, then, that merchants like Mahmud Gawan were attracted to ports like Dabhol, and that once on shore, they found willing buyers, agents, and transporters.

Gawan had planned to proceed from Dabhol up to Delhi. But first, he wished to visit Bidar, then the Bahmani capital, in order "to sit at the feet" of Shah Muhibb Allah Kirmani. This was a grandson of the same Shah Niʻmat Allah Wali whom Sultan Ahmad I had earlier tried to recruit to Bidar from Iran.[2] He also happened to be the reigning sultan's son-in-law and Bidar's most politically connected man of religion. Meeting such a person could only have enhanced Gawan's career prospects with the Bahmani state. Of course, commercial interests also drove Mahmud Gawan's desire to proceed to Bidar. Sitting one day in the shop of a fellow merchant shortly after his arrival in Dabhol, he observed a grand procession passing in great pomp and ceremony through the streets of the town. At its head, carried on a litter and holding a nightingale, was the town's governor. Aware of the prices his goods could fetch at the centers of political power further inland, Gawan arranged an interview with the man. In making his request to visit the Bahmani court, Gawan stressed to the governor that he was no ordinary horse merchant, but an Iranian of cultivated background who had traveled, among other places, through Anatolia, Syria, Egypt, and Turkistan.[3] He might also have mentioned that during his travels he had declined offers to serve as chief minister in the courts of Khurasan and Iraq.

As Gawan had hoped, his petition was favorably received at the court of Sultan Ahmad II Bahmani, who welcomed the newcomer not just because of the prospects of acquiring fine Arabian warhorses. Persian or Persianized men of talent had been in increasing demand ever since the Bahmanis' anti-Tughluq revolution more than a century earlier, in 1347. Cut off from north India both politically and commercially, the Bahmani court had to look across the Arabian Sea for both administrative talent and warhorses. Men of letters were

---

[2] Haroon Khan Sherwani, *Mahmud Gawan, the Great Bahmani Wazir* (Allahabad, 1942), 73.
[3] Rafiʼ al-Din Shirazi, *Tazkirat al-muluk*, extracts trans. J. S. King, "History of the Bahmani Dynasty," *Indian Antiquary* 28 (August 1899): 218.

also targeted for recruitment. As an early case in point, Sultan Muhammad II (r. 1378–97) had tried to entice Hafiz, the great poet of Shiraz, to come and adorn the Bahmani court at Gulbarga. In response, the poet traveled as far as the port of Hormuz on the Persian Gulf and even boarded a special Bahmani ship lying in anchor there. But when a storm arose, the apprehensive poet lost heart and stepped back ashore. Instead of receiving one of the greatest Persian poets of all time, the Bahmani sultan had to settle for a nicely crafted poem that Hafiz composed and arranged to be delivered to Bidar.[4]

Subsequent rulers were more successful in their search for overseas talent. Both sultans Firuz and Ahmad I, whose combined reigns spanned the years 1397–1436, lived under the long shadow cast over Asia by Timur (d. 1405). By patronizing dazzling architectural monuments in Central Asia and Iran, and by attracting the finest men of Persian letters to his court, Timur had established a model of imperial splendor that many potentates would emulate. Among these was Firuz. Fancying himself playing on a larger geo-political stage than had his ancestors, the Bahmani sultan embarked on a project of aggressively attracting to his court Iranians or Persianized men of talent. Annually, he sent ships from Konkani seaports to find and recruit to the Bahmani court the brightest stars of the Persian world.[5] The pace of immigration gathered even more momentum during the reigns of Firuz's two successors, his brother Ahmad and the latter's son 'Ala al-Din, who reigned as Ahmad II from 1436 to 1458. The elder Ahmad, in addition to recruiting the family of Shah Ni'mat Allah Wali from Kirman, recruited a body of 3,000 archers from the Persian Gulf and the Khurasan regions to form the kingdom's élite fighting corps.[6]

Known in contemporary sources as *gharbian*, or "Westerners" – i.e., people who had come from lands west of India – Persianized immigrants were given top positions in the Bahmani military and political apparatus. This is revealed in lists of prominent figures who served the Bahmani state, since Persian last names often indicate one's own or one's paternal ancestor's place of origin. Table 1 lists the names of such men active between 1422 and 1458, the period immediately preceding and following Gawan's own arrival. One sees that although some had come from the Arab Middle East (i.e., Basra, Karbala), the majority had originated in the Persian-speaking world of Khurasan, Afghanistan, Central Asia, or Iran. Possessing a population base roughly ten times that of the more sparsely populated Iranian plateau, South

---

[4] Firishta, *Tarikh*, I:302; John Briggs, *History of the Rise of the Mahomedan Power in India* (London, 1829: repr. Calcutta, 1966), II:215.

[5] Firishta, *Tarikh*, I:308; Briggs, *Rise*, II:227.   [6] Firishta, *Tarikh*, I:322; Briggs, *Rise*, II:249.

Table 1 *Some prominent Westerners in Bahmani service, 1422–58.*

Dilawar Khan Afghan	Iftikhar al-Mulk Hamadani
Khwaja Hasan Ardistani	Mir Abu'l-Qasim Jurjani
Khwaja-i Jahan Astarabadi	'Ubaid Allah Kabuli
Khalaf Hasan Basri	Saiyid Nasir al-Din Karbala'i
Mir Farrukh Badakhshi	Shah Khalil Allah Kirmani
Saiyid Husain Badakhshi	Mullah Qutb al-Din Kirmani
Jalal Khan Bukhari	'Abd Allah Kurd
Majnun Sultan Changezi	Rustam Khan Mazandarani
Quli Sultan Changezi	Mir Shams al-Din Qummi
Mahmud Gawan Gilani	Qasim Beg Safshikan
Saiyid Hanif Gilani	Khwaja 'Imad al-Din Simnani
'Imad al-Mulk Ghuri	Mir 'Ali Sistani
Saif Allah Hasanabadi	Khusrau Uzbek

Source: H. K. Sherwani, *Bahmanis of the Deccan*, 132–61, *passim.*

Asia generated a total wealth many times greater than that of Iran. As a result, the richer courts of South Asia could lavish far more patronage on rising literati or ambitious fortune-seekers than could the more meager courts of Iran or Central Asia.[7] The Konkan coast, moreover, had for centuries lured maritime merchants seeking the source of India's fabled textiles, pepper, and spices, as well as destination markets for the valuable horse trade.

Mahmud Gawan's own career exhibits the entire range of motives for mobile Iranians to come to the Deccan. In addition to "pull" factors such as his desire to sell horses to the Bahmani court and to take blessings from that kingdom's leading shaikh, "push" factors were also involved. Born into a family of aristocrats who had served as ministers to a small kingdom in Gilan (on the southwestern shores of the Caspian Sea), Gawan seemed destined to follow the family tradition and never leave home. But after his father's death, he grew disgusted with local politics on learning that both the kingdom's minister and the commander of the army had intrigued against him at court. Finally, his widowed mother advised her sons to leave Gilan and its nasty political environment, which they both did. His brother set out for Mecca, whereas Mahmud embarked on a journey that, combining study with trade, took him

---

[7] In 1563 Shaikh Husain al-Harithi, while living in Bahrain in self-imposed exile having been sacked from Iran's Safavid court, advised his son, "If you seek this world alone, then go to India. If you desire the next world, then you must come to Bahrain. But if you desire neither this world nor the afterlife, then stay in Iran." Devin J. Stewart, "The First *Shaykh al-Islam* of the Safavid Capital Qazvin," *Journal of the American Oriental Society*, 116, no. 3 (1996): 390.

through Khurasan, Iraq, Egypt, and Syria. While cultivating a taste for learning, which he indulged especially in Cairo and Damascus, Gawan also enjoyed success as a merchant. When he reached Dabhol's harbor in 1453, he brought with him, in addition to his consignment of goods and horses, a sum of 40,000 silver coins (*lari*) for purposes of investment.[8] He also joined the stream of other Westerners who for decades had been migrating to the Deccan and had taken up service in Bidar, the Bahmani capital.

GULBARGA AND BIDAR: TWO BAHMANI CAPITALS

How did Bidar become the capital? Residents of Delhi know that there is no one "Delhi," but many. Seeking to dissociate themselves from defeated or discredited predecessors, the founders of each new ruling dynasty following the slave kings – the Khaljis, the Tughluqs, the Lodis, the Suris, the Mughals, the British – built a new complex of buildings as their capital, spatially distinct from those of their immediate predecessors.

Something of this sort had happened in the Deccan when the Bahmanis shifted their capital from Daulatabad, which had been associated with the imperial Tughluqs against whom they had rebelled, to a new capital at Gulbarga. The process was repeated after Sultan Firuz's death in 1422. Even though sovereign rule in this instance passed directly from brother to brother, the change more closely resembled a dynastic revolution. Aware that four of his eight predecessors on the Turquoise Throne had been either assassinated or blinded, Firuz's brother Ahmad was well acquainted with Gulbarga's murderously vicious political atmosphere. Moreover, the city's spiritual continuity was broken with the passing of his own patron, Gisu Daraz, who died the same year his brother Firuz did.

Determined, then, to make a clean break with the past, Sultan Ahmad I abandoned Gulbarga altogether and built a new city. In 1424, two years after his accession, he transferred his capital to Bidar, a former Chalukya (974–1190) and occasional Yadava (1185–1317) or Kakatiya (1163–1323) fort located some sixty miles northeast of Gulbarga (see Map 3).[9] Occupying the heart of the Deccan plateau, this new site perfectly straddled the fault lines separating all three of the Deccan's major cultural regions – the Kannada-speaking southwest, the Marathi-speaking west and northwest, and the Telugu-speaking east. By not

[8] Sherwani, *Mahmud Gawan*, 21–26; Briggs, *Rise*, II:316.
[9] For a study of the full range of changes accompanying the shift of the capital – ideological, social, mystical – see Muhammad Suleman Siddiqi, "Ethnic Change in the Bahmanid Society at Bidar, 1422–1538," *Islamic Culture* 60, no. 3 (July 1986): 61–80.

being firmly nested within any single linguistic region, Bidar was ideally suited as the capital of an aspiring transregional sultanate on the model of Timur's own sprawling empire. The Bahmani state in its post-1424 phase thus marked the Deccan's first truly imperial formation since the eclipse of the Chalukyas in the late twelfth century.[10] Indeed, with Delhi's last capital, Tughluqabad, largely ruined by Timur's raids just several decades earlier, fifteenth-century Bidar could lay claim to being India's most imposing imperial center.

The new capital consisted of a city, a fort, and within the latter, a citadel.[11] Completed in 1432, the citadel measures some 300 by 500 yards and rests on the southern edge of a spacious plateau about two-and-a-half miles in circumference, bounded by natural escarpments to the north and east. The plateau is entirely enclosed by the fort's walls, with their thirty-seven bastions and seven gates. On its southern side, the citadel is entered from the town by a series of gates and draw-bridges (see Plate 4). The latter span three moats that are thirty feet deep, hewn from solid laterite rock.

Architecturally, Ahmad I's palaces clearly reflect the influence of Timur, whose capital at Samarqand projected an image of awesome splendor and might. Bidar's citadel included a Royal Chamber (Takht Mahal), a Hall of Public Audience, the Naubat Khana, the Lal Bagh, and the Tarkash Mahal, together with mosques, pavilions, kitchens, courtyards, gardens, cisterns, and ditches. Breaking from the tradition of low, squat, and stilted arches found in Gulbarga, architects at Bidar, influenced by the more sweeping vision of Timurid Samarqand and Herat, built structures reaching a height of over 100 feet. Timurid influence is especially clear in the entrance to the citadel's Royal Chamber, whose tall arches (thirty-five feet) and graceful spandrels with lion and sun motifs recall Timur's own Aq Saray palace at Shahr-i Sabz (1379–96), where the spandrels of the entrance-way arches also portrayed lion and sun images.[12] Similarly, the adjacent Hall of Public Audience, which measures 166 feet by 133 feet and housed the Turquoise Throne, was covered with a

---

[10] It is no coincidence that Kalyana, capital of the Chalukya empire whose boundaries roughly corresponded to those of the Bahmanis, is located on the same fault line, only forty miles west of Bidar.

[11] The classic architectural survey is G. Yazdani, *Bidar: its History and Monuments* (Oxford, 1947).

[12] For Timur's Aq Saray palace, see Thomas W. Lentz and Glenn D. Lowry, *Timur and the Princely Vision: Persian Art and Culture in the Fifteenth Century* (Los Angeles, 1989), 42–43. Appearing later than Timur's palace, but before Bidar's Royal Chamber, was another lion/tiger motif on the gateway spandrels of the entrance of the palace area at Firuzabad, built between 1399 and 1406 by Ahmad I's brother Sultan Firuz. Clearly, both brothers were under Timur's aesthetic spell. Though only faintly visible today, the artwork on the Firuzabad spandrel presents the earliest known use of an animal motif in all Indo-Islamic architecture. See George Michell and Richard Eaton, *Firuzabad: Palace City of the Deccan* (Oxford, 1992), 80–82.

dazzling profusion of polychrome tiled paneling – glazed tiles of blue, yellow, and green, with white borders – whose geometric and calligraphic designs appertain "specifically to the lands of the Timurid state."[13]

In 1453 Mahmud Gawan first beheld these tiles, together with the Turquoise Throne, as he passed through the arched entrance-ways leading to the Hall of Public Audience for his initial meeting with Sultan Ahmad II. Clearly impressed by Gawan's credentials, the court made him a noble with a rank of 1,000.[14] In 1457 the sultan placed him at the head of a squadron of royal cavalry and sent him to the fort of Nalgonda, a Bahmani possession in Telangana, where he successfully suppressed a minor rebellion. The following year, Gawan's fortunes soared higher when Ahmad II's successor, Sultan Humayun, presented him with a golden cap and belt and appointed him chief minister (*wakil-i sultanat*) with the title Prince of Merchants (*malik al-tujjar*). In 1466, having served as a regent for two successive boy-monarchs following Humayun's death, Gawan was entrusted by Humayun's powerful widow with the general supervision of all Bahmani provinces. She also confirmed his appointment as chief minister with a bodyguard of 2,000 Turkish troops. For the next twenty-five years Gawan would hold all these posts. In official documents he would be addressed with such lofty titles as Lord of the Habitants of the Globe, Secretary of the Royal Mansion, Amir of Amirs, and Deputy of the Realm.[15]

How can one explain this meteoric rise? Given the state's dependence on imported warhorses, Gawan's initial appointment as "Prince of Merchants" doubtless acknowledged his reputation as a successful long-distance merchant who possessed valuable commercial contacts overseas. He also had non-commercial contacts, for when Sultan Humayun promoted Gawan, the king stressed the need for a minister "who should be well known the world over and who should excel in wisdom among the Arabs as well as the Persians."[16] Having already studied in Cairo and Damascus after leaving his native Iran, Gawan clearly fit the bill. Over the course of the next twenty-three years, in fact, he remained in close touch with poets, scholars, and princes throughout the Persian-speaking world, as is evidenced by his 148 surviving letters.[17]

---

[13] Yolande Crowe, "Some Glazed Tiles in 15th-century Bidar," in *Facets of Indian Art*, ed. Robert Skelton *et al.* (London, 1986), 44. A description of the citadel's audience halls is found in Yazdani, *Bidar*, 62–77.

[14] The figure indicated both the amount of revenue a noble was expected to collect from specified districts, and the number of mounted horsemen he was expected to recruit, train, and maintain for royal service.

[15] Sherwani, *Mahmud Gawan*, 119.   [16] *Ibid.*, 81.

[17] See Khwaja 'Imad al-Din Mahmud Gawan, *Riyad al-insha'*, ed. Shaikh Chand bin Husain (Hyderabad, 1948).

Twenty-four of these were addressed to reigning sovereigns of the day, the most illustrious being the Ottoman sultan Mehmet II ("the Conqueror"), who had seized Constantinople the same year Gawan reached India. Under Gawan's ministry, the two courts exchanged envoys. He also corresponded directly with the sultans of Iraq and Egypt, to whose courts he also sent embassies.[18]

His most interesting letters, however, are those sent to distant scholars and poets, whose names read like a catalog of the "best and brightest" in the contemporary Persian world. Many of these he encouraged to come and settle in Bidar, though fewer came than were invited. In his seven letters to 'Abd al-Rahman Jami (d. 1492) of Herat, Gawan on several occasions urged the great poet to visit Bidar while making a planned pilgrimage to Mecca. Although he never did visit Bidar, Jami did praise Gawan, proclaiming in one poem that owing to Gawan India had become "the envy of Rum itself" (i.e., Europe).[19] Similar recognition came from the Shirazi philosopher Jalal al-Din Dawani (d. 1502), who dedicated his *Shawakil al-Hur*, a commentary on the mystical work of Shihab al-Din Suhurawardi, to the Bahmani statesman.[20] Gawan also corresponded with Jami's teacher, the Naqshbandi Sufi 'Ubaid Allah al-Ahrar (d. 1490) of Samarqand, and with Sharf al-Din Yazdi (d. 1454) of Yazd, who authored the famous history of Timur, the *Zafar-nama*. To Abu Bakr Tehrani, too, Gawan extended an invitation to settle in Bidar, boasting that "India is famous among all eminent persons of the world, and many learned persons live here."[21] Gawan spared no rhetoric in trying to lure Shaikh Sadr al-Din Rawwasi (d. 1466–67) from Herat, stating that "had our heart not been waiting for meeting you, it would have got burnt in despair," and that only the hope of meeting him was keeping him and his men at Bidar alive.[22]

Mahmud Gawan's greatest legacy is Bidar's college, or *madrasa*, whose construction, completed in 1472, he personally commissioned.[23] Only three-quarters of the damaged monument now survives, as does just one of its

---

[18] M. A. Nayeem, "Foreign Cultural Relations of the Bahmanis (1461–81 A.D.) (Gleanings from Mahmud Gawan's *Riyazul Insha*)," in *Studies in the Foreign Relations of India*, ed. P. M. Joshi and M. A. Nayeem (Hyderabad, 1975), 394–400.
[19] Haroon Khan Sherwani, *The Bahmanis of the Deccan* (2nd edn, repr. New Delhi, 1985), 228–29.
[20] Sherwani, *Mahmud Gawan*, 199.
[21] Nayeem, "Foreign Cultural Relations," 403.
[22] *Ibid.*, 402.
[23] Over the structure's eastern facade, in blue and white glazed tiles, is inscribed a Qur'anic verse (39:73–74) that quotes the words of the guards of Paradise as they greet the faithful, "Peace be on you! ye have been good: wherefore enter ye into paradise, to remain therein for ever." Chosen by Gawan himself, the verse suggests his ideas on the benefits of knowledge.

two original minarets (see Plate 5). And only traces remain of the brilliantly colored glazed tiles that once covered its walls and minarets. Yet the college's original splendor is unmistakable even in its present state, its arches and colorful glazed tiles recalling Timurid Central Asia, and its minaret and domes reminiscent of Mamluk Egypt. Moreover, the structure's sheer monumentality and its placement in the heart of the unwalled city – not in the heavily fortified citadel or near any royal palaces – confirms what we know from Gawan's prodigious correspondence with overseas scholars, namely, that he was determined to put Bidar on the map of the Persian-speaking world as a major center of learning. Its library originally held 3,000 volumes. Thirty-six suites of rooms on three storeys accommodated more than a hundred students, and in six suites of rooms resided some twelve professors, who lectured in four vaulted halls measuring forty feet by twenty-seven feet.[24] This extraordinary place, where the chief minister himself passed many hours in study and discussion, remains the most visible legacy of Gawan's cosmopolitanism and his devotion to scholarship.

DECCANIS AND WESTERNERS

Notwithstanding Bidar's cultural enrichment owing to the court's patronage of Westerners like Mahmud Gawan, that enrichment came at a heavy cost. This was the increasing alienation of that section of the nobility, the so-called "Deccanis," that had *not* come from overseas, and which resented the favoritism the court seemed to show to immigrant newcomers. As the two principal components of the socio-political order, Deccanis and Westerners in the end became totally polarized and, as is reflected in the epigram at the head of this chapter, ultimately fell on each other with deadly violence.

From an ethnic standpoint, the Westerners included men and their families who had migrated from, or had been recruited from, regions beyond the Konkan coast. Original sources refer to merchants, scholars, administrators, or soldiers hailing from the Persian-speaking world – Central Asia, Khurasan, Iran – although Persianized Arabs are also present. Enjoying favored status at the court and bound together by a common language, these elements intermarried, coalescing over time into a bloc politically, socially, and culturally distinct from the Deccanis.

The passage of time, however, often erodes the foreignness of immigrant groups. In the Deccan, too, foreignness was never intrinsic or fixed, but a fluid,

[24] See Yazdani, *Bidar*, 91–100.

even relational category. A case in point is found in an episode related by the sixteenth-century historian 'Ali Tabataba. In 1455–56 a prominent noble, Jalal Khan, raised an insurrection on hearing the rumor, which turned out to be false, that Sultan Ahmad II had died. Jalal Khan and his son Sikandar Khan, writes Tabataba,

> had with them two or three thousand well trained and experienced cavalry, but as they counted themselves among the number of the foreigners [*ghariban*] they feared to present themselves at court . . . Their enemies used to prevent their having an opportunity of speech, so that they were counted as rebels and infidels, and their traducers made the fact of their not presenting themselves at court to seem like a proof of the accusation.[25]

In the end, all was well. Upon learning that the sultan was not only alive but had mobilized a formidable army to suppress the movement, father and son prudently called off the revolt. Ultimately, the sultan received the two in court, pardoned their behavior, and even restored to them their family estates.[26]

Yet the incident reveals Bidar's Hall of Public Audience as a stage on which the heady and dangerous theatre of politics was publicly enacted. Ties of political loyalty were always tenuous; alliances could shift depending on what one said, to whom one said it, and in what language – Persian, Dakani, or one of the Deccan's older vernaculars. Above all, the incident suggests that the quality of being foreign – that is, a "Westerner" – was to some degree constructed and relational. Jalal Khan and his son are not described as being foreign by nature; rather, they had "counted themselves among the number of foreigners."[27] That is, whether or not one was foreign was related to the faction with which one allied oneself. To this extent, "Westerner" was a political category. Yet the term was also cultural, inasmuch as it implied identification with Persian language and culture, and overseas ancestry.

The category "Deccani" was similarly both political and socio-cultural. The term generally referred to families descended from those Muslims – many of them of part-Turkish ancestry – who had migrated down to Daulatabad in 1327, when Sultan Muhammad bin Tughluq declared that city the Tughluq empire's new co-capital. Within only twenty years of that event, however, that class of migrants, and the generation immediately following, threw off allegiance to Delhi and established the Bahmani sultanate. In that context,

---

[25] 'Ali Tabataba, *Burhan-i ma'athir* (Delhi, 1936), 85. J. S. King, trans., "History of the Bahmani Dynasty," *Indian Antiquary* 29 (August 1899), 240.

[26] Sherwani, *Bahmanis*, 169–70.

[27] "*Khud-ra dar a' dad-i ghariban mi-shumurdand.*" Tabataba, *Burhan*, 85. Tabataba's term *gharib*, "foreigner," refers to the same social class that his contemporary, Firishta, designated by the term *gharbi*, "Westerner."

"Deccani" referred to a north Indian immigrant who opposed Tughluq rule. By the end of the fourteenth century, however, people in this class had sunk roots in Deccani society and culture, acquiring the Marathi, Kannada, or Telugu languages while evolving their own vernacular: Dakani, or Dakani Urdu. As this happened, self-styled Deccanis saw themselves less in political terms – that is, as opponents of the Tughluqs as a ruling dynasty – and more in terms of natives of the Deccan as opposed to "Hindustan," or north India. By the fifteenth century, and especially after 1424 when the Bahmani capital was shifted to Bidar and the pace of overseas immigration quickened, the reference point for Deccani identity – in terms of what they were *not* – had shifted from north India to "the West," and in particular, the Persian world.

The court itself, finding it expedient to play one side against the other, was largely responsible for this viciously polarized situation. Indeed, overseas recruitment was apparently used as a tap that could be adjusted in order to maintain a balance between Deccanis and Westerners. By the mid-fifteenth century, a de facto apartheid system had become thoroughly institutionalized. Sultan Ahmad II (r. 1436–58) ordered that when the kingdom's nobles were assembled in the Hall of Public Audience and arranged according to their rank and influence, the Westerners would occupy the right-hand side of the throne and the Deccanis the left. That order followed more than two decades of factional strife that first erupted in 1430. In that year Ahmad I, hoping to exploit a quarrel between rulers of Gujarat and Malwa – and possibly trying to turn into reality Timur's gesture of "bestowing" both regions on his brother Firuz – sent armies from Daulatabad north to the Tapti valley and west to Mahim on the Konkan coast. But during the campaign, Deccani and Westerner officers intrigued against each other, to the point that some Deccanis resolved not to take part in the fighting. As a result, when the Gujaratis inflicted a complete rout of their forces at Mahim, the Deccanis and Westerners blamed each other for the defeat. Seven years later, when the court became alarmed over an anticipated attack by the ruler of neighboring Khandesh, Westerners at court persuaded Sultan Ahmad II to send out an army commanded exclusively by their group. This time, Bahmani arms routed the army of Khandesh together with allied armies from Gujarat and Malwa, an outcome that enhanced the position of Westerners in state politics while diminishing that of the Deccanis.

Relations between the two factions reached their lowest point in 1447, when a mixed force marched to subdue local rebels in the Sahyadri Mountains. Making their headquarters at Chakan, just north of modern Pune, the two parties again split up, the Deccanis remaining behind while the Westerners advanced through the dense jungles and hills toward Sangameshwar (in Ratnagiri

District). When the raja of Sangameshwar routed the Bahmani army, the Deccanis, who were the first to report the affair to the court, blamed the disaster on reckless and foolhardy Westerners. Upon hearing this, an enraged Sultan Ahmad II ordered the massacre of all Westerner survivors who managed to return to Chakan. Then, on learning that the Westerners alone had done the fighting, the sultan turned with equal fury on Deccanis. Those still at Chakan were ordered to be brought to Bidar in chains; many others were executed.

THE CAMPAIGN OF 1469–72 AND AFTER

Such was the poisoned political atmosphere that greeted Mahmud Gawan when he reached Bidar in 1453, just five years after the debacle at Chakan. Within another five years, in 1458, he was promoted to chief minister. How would he use this power, and how could he, himself very much a Westerner, deal with the kingdom's bitter socio-political rivalries?

We find an early answer to this in 1462, when the kingdom was ruled by a council of regents for the youthful Muhammad III. Seeking to exploit the state's political vulnerability, the sultan of Malwa invaded the kingdom and marched clear to the capital, which he besieged. In these dire straits Mahmud Gawan advised that the defense of the citadel be entrusted to a prominent Deccani, Mallu Khan, while the entire court be evacuated to Firuzabad, the second capital built by Sultan Firuz seventeen miles south of Gulbarga. In the 1470s Gawan again showed such conciliatory sentiments when, as chief minister, he divided the kingdom's eight governorships equally between Deccanis and Westerners. By this time, the realm had expanded to embrace the entire plateau from coast to coast, i.e., from Goa and Dabhol in the west to Masulipatnam in the east. To accommodate this growth, Gawan doubled the number of internal provinces from four to eight. He also curbed the power of both Westerner and Deccani nobles by reducing the size of their estates, increasing the amount of land classified as royal domain, and forbidding governors from controlling more than a single fort. Finally, with a view to normalizing and enhancing the land revenue, he ordered that the demand be based on a systematic measurement of all lands in agricultural production.[28]

What enabled the chief minister to implement these sweeping reforms was the power and prestige he had derived from leading an exceptionally successful military expedition in western Maharashtra. The expedition had both political

[28] P. M. Joshi and H. K. Sherwani, eds., *History of Medieval Deccan (1295–1724)* (Hyderabad, 1973), 1:189–90.

and commercial objectives. Afanasy Nikitin, a Russian horse-merchant residing in Bidar in the early 1470s, remarked that as many as 20,000 horses were sold at markets close to Bidar,[29] suggesting both the degree to which the state relied on imported warhorses, and the government's need to maintain secure overland and maritime trade routes to facilitate the horse trade. Yet ever since the rise of Bahmani power, these routes lay exposed to attack by highwaymen and pirates. Himself a former horse merchant, Gawan was keenly aware of this vulnerability, and his correspondence betrays his anxieties in the matter. In one letter he noted that coastal chieftains were deploying more than a hundred vessels to raid Muslim-operated ships along the Konkan coast, and in another he argued that "travelers by land and sea should be free from the fear of marauders and pirates."[30]

Gawan's protracted expedition, which lasted from 1469 to 1472, thus aimed at subduing both the hill-forts and the sea forts from which local chieftains had been harassing strategic trade routes. Reinforced by units sent from Bahmani strongholds in Junnar, Chakan, Dabhol, and Chaul, his army systematically reduced hill-forts in the thickly forested interior of modern Ratnagiri district, working his way from south to north. His first conquest was Raingna, located in the Savantwadi region some twenty-five miles north of Goa (mid-July 1470), followed by Machal, a large fort near Vishalgarh further north (January 1471), and finally, Sangameshwar (December 1471). Having secured the land routes leading from the plateau to the coast, Gawan turned to the shipping lanes of the southern Konkan coast, then dominated by the important sea fort of Goa, a protectorate of Vijayanagara. In a coordinated land and sea assault, Gawan captured that city in February 1472.[31]

Soon thereafter, however, the raja of Vijayanagara persuaded Parketa, the chief of Belgaum, to try to retake Goa. In response, Gawan subjected the fort of Belgaum to a siege that was remarkable on two counts. First, it saw the earliest recorded use of gunpowder in the Deccan. Bahmani engineers mined Belgaum's walls and laid charges that blasted open breaches in the fort's defenses, leading to Parketa's surrender in March 1472. And second, rather than punish the defeated Parketa in any way, Gawan made him an *amir*, presumably leaving him in charge of the Belgaum fort.[32] Firishta's casual way of mentioning this outcome suggests that by this time the integration of chiefs like Parketa into Bahmani service had become common.

---

[29] Athanasius [Afanasy] Nikitin, "The Travels of Athanasius Nikitin of Twer," in *India in the Fifteenth Century*, ed. R. H. Major (Hakluyt Society, First Series no. 22; repr. New York, 1970), 12.

[30] Sherwani, *Bahmanis*, 213, 217.   [31] *Ibid.*, 213–19.   [32] Briggs, *Rise*, II:303.

On May 19, 1472, after an absence of nearly three years, Gawan returned in triumph to the capital, an event witnessed by Afanasy Nikitin. Referring to Gawan by his title "*malik al-tujjar*," Prince of Merchants, the Russian merchant wrote:

Melikh Tuchar took two Indian towns, whose ship's pirated on the Indian Sea, captured seven princes with their treasures, a load of precious stones, a load of diamonds and *kirpuks* [= *kirpas*, "fine linen"?], and a hundred loads of valuable goods; while the army took an immense quantity of various merchandize. The town had been besieged for two years by an army of two hundred thousand men, one hundred elephants, and three hundred camels.

Melikh Tuchar came with his army to Beder . . . in the Russian Calendar Peter's day; and the sultan sent ten viziers to encounter him at a distance of ten kors [twenty miles] . . . each at the head of ten thousand warriors, and of ten elephants in full equipment.[33]

Yet the more impressive the chief minister's successes, the more envious grew sections of the nobility, especially Deccanis, whom the Westerner chronicler Firishta compared to "wounded vipers, writhing in the torment of jealousy."[34] Even while he and his men had been on campaign, hacking their way through the Konkan's dense forests, Gawan knew of the groundswell of enmity against him that was growing in the capital. "Untruths are being made to hide the faint sparks of truth," he wrote in one letter, "and these are sent up as the food to the Royal Throne." And in another: "Out of sheer malice they would kill each other and make me the object of all the wrongs which it is in their power to perpetrate."[35] The ill will directed toward Gawan while still on campaign only deepened once he returned to the capital and enacted the reforms that would further curb the power of nobles. Once those reforms were enacted, the tragic climax followed.

Several disaffected officers, one a Deccani and the other an Ethiopian, plied Gawan's seal-bearer with gifts and then presented him with a blank sheet of paper that required the chief minister's seal. Told that it was but a routine document, the seal-bearer willingly obliged by stamping it. The conspirators now wrote on the document a letter purporting to be Gawan's, in which the addressee, the raja of Orissa, was invited to invade Bahmani territory and share the spoils with the chief minister. This done, the conspirators presented the letter to Sultan Muhammad III, claiming that the document had been intercepted and that it confirmed Gawan's treasonous behavior. Enraged, and his senses addled by wine, the sultan immediately summoned his chief minister, who went straight to court, despite the warnings voiced by suspicious friends.

---

[33] Nikitin, "Travels," 26.   [34] Briggs, *Rise*, ii:302.   [35] Sherwani, *Bahmanis*, 217.

When shown the document with his own seal affixed, a shocked Gawan pleaded innocence, which the sultan merely ignored. Standing up and turning to leave, he ordered his executioner to do his work. Remarked Gawan, "The death of an old man like me is, indeed, of little moment, but to your Majesty it will be the loss of an empire, and the ruin of your character."[36] These words, too, were ignored by the king, who proceeded to his chambers. Gawan, kneeling down and facing Mecca, was reciting the Islamic credo when the broad sword struck his neck.

That night, April 5, 1481, a waxing quarter moon set over the Deccan skies, tracing a kingdom that was already waning, and about to be totally eclipsed. When he realized what he had foolishly done, Sultan Muhammad III, consumed with remorse, fell into a deep melancholy from which he never recovered. He let his generals disperse with their armies, while he himself – unwilling even to reside in the capital – retired to Firuzabad. There, in that formerly splendid palace-city built by his illustrious forebear, the despondent sultan spent three months drowning himself in drink and pleasure. But it was a self-destructive effort that only hastened his decline. Inwardly he was stricken with grief; in fact, he was dying. While still in Firuzabad, the infirm sultan formally entrusted the kingdom to his twelve-year-old son, Prince Mahmud. But even while the document was being drawn up, the rueful king was heard to say, "If they do not obey me, who reigned gloriously for many years, and conquered nations with my sword, how will they submit to a child?"[37] The sultan then returned to Bidar. There he died within months, exactly one lunar year to the day after Mahmud Gawan's execution.

SUMMARY

Focused on its glittering Royal Chamber and Hall of Public Audience, Bidar in the fifteenth century came close to becoming what Delhi had long been – an imperial center. One cannot explain this rare moment of extensive and centralized rule by invoking the "gunpowder thesis," i.e., the notion that states that can afford substantial investments in cannon and impregnable forts achieve their reach by prevailing over those that cannot. Although Gawan himself presided over the Deccan's earliest known use of gunpowder, in 1472, the new technology clearly failed to enhance Bahmani power, which vanished only several decades later. What was it, then, that allowed the Bahmanis to attain their impressive degree of stability and territorial reach?

[36] Briggs, *Rise*, II:313.　　[37] *Ibid.*, 319.

For one thing the Bahmanis, unlike most Indo-Muslim states, practiced royal primogeniture. Kings were normally succeeded by their eldest sons, an exception being Firuz's succession by his brother. Consequently we do not find self-destructive wars of succession or fratricidal struggles of the sort that the Delhi sultans or the Mughals, among others, repeatedly experienced. On the other hand, the periodic strife avoided by royal primogeniture was more than canceled out by the strife caused by the kingdom's chronic Deccani–Westerner conflict.

More importantly, by inducing neighboring rulers to give their daughters to the Bahmani court, and by preventing their own women from marrying outside the kingdom, the Bahmanis briefly made themselves the hub of an imperial network in which their neighbors were, at least symbolically, political satellites. Thus, in 1406 Sultan Firuz married a daughter of Deva Raya I of Vijayanagara. He also married his son to a woman who resided in a border region disputed by the Bahmani and Vijayanagara states, and whom the raja of Vijayanagara had *wished* to marry. While still a prince, Ahmad II was married to the daughter of Sultan Nasir Khan Faruqi of Khandesh, which lay on the Bahmanis' northern frontier. Later, as sultan, he married the daughter of the raja of Sangameshwar, the Konkani state that was finally reduced by Mahmud Gawan.[38] By a similar logic, a court's imperial pretensions correlated with the number of women from surrounding states who were in its royal harem. Firuz's harem had women not only from Telangana and Maharashtra, but also, reportedly, from Gujarat, Rajasthan, Bengal, Arabia, Afghanistan, Central Asia, the Caucasus, Russia, China, and western Europe[39] – in short, anywhere that mattered in the Bahmanis' image of the world. Conversely, the Bahmanis endeavored to prevent royal daughters from marrying beyond the ranks of their own nobility; some were married to the sons of Bidar's saintly Ni'mat Allahi family (see Chart 1).

Perhaps most critical in enabling the state to build up territory was the power and wealth derived from its long-distance trade, a phenomenon that inevitably drew the Deccan into the global economy. By the end of the Bahmani era, the dynasty was able to field a cavalry of approximately 30,000.[40] Considering that 20,000 horses were sold in markets near Bidar, as Nikitin noted, and that virtually all of these would have arrived via Konkani ports, and considering, too, that the sultan used duties collected on imported horses to pay government

---

[38] Sherwani and Joshi, *History*, i:162, 169, 171.   [39] Briggs, *Rise*, ii:228.

[40] Tomé Pires, *The Suma Oriental of Tomé Pires: an Account of the East, from the Red Sea to Japan, Written in Malacca and India in 1512–1515*, trans. Armando Cortesão (London, 1944; repr. New Delhi, 1990), i:52.

servants,[41] one realizes how dependent the state was on international trade. With long-distance merchants so tightly woven into the Bahmani political economy, it is hardly surprising that its chief minister was generally known as "Prince of Merchants."

Apart from Bidar's horse-markets, a great variety of locally produced textiles attracted long-distance merchants to the Konkan coast. Around 1512 a Portuguese officer wrote that the calicoes and turban material produced in the Deccan were enough "to furnish the world."[42] Satin, taffeta, and dungaree were some of the other woven fabrics produced in the Deccan and exported from Konkani ports. In Bahmani times the silk industry in Chaul and Thana had become thoroughly globalized: silk procured in cocoon stage from China was brought to the Konkan, where it was reeled, dyed, and woven before being exported to Middle Eastern markets. Similarly, the technique for velvet production, though imported from Central Asia, became indigenized in this region.[43] The bulk of the Deccan's textile goods went to Egypt, owing to a combination of Mamluk initiatives and the expertise of the Karimis, a powerful mercantile organization that dominated the India–Egypt trade. One member of the Karimi group, Shihab al-Din Malakki (d. 1446), even resided in Gulbarga where he functioned as the agent of the Mamluk court in Cairo.[44] The Textile Museum in Washington DC has a large collection of fragments of cotton textiles produced in fifteenth-century western India and found in Fostat, near Cairo.[45] Radiocarbon dating techniques applied to cotton textile fragments in the Ashmolean Museum, Oxford, have also confirmed the active trade in such fabrics from western India to Egypt at that time.[46]

Mahmud Gawan himself organized regular commercial relations between Bidar and markets throughout the Middle East, illustrating Sanjay Subrahmanyam's point that "trade and politics often went together in [the early modern] period, rather than being separated into hermetically sealed social spaces."[47] Although Gawan never returned to his native Gilan in northern Iran,

---

[41] *Ibid.*, II:53. [42] *Ibid.*

[43] Lotika Varadarajan, "Konkan Ports and Medieval Trade," *Indica* 22, no. 1 (March 1985): 14–15.

[44] *Ibid.*, 11.

[45] Mattiebelle Gittinger, *Master Dyers to the World: Technique and Trade in Early Indian Dyed Cotton Textiles* (Washington DC, 1982), 31–57.

[46] Ruth Barnes, "From India to Egypt: the Newberry Collection and the Indian Ocean Textile Trade," in *Islamische Textilkunst des Mittelalters: Aktuelle Probleme*, ed. Muhammad Abbas Muhammad Salim (Riggisberg, Switzerland, 1997), 79–92. See also Ruth Barnes, *Indian Block-Printed Textiles in Egypt: the Newberry Collection in the Ashmolean Museum, Oxford* (Oxford, 1997), vol. 1.

[47] Sanjay Subrahmanyam, "Iranians Abroad: Intra-Asian Elite Migration and Early Modern State Formation," *Journal of Asian Studies* 51, no. 2 (1992): 341.

his son 'Abd Allah continued in the 1470s to act as his father's agent in the trade between the Deccan and Iran.[48] Reaching deep into Central Asia, the chief minister also transacted business with agents in Samarqand.[49] Other agents ranged still further, moving along established trade routes from Mamluk Egypt to Ottoman domains, namely Bursa, in western Anatolia. In 1479, Gawan sent three commercial agents to Bursa with consignments of textiles. And in February 1481, just months before his execution, six of his salaried agents, traveling via Arabia, reached their regional headquarters in Bursa. Some of these then moved on to the Balkans (i.e., Rumelia), where they marketed their fabrics.[50]

Yet even while these global linkages were being forged, at home the Westerner–Deccani conflict was tearing apart the Bahmanis' social and political fabric. This vexing issue was inherently unsolvable. On the one hand, the court was obliged to patronize the descendants of those north Indian settlers who had migrated to the Deccan in the fourteenth century and who, rebelling against Delhi, had launched the dynasty. But, on the other, in order to obtain the talent and prestige associated with the Timurid power-state, thereby to get on the big chessboard of global politics, the court wished to recruit immigrants from the Persian or Persianized world. Deccanis and Westerners, then, represented more than just two competing factions jostling for influence in the Hall of Public Audience; they stood for differing conceptions of state and society. If the Deccanis manifested a *colonial* idea, namely, a society composed of transplanted settler-founders and their descendants, the Westerners represented a *cultural* idea: a refined style of comportment, an eminent tradition of statecraft, a prestigious language. Since each class was legitimate in its own way, neither could be dislodged; nor could either one totally dominate the other. The only apparent solution was to balance them politically, which Mahmud Gawan accomplished by placing representatives of the two classes in the same districts, or by sending them on joint military expeditions. But only a man of consummate ability could manage this juggling act. Absent that man and there is no such act.

Despite, however, the disintegration of the Bahmani state so soon after Mahmud Gawan's tragic execution, the chief minister's spirit long survived

---

[48] Jean Aubin, "Le royaume d'Ormuz au début du XVIe siècle," *Mare Luso-Indicum* 2 (1973): 134–35, cited in Subrahmanyam, "Iranians Abroad," 342.

[49] Jo-Ann Gross and Asom Urunbaev, *The Letters of Khwaja ' Ubayd Allah Ahrar and his Associates* (Leiden, 2002), 245–46.

[50] Halil Inalcik, "Bursa and the Commerce of the Levant," *Journal of the Economic and Social History of the Orient* 3 (1960): 141.

the state he had served. By the dawn of the twenty-first century a cyber-cafe with full internet access – the "Mahmud Gawan Internet Cafe" – had opened for business directly across from the entrance to the chief minister's famous *madrasa*. One suspects that Gawan, always in touch with the wider world, would have approved.

CHAPTER 4

RAMA RAYA (1484–1565): ÉLITE MOBILITY
IN A PERSIANIZED WORLD

Prince Ibrahim [of Golkonda], accompanied by Saiyid Hayy, Hamid Khan [an Ethiopian], . . . and Kana-ji, a Brahmin, besides a few personal attendants, left the camp of [Sultan] Qasim Barid Shah [of Bidar] and proceeded to Vijayanagara. On his arrival, the Prince was received according to his rank and treated with the utmost respect and attention . . . At some former period Malik 'Ain al-Mulk Gilani, having offended [Sultan] Ibrahim 'Adil Shah [of Bijapur], left his service and entered that of Rama Raya, with four thousand cavalry. 'Ain al-Mulk had on many occasions so distinguished himself by his bravery that the Raja [Rama Raya] used to call him brother.[1]

Tarikh-i Muhammad Qutb Shah (1617)

THE YEARS 1510–12

In the above extract, the chronicler alludes to a number of men who migrated from the northern to the southern Deccan in the first half of the sixteenth century. By this time the Bahmani Sultanate had fractured into five successor-states, including the above-mentioned Golkonda, Bidar, and Bijapur (see Map 4). The men – a prince, a Saiyid, an Ethiopian, a Brahmin, and a high-ranking Westerner – found refuge and even patronage in the sprawling metropolis of Vijayanagara, or "City of Victory," the capital of the great kingdom of the same name that had dominated the southern Deccan since 1347.

Notices that casually record internal migrations such as these might seem unremarkable. In fact, though, they challenge us to rethink stereotypes found in much modern history-writing about Vijayanagara, a state often cast as a bastion of Hinduism against an advancing tide of Islam from the north. In this view the Krishna River, which formed the political frontier dividing Vijayanagara from the Bahmani Sultanate and its successor-states, is construed as something of a "Maginot Line" that walled off a "Hindu" southern Deccan from a "Muslim" north. But the quoted extract suggests a very different sort of space. It presents the Deccan as a single terrain on which élite actors enjoyed considerable mobility, moving about from patron to patron according to changes in political winds. Rama Raya, the Vijayanagara generalissimo who received these

---

[1] Anonymous, *Tarikh-i Muhammad Qutb Shah*, in *History of the Rise of the Mahomedan Power in India*, trans. John Briggs (London, 1829; repr. Calcutta, 1966), III:229.

northern exiles, and who even referred to one of them as "brother," had himself crossed the Krishna some years earlier, having exchanged political service to the north of that river for service to the south.

Rama Raya first appears in recorded history in 1512, when Sultan Quli Qutb al-Mulk enrolled this Telugu warrior as a military commander and holder of a land assignment in the newly emerged sultanate of Golkonda. It is useful to frame this moment in a larger, international context. About the same time that Rama Raya took up service in Golkonda, in far-off Central Asia, the Timurid prince Babur had just made a last, failed bid for control of Timur's illustrious capital city of Samarqand. Driven out by his arch-enemies the Uzbeks, he and his band of loyal retainers abandoned their dreams of a Central Asian dominion and in early 1512 marched through the snowy passes of central Afghanistan to their base in Kabul. From there, Babur would soon redirect his imperial ambitions toward north India, culminating in his defeat of the last of the Delhi Sultans, which launched the Mughal Empire.

As Babur was advancing from Samarqand to Kabul, the new viceroy for Portuguese operations in Asia, Afonso de Albuquerque, was busy building a string of fortified maritime bases at strategic ports between Africa and China. In March 1510 the viceroy seized from Bahmani successors the port of Goa, henceforth the Portuguese administrative hub in Asia, and took over the lucrative horse trade that passed through it into the Deccan. The conquest of Goa advanced a Portuguese agenda that grew ever clearer in subsequent decades: armed supremacy over the Indian Ocean, commercial monopoly on targeted commodities, and a religious mission that carried the energy and anti-Muslim zeal of Europe's Counter-Reformation.

The year 1510 also witnessed a terminal stage in the progressive decline of Bahmani authority and power, a process that had accelerated soon after the execution of Mahmud Gawan nearly three decades earlier. In 1510 Sultan Mahmud Bahmani (1482–1518), only a child when his father executed Gawan in 1481, found himself imprisoned in Bidar fort by Amir Barid, one of five nobles who had been carving out independent sultanates from the decaying Bahmani state since 1490. To be sure, a flicker of Bahmani authority lingered on until Mahmud's own demise in 1518, as the rulers of these new states continued to make formal obeisances to the nominal king whenever it suited their purposes. Yet the Bahmani state had effectively disappeared in 1510 when its last sultan became a captive puppet, immured behind the massive walls of Bidar's fort.

Finally, 1510 saw the first full year of rule by Vijayanagara's most renowned king, Krishna Raya, who had come to power the previous year and would reign until 1529.[2] It was this king who employed Rama Raya when he left the service of Sultan Quli Qutb al-Malik of Golkonda. And it was one of this king's daughters whom Rama Raya would marry, forging a link between patron and client that in popular memory survives to this day.

In short, Rama Raya appeared in Vijayanagara's service at a critical moment in Indian history, since during the period 1510–12 outsiders – the Timurids by land, and Europeans by sea – were about to connect the subcontinent with larger regimes of global contact and exchange.

DYNAMICS OF VIJAYANAGARA'S HISTORY

Rama Raya also lived during a decisive moment in the cultural and political evolution of the Vijayanagara state. Owing to the recent profusion of fine scholarship on the kingdom (and especially on the city), it is no longer possible – as it seemed to some in the past – to characterize Vijayanagara in totalizing or synchronic categories such as "Asiatic state," "feudal state," "theatre state," "war state," or "segmentary state." New scholarship has replaced such static notions with more dynamic understandings of the Vijayanagara kingdom.[3]

Consider architecture. By the early sixteenth century, royal patrons at Vijayanagara were building the monumental temples that have become today, in the popular imagination, iconic images of the state. At this time, kings regularly sponsored huge public processions and multi-day ceremonies that were enacted in spacious halls near their palaces and in elaborate temple complexes. These complexes exhibit long chariot streets, tanks, 100-pillar halls, and colonnades lining their inner enclosure walls. The capital's ornate architecture

---

[2] In the secondary literature this famous monarch is usually called Krishna Deva Raya, or Krishnadeva Raya, an innovation that seems to have been introduced in the nineteenth century.

[3] Examples include A. L. Dallapiccola and M. Zingel Ave-Lallemant, eds., *Vijayanagara: City and Empire*, 2 vols. (Wiesbaden, 1985); Anna L. Dallapiccola and Anila Verghese, *Sculpture at Vijayanagara: Iconography and Style* (New Delhi, 1998); Dominic J. Davison-Jenkins, *The Irrigation and Water Supply Systems of Vijayanagara* (New Delhi, 1997); John M. Fritz and George Michell, eds., *New Light on Hampi: Recent Research at Vijayanagara* (Mumbai, 2001); Noburu Karashima, *Towards a New Formation: South Indian Society under Vijayanagara Rule* (New Delhi, 1992); Alexandra Mack, *Spiritual Journey, Imperial City: Pilgrimage to the Temples of Vijayanagara* (New Delhi, 2002); George Michell, *Architecture and Art of Southern India: Vijayanagara and the Successor States* (Cambridge, 1995); Kathleen D. Morrison, *Fields of Victory: Vijayanagara and the Course of Intensification* (Berkeley, 1995); Kathleen D. Morrison and Carla M. Sinopoli, "Dimensions of Imperial Control: the Vijayanagara Capital," *American Anthropologist* 97 (1995): 83–96; Vijaya Ramaswamy, *Textiles and Weavers in Medieval South India* (Delhi, 1985); Carla M. Sinopoli, *The Political Economy of Craft Production: Crafting Empire in South India, c. 1350–1650* (Cambridge, 2003); Burton Stein, *Vijayanagara* (Cambridge, 1989); Sanjay Subrahmanyam, "Reflections on State-Making and History-Making in South India, 1500–1800," *Journal of the Economic and Social History of the Orient* 41, no. 3 (1998): 382–416; Anila Verghese, *Archaeology, Art, and Religion: New Perspectives on Vijayanagara* (New Delhi, 2000).

of this later period, which has inspired numerous scholarly monographs and lavishly illustrated coffee-table albums, recalls Clifford Geertz's notion of the "theatre state" – that is, a state whose primary function is not so much to govern as grandly to display cosmic and moral order.[4] As a characterization of Vijayanagara's 300-year history, however, the static "theatre state" notion, like the other characterizations mentioned above, fails to capture the dynamics of Vijayanagara's social history.

Indeed, the elaborate temple complexes commonly thought to typify the whole of the Vijayanagara era, reflect in fact only a single, and very late, phase of the kingdom's socio-cultural evolution. Stylistically, the city's earliest temples conformed to a local, Deccani idiom, which by the early fifteenth century had begun to incorporate southern elements such as entrance towers with barrel-vaulted roofs.[5] In the city's "Sacred Center," progressively greater Tamil influence is seen in a cluster of temples associated with each of the first four Sangama rulers, spanning the period from the mid-fourteenth to the early fifteenth century.[6] This is readily understandable. Very early in the kingdom's history, between 1352 and 1371, royal armies from the upland plateau conquered much of the fertile and prosperous Tamil country to the south and east of the dry interior that formed the core of the Vijayanagara state. Prolonged contact between Vijayanagara's political core and its wealthy coastal provinces led, among other things, to the imperial city's gradual assimilation of the rich heritage of classical Tamil architecture.

A similar evolution is found in the kingdom's religious history. We have already seen how Vijayanagara emerged as a regional power in the second quarter of the fourteenth century as part of a Deccan-wide rebellion against Tughluq imperial rule, in tandem with the rise of the Bahmani Sultanate. If the two states shared common political origins, however, they pursued very different means of religious legitimation. Whereas the sultans in Gulbarga and Bidar patronized eminent Sufis who conferred blessings on the sultans' rule, the Sangama rulers associated themselves with an important regional cult that had already taken root along the southern banks of the Tungabhadra River. From at least the seventh century, this cult had focused on the river goddess Pampa – the origin of the modern site-name "Hampi" – to whom passing local chiefs would make periodic donations. In the eleventh century a temple to Pampa

---

[4] See Clifford Geertz, *Islam Observed* (New Haven, 1968), and *Negara: the Theatre State in Nineteenth-Century Bali* (Princeton, 1980).
[5] Verghese, *Archaeology, Art, and Religion*, 59.
[6] Phillip B. Wagoner, "Architecture and Royal Authority under the Early Sangamas," in *New Light on Hampi*, ed. Fritz and Michell, 19.

appeared at the site, a clear sign that the cult was becoming institutionalized. By the end of the twelfth century there had appeared a temple dedicated to the male god Virupaksha, locally understood as Pampa's husband and lord. In time, Virupaksha also became identified as a form of Śiva, and Pampa as a form of Devi, affording a classic instance of "Sanskritization," i.e., the process by which local deities became assimilated into the wider Indian pantheon.

These changes had already occurred before the rise to prominence of the Sangama family, Vijayanagara's first dynasty, whose members had named Virupaksha as their *kulu-devata*, or family deity, as early as 1347. Indeed, it appears that the Sangamas chose the Virupaksha–Pampa cultic center as the site for their capital largely because of the ritual and political benefits they could derive from being the "protectors" of the cult. In this way Virupaksha, the Sangamas' family deity, became the new kingdom's state deity. Accordingly, important state transactions were formalized in the presence of the icon of Virupaksha, whose Kannada "signature" appeared directly below the Sanskrit text in copperplate inscriptions recording those transactions.[7]

By the end of the fourteenth century, kings of the Sangama dynasty had extended the city's walls far beyond the Virupaksha temple complex, through the maze of jumbled boulders that comprise the area's extraordinary topography, to embrace a series of newly built palaces several miles to the south. Here, in a quarter scholars call the "Royal Center," they built a smaller temple to Virupaksha (the Prasanna Virupaksha), intended evidently for the ruling family's personal use. And in the early fifteenth century they built the richly carved Ramachandra temple, dedicated to the Vaishnava deity Rama, in the very heart of the Royal Center. It is notable that the temple's perfect north–south alignment with one of the city's most prominent topographical features, Matanga Hill, linked the temple to pre-Vijayanagara traditions pertaining to episodes from the great Vaishnava epic, the *Ramayana*.[8] Yet the temple's appearance did not indicate a departure from the court's traditional ties to Pampa and her lord,

---

[7] See Phillip B. Wagoner, "From 'Pampa's Crossing' to 'The Place of Lord Virupaksa': Architecture, Cult, and Patronage at Hampi before the Founding of Vijayanagara," in *Vijayanagara: Progress of Research, 1988–1991*, ed. D. Devaraj and C. S. Patil (Mysore, 1996), 141–74. See also Verghese, *Archaeology, Art and Religion*, 94–104.

[8] This was the tradition concerning the struggle between the brothers Sugriva and Vali for control of the kingdom of Kishkindha, a conflict ultimately resolved by the intervention of Rama. Inasmuch as Matanga Hill was traditionally identified as the very spot where Sugriva found security from his brother, it is likely that the Sangamas endeavored to benefit from the hill's protective power by placing both their political and their religious structures in axial alignment with it. See Phillip B. Wagoner, *Tidings of the King: a Translation and Ethnohistorical Analysis of the* Rayavacakamu (Honolulu, 1993), 45–47; J. M. Malville, "The Cosmic Geometries of Vijayanagara," in *Ancient Cities, Sacred Skies: Cosmic Geometries and City Planning in Ancient India*, ed. J. M. Malville and L. M. Gujral (New Delhi, 2000), 100–18.

the Śaiva deity Virupaksha. For the royal patron of the Ramachandra temple, Deva Raya I (1406–22), recorded in its dedicatory inscription that "Devaraya, too, is blessed by Pampa."[9] In reality, the Ramachandra temple signaled royal patronage of multiple traditions – the goddess Pampa (and through her, the Śaiva god Virupaksha), and both local and pan-Indian Vaishnava traditions respecting the deeds of Rama.

In the fifteenth century, as the state expanded over the southern Deccan to embrace peoples of varying cultural backgrounds, Vijayanagara's rulers patronized an ever-widening range of religious traditions, which included not only Śaiva and Vaishnava, but also Jain and Islamic institutions. Especially striking was the growing attention they paid to Vaishnava deities and institutions. The trend began soon after the Sangamas were overthrown by a new family, the Saluva, whose founder Saluva Narasimha (1485–91) favored the Vaishnava deity Venkateśvara, the lord of the great shrine at Tirupati in southern Andhra. For several decades, important transactions continued to be issued in the presence of Vijayanagara's original state deity, Virupaksha, in his great temple near the banks of the Tungabhadra River. However, from 1516 until the decisive Battle of Talikota in 1565, most such transactions were witnessed by the Vaishnava deity Vitthala in a magnificent new temple complex dedicated to that god, located by the river-front to the northeast of the Virupaksha complex.[10]

In short, when Rama Raya took up service in the court of Krishna Raya in 1515, the Vijayanagara state had entered a late stage in its religious evolution: the Vaishnava god Vitthala was receiving increasing attention at the expense of the Śaiva god Virupaksha, while in the sprawling, cosmopolitan capital the government was lending public support to a range of non-Hindu religious traditions.[11]

---

[9] Anna L. Dallapiccola, John M. Fritz, George Michell, and S. Rajasekhara, *The Ramachandra Temple at Vijayanagara* (New Delhi, 1992), 20.

[10] Verghese, *Archaeology, Art and Religion*, 5–7, 103–4, 195. The elaborate Vitthala complex was built in stages. While the core of the temple appears to have been built in the fifteenth century, the entrance towers (*gopuras*) were constructed in 1513, the 100-pillar pavilion in 1516, the Narasimha shrine in 1532, the Lakshmi-Narayana shrine in 1545, and the "swing pavilion" in 1554. See Pierre Filliozat, "Techniques and Chronology of Construction in the Temple of Vithala at Hampi," in *Vijayanagara – City and Empire*, ed. Dallapiccola, 296–316; Anila Verghese, *Religious Traditions at Vijayanagara as Revealed through its Monuments* (New Delhi, 1995), 59–66.

[11] Verghese, *Archaeology, Art and Religion*, 185. These changes are also reflected in the images found on the obverse side of Vijayanagara's gold coins. From 1347 to 1377 the emphasis was on Hanuman; from 1377 to 1424 coins bore mixed Śaiva and Vaishnava images. From 1424 to 1465 no deity – only an elephant – appeared, whereas from 1509 to 1614 the coins bore predominantly Vaishnava motifs. See A. V. Narasimhamurthy, *Coins and Currency System in Vijayanagara Empire* (Varanasi, 1991).

Table 2 *Reservoirs built in*
Vijayanagara's core

1300–1350	2
1350–1400	16
1400–1450	19
1450–1500	3
1500–1550	20
1550–1600	3
1600–1650	2
1650–1700	3

Source: Morrison, *Fields of Victory*, 132. The districts surveyed, constituting the state's core hinterland, are Raichur, Dharwar, Bellary, Shimoga, Chitradurga, Chikmagalur, Hassan, Tumkur, Mandhya, Bangalore, and Kolar.

Other evidence reveals dramatic shifts in the kingdom's economic history. The pattern of reservoir construction, vital to an agrarian society based on land as arid as the Deccan plateau, reflects two distinct periods of growth. The first was the hundred years that followed the state's founding; the second was the first half of the sixteenth century (see Table 2). Between those two peaks of activity was a half-century lull, the period 1450 to 1500, when only three reservoirs are known to have been built in the kingdom's core. Nor are any major temples known with certainty to have been built during that half-century. The same pattern is found in the chronological distribution of stone or copperplate inscriptions, which reflect the level of publicized donations and commercial transactions occurring within the state's borders. Here, too, a relatively stagnant period – the late fifteenth century – is sandwiched between two peaks of vigorous activity.[12] Likewise with coinage. Whereas the state continuously minted gold and copper coins for a century between *c.* 1347 and 1446, only copper coins were issued from 1446 to 1465. Then for nearly four decades no coins of any sort are known to have been minted, until Krishna Raya (1509–29) resumed the minting of both gold and copper coins, which then continued through the early 1600s.[13] Although the four-decade interruption of minting does not imply a complete

[12] Morrison, *Fields of Victory*, 123.   [13] See Narasimhamurthy, *Coins and Currency System*.

cessation of economic activity – existing stocks from earlier regimes would have continued to circulate – an inelastic money supply would certainly have precluded any expansion of such activity above mid-fifteenth-century levels.

What caused this apparent lull in cultural and economic activity during the second half of the fifteenth century? Kathleen Morrison has found that the most devastating drought-induced famines that struck the Deccan in the Vijayanagara era – those of 1396, 1412–13, 1423–24, and 1471–72 – clustered towards its middle and not its early or later periods.[14] It is therefore possible that early fifteenth-century famines, which would have triggered population reduction, declining harvests, and falling land revenue, led to overall stagnation in the second half of that century.

Such stagnation could also have been related to the state's chronic inability to harmonize the agrarian economy of the dry, upland plateau with the commercialized economy of the rich Tamil coast. Until the early 1500s, the plateau and the coast effectively lived in two separate economic worlds, as is seen in patterns of textile production and consumption. Along the coast, the port of Pulicat had emerged in the fifteenth century as a major center for the export of textiles produced along both the Coromandel low country and the Kaveri delta. By the early sixteenth century, Pulicat's annual textile exports to the southeast Asian port of Melaka were estimated to be worth 175,000 Portuguese *cruzados*[15] – reflecting the integration of the heavily commercialized coast with the trading world of the wider Indian Ocean. The boom had also led to a rise in the social status of Tamil weavers, who in the course of the fifteenth and sixteenth centuries won the right to ride palanquins and blow conch shells on ritual occasions.[16]

Notably, the Coromandel coast's manufacturing and commercial boom coincided in time – the late fifteenth century – with the general economic stagnation in Vijayanagara's agrarian heartland. Although the court itself appears in this period to have been consuming increasing amounts of cloth, much of it

---

[14] See Kathleen D. Morrison, "Naturalizing Disaster: from Drought to Famine in Southern India," in *Environmental Disaster and the Archaeology of Human Response*, ed. Garth Bawden and Richard M. Reycraft (Albuquerque, 2000), 30.

[15] Sanjay Subrahmanyam, *The Political Economy of Commerce: Southern India, 1500–1650* (Cambridge, 1990), 94–98.

[16] Vijaya Ramaswamy, "Artisans in Vijayanagar Society," *Indian Economic and Social History Review* 22, no. 4 (1985): 435. Nor were weavers alone among artisans benefiting from the boom; smiths were allowed to bear insignia (banners, fans), use specific musical instruments, and cover their homes with plaster.

produced on the Coromandel coast,[17] the kingdom's upland core proved unable to profit fiscally from the coastal boom. In 1513 coastal weaving communities even got the government to rescind an order that would have increased taxes on their looms.[18] The court's inability to impose taxes on such a critical sector of the economy points to the central government's structural weakness vis-à-vis its coastal provinces. An early sign of this weakness appeared in the form of a major tax revolt. In 1429 communities of cultivators and artisans of the Kaveri delta, which Vijayanagara had conquered and annexed sixty years earlier, rose up in a widespread rebellion against the oppressive taxes imposed by imperial administrators.[19] Following that revolt, Vijayanagara's central administration maintained only a loose grip over its Tamil province.[20] One consequence of the central government's devolution of power in the region was that the core upland region failed to benefit from the economic boom then occurring in the Tamil country. As Burton Stein put it, "the Kaveri milch-cow of resources for a central Vijayanagara exchequer proved difficult to milk."[21]

What is more, the eastern coastal strip and its considerable wealth went on to serve as a power-base for a succession of military commanders who ultimately determined the destiny of the state. The pattern already began in the reign of Deva Raya II (1424–46), who granted considerable autonomy to powerful military commanders after the Kaveri delta tax revolt of 1429. Soon after that king's death, the first of several great generalissimos, Saluva Narasimha, appeared in Vijayanagara's history. From his political base at Chandragiri, the great hill-fort that controlled the northern Tamil plain, the general in 1456 started making generous endowments to the nearby Tirupati temple complex. Dedicated to the Vaishnava deity Venkateśvara, this shrine had already become the most important pilgrimage center in south India.[22]

---

[17] Vijayanagara's metropolitan center exhibited an increasingly voracious appetite for cloth between the early fifteenth and early sixteenth centuries. Contemporary sculptures reveal that in the early fifteenth century, courtly male dress was confined to *dhotis*, while the upper body and head remained bare. By the mid-fifteenth century men appear wearing shawls, long scarfs, and tall caps. By the early sixteenth century their upper bodies, too, were covered – with close fitting, high-necked, full-sleeved shirts or jackets that were usually buttoned down the front – while over the lower body *dhotis* were covered by broad girdles and waistbands, the whole ranging from knee-length to ankle-length. Anila Verghese, "Court Attire of Vijayanagara (From a Study of Monuments)," *Quarterly Journal of the Mythic Society* 82 (1991): 43–61.

[18] *Ibid.*, 427, 435.   [19] See Sinopoli, *Political Economy*, 285–90.

[20] Karashima, *Towards a New Formation*, 49–50, 59, 64–65, 152–54. Venkata Raghotham, "Religious Networks and the Legitimation of Power in 14th c. South India: a Study of Kumara Kampana's Politics of Intervention and Arbitration," in *Studies in Religion and Change*, ed. Madhu Sen (New Delhi, 1983), 154–55.

[21] Stein, *Vijayanagara*, 51.   [22] *Ibid.*, 89.

In the 1470s Saluva Narasimha, gathering power to himself through his military command and his continued patronage of the Tirupati shrine, seized control over the entire eastern coast from the hill-fort of Udayagiri in modern Nellore district down to Rameśvaram, adjacent to Sri Lanka. Although he remained for some time nominally subordinate to his royal overlord, in 1485 Narasimha became the first Vijayanagara general to overthrow the ruling dynasty and install himself on the throne. A new pattern now set in. The descendants of two of his subordinate commanders later rose to become generalissimos themselves, and each of these repeated the path to power pioneered by Saluva Narasimha, in 1505 and 1542 respectively. The second of these emerged as the most powerful general of them all, and also one of Vijayanagara's most vivid figures – Rama Raya.

RAMA RAYA AND ÉLITE MOBILITY, 1512–42

Born in 1484 in modern Kurnool district, in southwestern Andhra, Rama Raya was only a year old when Saluva Narasimha seized the throne from the last Sangama king. By 1505, when only twenty-one years of age, he had already lived through two dynastic changes – from Sangama to Saluva, and from Saluva to Tuluva – and had witnessed a good deal of raw power politics. Seven years later he enlisted in the service of the sultan of Golkonda, the easternmost of the five new successor-states to the erstwhile Bahmani kingdom. It seems that in 1512 the sultan had invaded and seized several districts of Vijayanagara territory – very possibly Racakonda, some twenty-five miles southeast of modern Hyderabad. But because the sultan was unwilling to leave one of his Muslim officers in charge of the fort there, he recruited Rama Raya to administer the districts while he himself returned to Golkonda.[23]

That the son of a prominent Vijayanagara general could so readily take up service in the army of the sultan of Golkonda suggests that for élite soldiers, at least, the entire Deccan constituted a seamless arena of opportunity, and not, as many historians have imagined, a land divided into a "Muslim" north and "Hindu" south, with the Krishna River running between them. An inscription dated 1430 records that Deva Raya II had recruited 10,000 "Turkish" cavalry into Vijayanagara's armed forces.[24] Whether the term "Turkish" referred to Deccani Muslims from anywhere in the Deccan or to

---

[23] Anonymous, *Tarikh-i Muhammad Qutb Shah*, in Briggs, *Rise*, III:212, 228–29; M. H. Rama Sharma, *The History of the Vijayanagar Empire: Beginnings and Expansion (1308–1569)* (Bombay, 1978), I:121, 161 n. 47.

[24] T. V. Mahalingam, *Administration and Social Life under Vijayanagar*, 2nd edn. (Madras, 1975), 211.

Westerners from beyond the Arabian Sea (both are possible), the inscription reveals the permeability of the Vijayanagara–Bahmani frontier. It also signals the advent of a political environment in which loyalty to family, faction, or paymaster counted for more than loyalty to land, religion, or ethnic group. Formerly, states of the early medieval Deccan such as the Hoysalas, Yadavas, or Kakatiyas had recruited their armies mainly from local kin groups. But by Deva Raya II's reign, Vijayanagara had adopted policies already practiced in the Middle East, Central Asia, and north India. From Mamluk Egypt to Timurid Samarqand to Tughluq Delhi, armies were composed largely, though not exclusively, of distant recruits, whether as slaves (*mamluk, ghulam*) or as free men. By the 1430s, the same thing was happening on both sides of the Krishna River, for we have already noted that Deva Raya II's contemporary to the north, Sultan Ahmad Shah I (1422–36), had recruited 3,000 archers from the Persian Gulf and northeastern Iran into Bahmani service.

By taking up service for the sultan of Golkonda, then, Rama Raya was adhering to a widespread and long-standing practice. But his service in the neighboring sultanate was brief. In 1515 armies of Bijapur, one of Sultan Quli's rivals to the west and another Bahmani successor-state, invaded the districts under Rama Raya's charge. Instead of defending his fort, Rama Raya fled to the court of his royal patron in Golkonda. Viewing this as an act of cowardice, the sultan dismissed the Telugu warrior, who then returned to Vijayanagara and entered the service of Krishna Raya.[25]

The timing of Rama Raya's return to Vijayanagara is noteworthy, for his new patron had just embarked on an unbroken string of stunning conquests that brought enormous wealth to the capital, which appears to have helped end the state's half-century of economic stagnation. The string began in 1509, when at Koilkonda, sixty miles southwest of Hyderabad, Krishna Raya defeated the last remnant of Bahmani power, Sultan Mahmud, along with Yusuf 'Adil Shah of Bijapur, who was killed in the engagement. Soon thereafter the king turned south and seized Penukonda, Śrirangapattan, and Śivasamudram from the chiefs of the powerful Ummattur family. In 1513, turning to the southern Andhra coast, he reconquered the great fort of Udayagiri, which had fallen into the hands of the Gajapati kings of Orissa. Two years later his armies seized from the Gajapatis the fort of Kondavidu in the Krishna delta. In 1517 he took Vijayavada and Kondapalli, also in the Krishna delta, and then Rajahmundry, up the coast in the Godavari delta. In 1520, with the help of Portuguese mercenary musketeers, he reconquered the rich Raichur region which, lying

[25] Briggs, *Rise*, iii:229.

Chart 2 Tuluva and Aravidu dynasties of Vijayanagara

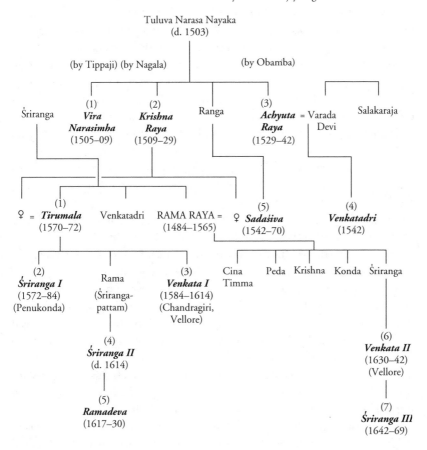

Tuluva Narasa Nayaka
(d. 1503)

(by Tippaji) (by Nagala)   (by Obamba)

Śriranga

(1)
*Vira
Narasimha*
(1505–09)

(2)
*Krishna
Raya*
(1509–29)

Ranga

(3)
Achyuta = Varada
Raya   Devi
(1529–42)

Salakaraja

♀ = *Tirumala*
(1570–72)

(1)
Venkatadri

RAMA RAYA = ♀ *Sadaśiva*
(1484–1565)   (1542–70)

(5)

(4)
Venkatadri
(1542)

(2)
Śriranga I
(1572–84)
(Penukonda)

Rama
(Śriranga-
pattam)

(3)
Venkata I
(1584–1614)
(Chandragiri,
Vellore)

Cina
Timma

Peda Krishna Konda Śriranga

(4)
Śriranga II
(d. 1614)

(6)
Venkata II
(1630–42)
(Vellore)

(5)
Ramadeva
(1617–30)

(7)
Śriranga III
(1642–69)

between the Krishna and Tungabhadra rivers, had been perennially contested by his Sangama predecessors and the Bahmani sultans. In 1523 he penetrated further north and seized, but chose not to hold, Gulbarga, the former Bahmani capital and city of Gisu Daraz.[26]

Thus ended fourteen years of unparalleled and uninterrupted military success. Especially remarkable was Krishna Raya's brief capture of Gulbarga, for long a potent symbol of "Turkish" power in the Deccan. On seizing that venerable seat of former Bahmani authority, Krishna Raya took the liberty of "appointing" one of the sons of the late Sultan Mahmud Bahmani as the new Bahmani sultan, even though the state was defunct by then. He also

[26] P. M. Desai, *A History of Karnataka* (Dharwar, 1970), 368–70.

provocatively styled himself *Yavana-rajya-sthapanacharya*, or "the one who brings about the (re)establishment of Yavana [i.e., Turkish] rule,"[27] probably in retaliation for the occasions when, a century earlier, the Bahmani kings had treated Vijayanagara as a mere tributary state.[28] The title also advertised the boast that he, Krishna Raya, was now the political arbiter of *all* the Deccan, capable of establishing – or in this case, renewing – even Turkish power. Never before had a ruler of Vijayanagara so intruded in the affairs of the northern Deccan. Significantly, the king's bold actions and claims anticipated the even more audacious steps that Rama Raya would take in the north several decades later.

Riding the coat-tails of Krishna Rama's military success, Rama Raya so distinguished himself on his patron's campaigns that the king, as a sign of royal favor, gave him one of his daughters in marriage.[29] His younger brother Tirumala, also an accomplished commander, was given another of the king's daughters, indicating the close alliance between Rama Raya's kin, the Aravidu family, and the ruling Tuluva dynasty. But Krishna Raya never planted his own kinsmen in central ministries or in command of major forts. Rather, he continued the earlier practice of hiring large numbers of mercenary troops – Portuguese gunners, Deccani and Westerner cavalry – and of placing Brahmins, not kinsmen, in command of the kingdom's great forts. Such measures served to check, temporarily, the power of quasi-independent generalissimos and to centralize the state to a greater degree than ever before.[30]

The king's efforts were ultimately subverted, however, by his ambitious son-in-law, Rama Raya, who quietly but systematically gathered power around himself and his family, the Arividu clan. Gradually, he emerged as Vijayanagara's supreme generalissimo, if not quite king. But this happened in stages, the first occurring immediately after Krishna Raya's death in 1529. Although Krishna Raya had named his half-brother Achyuta to succeed him on the throne, and Rama Raya to be chief minister, upon the king's death the impatient son-in-law tried to outmaneuver Achyuta by having the late king's infant son proclaimed king and himself regent. But the effort met stiff resistance from

---

[27] *Ibid.*, 370.

[28] In 1407, Firuz Bahmani concluded a treaty with Deva Raya I stipulating that the raja remit an annual payment of 100,000 *huns*, five maunds of pearls, and fifty elephants. In 1417, the sultan launched a war with Vijayanagara over nonpayment of the tribute. In 1436 his brother Sultan Ahmad I went to war on the grounds that Vijayanagara had fallen five years in arrears in its tribute. In 1443, Deva Raya II fell in arrears by 700,000 coins. The raja even attacked the Bahmanis; but after being defeated, he again promised to pay his tribute. See Haroon Khan Sherwani, *The Bahmanis of the Deccan*, 2nd edn. (1977; repr. New Delhi, 1985), 113, 115, 159, 164–65.

[29] Stein, *Vijayanagara*, 113.   [30] *Ibid.*, 43.

the nobility, which rallied behind Achyuta. The latter, having already crowned himself at the great Tirupati shrine, marched in triumph to the capital where he celebrated, for good measure, a second coronation ceremony.

Though temporarily checked, Rama Raya quietly prepared for another power play by exploiting both his position as minister and his marital connection to the late Krishna Raya, the memory of which survives to this day in his popular sobriquet Aliya, or the "son-in-law." First, he arranged for key forts in the heartland – i.e., Adoni, Kurnool, and Nandyal – to be transferred to his own kinsmen, marking an important step in Vijayanagara's transition to a patrimonial state. Second, he lavishly patronized the popular Venkateśwara temple at Tirupati, by now a well-trod stepping stone to the throne. Whereas Achyuta Raya had granted forty-three villages for the benefit of the shrine, Rama Raya, by contrast, granted sixty villages for this purpose.[31]

Third, Rama Raya skillfully benefited from a social revolution then playing out north of the Krishna River. Immediately upon succeeding to the throne of Bijapur in 1535, Sultan Ibrahim ʿAdil Shah I replaced Persian with Marathi and Kannada ("Hindawi") as the languages of Bijapur's public accounts, the management of which he gave to local Brahmins, who soon acquired great influence in the government. At the same time, Ibrahim dismissed all but 400 of his Westerner troops, most of whom were Shiʿi immigrants from Iran, and replaced them with Deccanis. Owing to his prior service at Golkonda, Rama Raya would surely have been familiar with the perennial tension between Westerners and Deccanis that had plagued the northern Deccan for many decades. So, in another illustration of élite mobility across the Krishna River, Rama Raya recruited into his own service 3,000 Westerners who had been dismissed from Bijapur's service.[32]

These maneuvers considerably improved Rama Raya's position when Achyuta Raya died in 1542 and was succeeded by his youthful son. However, the coronation ceremony was hardly over when Salakaraja, the late king's brother-in-law and regent, rashly wiped out nearly the entire Tuluva family, including his royal charge, in a mad effort to seize the throne for himself. This heinous act so alienated the nobility that Rama Raya, who had fled to one of his estates with his brother Tirumala, suddenly emerged as the rallying point for the kingdom's salvation. The tables had turned. In a rare public display of their covert power, the queens of the royal harem ordered the nobles to hand over the city to Rama Raya, who in the meantime had consolidated his grip over the

---

[31] *Ibid.*, 89–90.
[32] Muhammad Qasim Firishta, *Tarikh-i Firishta* (Lucknow, 1864–65), II:27; trans. Briggs, *Rise*, III:47–48.

major forts of the interior uplands – Penukonda, Adoni, Gutti, Gandikota, and Kurnool. Gathering together large armies from these regions, he now marched on the capital, softening up his opposition by bribing Salakaraja's troops stationed near the capital. Seeing his support evaporate, a cornered and desperate Salakaraja fell on his own sword.[33]

Now it was Rama Raya's turn to march triumphantly to the capital and be hailed as Vijayanagara's savior. This he did; nothing and nobody stood in his way.

KALYANA AND THE ROAD TO TALIKOTA, 1542–65

As he rode in triumph through the gates of the great capital city, Rama Raya possessed much more than public support. By his side were his two loyal brothers, Tirumala and Venkatadri, and the sole remnant of the ruling dynasty to have escaped Salakaraja's general massacre. This was the prince Sadaśiva, a sixteen-year-old nephew of Krishna Raya and Achyuta Raya whom Rama Raya had spirited away to an interior fort during the turmoil in the capital. He would now serve as Rama Raya's ticket to supreme power. Abandoning the notion of seizing the throne for himself, Rama Raya arranged for Sadaśiva to be formally crowned as king, with himself as regent.[34]

This arrangement lasted until 1550, when Sadaśiva tried to assert his own right to rule. In response, Rama Raya simply imprisoned his charge, allowing him to make a public appearance but once a year. Whereas inscriptions now identified the former regent as co-ruler with Sadaśiva, in fact the kingdom had become a patrimonial state, with Rama Raya appointing his own kinsmen as commanders of the principal forts in the realm, as high officials at court, and as governors over territories as distant as Sri Lanka. The final stage was reached around 1562, when Rama Raya discontinued even the formality of allowing the hapless Sadaśiva his annual public viewing. Though he stopped short of having himself crowned, Rama Raya had emerged as autocrat.[35]

In the days of Rama Raya's autocratic rule, Vijayanagara's external relations were dominated by its involvement with the sultanates of the northern Deccan. The conventional view is that after decades of mutual rivalry and warfare, those sultanates set aside their differences and, in the name of Islamic solidarity, combined to invade their "Hindu" enemy to the south. This in turn led to the fateful Battle of Talikota (1565), the destruction of Vijayanagara's sprawling capital city, and the end of the most glorious phase of the state's history (see Map 4).

---

[33] Henry Heras, *The Aravidu Dynasty of Vijayanagar* (Madras, 1927), 5–11.
[34] *Ibid.*, 29–30.   [35] *Ibid.*, 32–38.

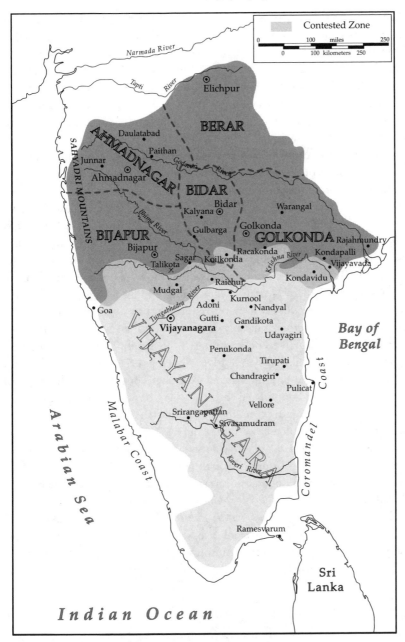

Map 4. The Deccan in 1565.

The view of Vijayanagara as the victim of Islamic aggression, and therefore of Talikota as some sort of titanic "clash of civilizations," is informed by a highly reductionist view of the presumed essential character of both Vijayanagara and the northern sultanates. Writing in 1900 during the height of Orientalist scholarship, the historian Robert Sewell perfectly articulated this view when he characterized Vijayanagara as "a Hindu bulwark against Muhammadan conquests."[36] From this perspective, it would follow that Talikota represented a decisive moment in India's religious history, since that battle saw Sewell's "Hindu bulwark" overwhelmed by an advancing tide of "Muhammadans."

But a scrutiny of the relations between Rama Raya and his northern neighbors reveals two important points. First, no party appears to have been motivated by religious concerns. And second, the Battle of Talikota, far from being a sudden, isolated event, possessed a very deep history. In fact, the battle grew out of several decades of conflict in which Rama Raya had chosen to ally himself with one or another of his neighbors. One might then ask why, from 1543 on, Rama Raya actively involved himself in the wars between the dynastic houses of the northern Deccan. A clue is found in his own growing dynastic identity. Departing radically from the traditions of any of the three houses that had theretofore governed Vijayanagara – the Sangama, Saluva, and Tuluva – Rama Raya increasingly associated himself, his family, and the state he governed with the Chalukya dynasty of Deccani kings (974–1190), and also with that dynasty's capital city of Kalyana. Although long-defunct, the imperial Chalukyas, who had dominated the peninsula from the Narmada River clear down to the Tamil country from the late tenth to the late twelfth century, were in Rama Raya's day still a powerful memory.

Consider the rhetoric of Vijayanagara's court poets and genealogists. Between 1543 and 1547, during his early years as regent, the poet Konerunatha Kavi praised members of Rama Raya's family with the extraordinary titles "Chalukya Emperor" (*Calukya-cakravarti*), "Founder of the Kingdom of Kalyana" (*Kalyana-rajya-sthapanacaryundu*), and "born in the Chalukyan line" (*Calukya-anvaya-bhava*).[37] A stone Sanskrit inscription at the great temple of Tirupati, dated 1561, publicly records a genealogy of the Aravidu family that describes Rama Raya's father as "Lord of the excellent city of Kalyana"

---

[36] Robert Sewell, *A Forgotten Empire (Vijayanagara): a Contribution to the History of India* (1900; repr. Delhi, 1962), 1.

[37] Konerunatha Kavi, *Padya Balabhagavatamu*, in *Andugula Vengakavi Ramarajiyamu leka Narapati Vijayamu mariyu Doneru Konerunatha-kavi Padya Balabhagavatamu, Dvipada Balabhagavatamu (Araviti Rajula Prasamsa)*, ed. C. V. Ramachandra Rao (Nellore, 1995), 67, 73. My thanks to Phillip Wagoner for drawing my attention to this work.

(*Kalyana-pura-varadhisah*) and Rama Raya himself as "A Narayana of the Chalukyas" (*calikki-narayana*).[38] Yet these boasts had no basis in fact since Kalyana is located far to the north of Vijayanagara and had for several centuries been controlled by Muslim rulers – first by the Tughluqs, then by the Bahmanis, and from 1543 by the sultan of Bidar, one of the five successor-states of the Bahmanis (see Map 4). Remarkably, Rama Raya's family was thus identified as lords over a city that for more than two centuries had been ruled by "Turks," as they were known in Vijayanagara.

In the late seventeenth century the Telugu poet Andugula Venga Kavi even claimed that Rama Raya was genealogically descended from the Kalyana Chalukyas. The same poet also made specific claims as to the territorial reach of Rama Raya's authority. Heading all the titles assigned him by the poet was the exalted "Radiant King of Kalyana" (*Kalyana mahipalabhaswari*), followed by "Lord of the Excellent City of Kalyana" (*Kalyana puravaradhisvara*) and "The One who Captured the City of Kalyana" (*Kalyananagara sadhaka*). Respecting cities to the north of the Krishna River other than Kalyana – that is, cities lying beyond Vijayanagara's actual reach – Rama Raya is said to have "protected" (*poshana*) Warangal, "captured" (*harana*) Sagar, "occupied" (*samakranti-dhira*) Daulatabad, "chastised" (*dushana*) Golkonda, and "terrified" (*bhishana*) Bijapur, Bidar, and even Delhi. By contrast, with respect to forts that Vijayanagara had controlled for a long time, such as Udayagiri, Kondavidu, Gutti, or Mudgal, the same poet described Rama Raya as only a "ruler" (*rajyapalaka, dharandhara, nayaka*), and not a "lord." In sum, among all the important political centers on either side of the Krishna, apart from metropolitan Vijayanagara itself, the only cities over which Rama Raya was declared "lord" were Kalyana (*puravaradhisvara*) and his family's power base in the Tamil plain, Chandragiri (*rajyadhisvara*).[39]

We should not dismiss as mere hyperbole Rama Raya's titles such as "Chalukya Emperor" or "Lord of Kalyana," as trumpeted by court poets, whether they were contemporary with Rama Raya or not. For, turning from the rhetoric of his poets to the record of his own deeds, we find that his actions in fact confirmed their words. As a general principle, for more than twenty years, Rama Raya endeavored to ensure that whichever northern sultan he was at the moment allied with *also* controlled Kalyana, as though that sultan were an intermediary between himself and the old Chalukya capital.

---

[38] Sadhu Subrahmanya Sastry and V. Vijayaraghavacharya, eds., *Tirumala Tirupati Devasthanam Inscriptions* 6, part 1: Inscriptions of Venkatapatiraya's Time (Tirupati, 1930; repr. 1998), no. 1.

[39] Andugula Venga Kavi, *Ramarajiyamu* [also known as *Narapati Vijayam*]. Extracts in S. Krishnaswami Aiyangar, ed., *Sources of Vijayanagar History* (1919; repr. Delhi, 1986), 182–83.

Thus, soon after his triumphant return to the capital in 1543, Rama Raya was invited by the sultan of Ahmadnagar to participate in a joint invasion of Bijapur, then allied with the sultan of Bidar, who in turn controlled the nearby fort of Kalyana. Agreeing to the proposition, he sent his brother Venkatadri at the head of a large army to join the action, out of which Vijayanagara gained both land and treasure. Kalyana, however, remained in Bidar's control. Three years later, Rama Raya induced his ally in Ahmadnagar again to invade Bijapur, but that campaign failed. Then in 1549 the sultan of Bijapur, angry at Rama Raya's intrigues against him, threatened Vijayanagara's ambassadors residing at his court, whereupon these men fled to their capital and complained to their master of their mistreatment. An enraged Rama Raya now resolved on punishing Bijapur by urging Ahmadnagar very specifically to attack Kalyana, which several years earlier had been ceded to Bijapur by Bidar. Following these urgings, the sultan of Ahmadnagar launched a dawn attack on the fort, and in line with Rama Raya's intentions, the former Chalukya capital fell into the hands of his ally.[40]

In 1558, when the sultan of Bijapur died and his successor 'Ali 'Adil Shah I resolved to recover Kalyana, the new sultan appealed to Rama Raya for help in the project. The two men formed a personal bond when the sultan rode virtually alone down to Vijayanagara to make his case and also to convey personal condolences on the death of Rama Raya's son. On this occasion the two men exchanged robes and feasted; Rama Raya's wife even called the sultan her own son (*farzand*). The upshot of their friendly meeting was that Rama Raya agreed to take his entire army north with a view to attacking the new ruler of Ahmadnagar, Sultan Husain Nizam Shah, and to restoring to Bijapur both Kalyana and the fort of Sholapur.[41] So in 1559 'Ali 'Adil Shah and Rama Raya joined forces and marched straight to Kalyana, which they besieged.

Outnumbered, Husain retreated to his capital at Ahmadnagar, which the invaders now besieged with a combined force of 100,000 cavalry. Husain then retreated to the town of Paithan on the Godavari River, only to be pursued by one of Rama Raya's generals. From Paithan the fugitive king sent an urgent message to the sultan of Berar pleading for help, and in response the latter sent his intrepid general Jahangir Khan to relieve the siege of Ahmadnagar. In late 1561, with Kalyana threatened, Ahmadnagar besieged, and himself holed up in Paithan, a desperate Husain sued for peace with Rama Raya. But Vijayanagara's stubborn generalissimo informed Husain that he would agree to peace only

---

[40] Briggs, *Rise*, III:56, 62–63, 141–43.
[41] Firishta, *Tarikh*, II:36; trans. Briggs, *Rise*, III:71, 145–46.

when three conditions were met. The first of these, significantly, was that Kalyana be ceded to his ally 'Ali 'Adil Shah I of Bijapur. Second, that Jahangir Khan be executed for interfering with the siege operations at Ahmadnagar. And finally, that Husain himself personally come to Rama Raya's headquarters and eat *pan* (betel nut) from his hand.[42]

Swallowing his pride, Husain submitted to each of Rama Raya's humiliating demands. First, he ordered Jahangir Khan executed. Then he proceeded to the Vijayanagara camp outside Ahmadnagar's fort and entered Rama Raya's tent. Rising to his feet, Rama Raya took the defeated sultan by the hand. But Husain, offended at having to touch the skin of his enemy, called for a basin of water to wash his hands. Enraged at this breach of etiquette, Rama Raya turned aside and muttered in Kannada, "If he were not my guest, I would cut off his hands and hang them round his neck." Calling for water, he too washed his hands. Husain then gave the keys to Kalyana fort to Rama Raya. At that moment the Vijayanagara ruler was indeed, if only briefly, the "lord" of Kalyana, his sovereignty unmediated by any other ruling authority. But, with no thought of actually annexing territory so far from Vijayanagara, and desiring only a symbolic sovereignty over his northern "vassal," Rama Raya immediately sent the keys to his ally 'Ali 'Adil Shah I of Bijapur. Then, for his final and most humiliating act of submission, Husain ate *pan* from the hand of Rama Raya.[43]

If the city and fort of Kalyana had all along been the focus of Rama Raya's policies in the northern Deccan, it now became an obsession for an embittered and humiliated Husain Nizam Shah. In 1562, determined to recover Kalyana from Bijapur, but also needing allies for the project, Husain cemented an alliance with Golkonda by offering his daughter in marriage to the sultan of that kingdom. To dramatize the centrality of the issue of Kalyana, the wedding ceremony was actually held beneath the walls of that fort, just beyond range of its cannon. As soon as the marriage celebrations were over, the forces of Ahmadnagar and Golkonda set about laying siege to the fort. Again 'Ali 'Adil Shah I of Bijapur marched to Vijayanagara to request assistance, and again Rama Raya mobilized and marched to Kalyana, this time to help his northern ally defend the fort.

For a second time Husain was forced to lift his siege of Kalyana and retreat to Ahmadnagar. Rama Raya pursued his adversary to the walls of Ahmadnagar, and again Husain was forced to abandon his capital, this time fleeing to the fort of Junnar, north of Pune. Rama Raya pursued him there as well, but in June

---

[42] Briggs, *Rise*, III:146–47, 241. 'Ali Tabataba, *Burhan-i ma'athir*, extracts trans. T. W. Haig, "The History of the Nizam Shahi Kings of Ahmadnagar," *Indian Antiquary* (April 1921): 105–06.
[43] Briggs, *Rise*, III:147–48.

1563 monsoon rains forced him to turn back to Vijayanagara. En route he gratuitously plundered and seized several districts of Golkonda and even some others belonging to his "ally," Bijapur.[44] This perfidious behavior snapped whatever tolerance the rulers of those kingdoms might still have had for their powerful neighbor to the south. Meanwhile Sultan Husain of Ahmadnagar, whom Rama Raya had repeatedly humiliated and hunted, burned with a desire for revenge, which he would soon find.

Such was the background to the Battle of Talikota of 1565, in which four kingdoms of the north – Ahmadnagar, Bijapur, Golkonda, and Bidar[45] – combined to challenge the grand army of Vijayanagara. During the winter of 1563–64, leaders of the four states cemented their cause through more inter-dynastic marital ties, resolving to merge forces a year later. Gathering in late December 1564 at the town of Talikota, just north of the Krishna River, the four armies forded that river and in late January 1565 engaged an immense Vijayanagara army near its southern shores. It was Rama Raya's last battle. During the conflict the octogenarian suffered a spear wound and fell from his horse. Captured by some Nizam Shahi troops, he was taken to Husain who, confronting his bitter adversary for the last time, ordered him beheaded on the spot, and his head stuffed with straw (see Plate 6).[46]

Vijayanagara's army now completely disintegrated. Rama Raya's brother Venkatadri was never heard from again. His other brother Tirumala, blinded in one eye, hastened from the battlefield to the capital, where he released Sadaśiva from prison, picked up his family, and quit the city just before the arrival of the advancing allies. While Sadaśiva and Tirumala busied themselves reconstituting the state and transferring the capital to the fort of Penukonda, some 120 miles to the southeast, the victorious allies spent six months looting the Vijayanagara metropolis. Two years later, the Venetian traveler Cesare Federici reported that the great city, twenty-four miles in circumference, "is not altogether destroyed, yet the houses stand still, but emptie, and there is dwelling in them nothing, as is reported, but Tygres and other wild beasts."[47] An era had ended. Rama Raya's

---

[44] *Ibid.*, III:74, 148–50, 243–44.

[45] The sultan of Berar abstained from joining the expedition, owing to his bitterness over Husain Nizam Shah's execution of his general, Jahangir Khan.

[46] Briggs, *Rise*, III:248. The battle scene depicted in Plate 6 is one of twelve miniatures that illustrate a Persian historical poem composed in the year of the battle by Aftabi, a Nizam Shahi court poet. See G. T. Kulkarni and M. S. Mate, eds. and trans., *Tarif-i-Husain Shah Badshah Dakhan* (Pune, 1987), 199–205.

[47] Cesare Federici, "Extracts of Master Caesar Frederike his Eighteene Yeeres Indian Observations," in *Hakluytus Posthumus, or Purchas his Pilgrimes*, by Samuel Purchas (1625; repr. Glasgow, 1905), x:92–93, 97.

obsessive preoccupation with Kalyana had played a decisive role in the wars leading to Talikota, to his own death, and to the destruction of the capital.

Why was Rama Raya so preoccupied with possessing "lordship" over Kalyana, even if only a symbolic or indirect lordship? For one thing, that city, occupying the very center of the plateau, had been ideally situated for the imperial ambitions of Chalukya kings. With their capital straddling the fault lines between the Marathi, Telugu, and Kannada linguistic zones, Chalukya sovereigns had made claims to imperial rule that transcended the linguistic space defined by any one of those vernacular languages. In fact, all three kingdoms that ruled the Deccan from the twelfth to the fourteenth century – the Hoysalas, Kakatiyas, and Yadavas – carved out linguistically based regional kingdoms by rebelling against their imperial Chalukya overlords. Rama Raya's claimed ties to the Chalukyas therefore signaled a return to a much earlier conception of authority, one whose spatial reach had extended from Kalyana over the *entire* Deccan plateau, both north and south of the Krishna River.

It is also likely that Rama Raya's claims to having conquered and ruled Kalyana evoked the memory of the bitter rivalry between two of the mightiest empires of medieval India – the Chalukyas of the central Deccan and the Cholas of the Tamil coast. In 1045 Rajadhiraja Chola had attacked and plundered Kalyana, taking back to his own capital a large stone door guardian as a trophy of war; subsequent Chola rulers made similar claims of having mastered or humiliated the Chalukya rulers of Kalyana.[48] Inasmuch as Rama Raya's own power-base was centered on the fortress of Chandragiri, on the northern Tamil plain near the Chola heartland, his claims to lordship over both Kalyana *and* the Tamil heartland would have recalled Chola deeds of glory vis-à-vis their perennial adversaries to the north. Moreover, Rama Raya, who lacked royal blood of his own, had usurped power, and had withheld the state's reigning sovereign from public view, needed some means to legitimate his rule. By mimicking Chola claims of mastery over their Chalukya adversaries, while also claiming genealogical descent from the Chalukya house, he attained at least a vicarious connection with two of the most powerful dynasties of recent memory.

THE PERSIANIZED WORLD OF THE EARLY MODERN DECCAN

There is no denying that the debacle at Talikota caused a political rupture for the Vijayanagara state. The destruction of the city deprived its rulers, now uprooted to Penukonda, of their status as "protectors" of Pampa and

---

[48] Richard H. Davis, *Lives of Indian Images* (Princeton, 1997), 51–3, 76–82.

Virupaksha, whose cults were inseparably tied to their ancient shrines by the banks of the Tungabhadra River. Nor could its rulers continue to patronize the many monuments with which the kingdom's sovereignty had become closely associated – most importantly, the Vitthala temple complex, whose central shrine and image were apparently desecrated in the course of the city's destruction that followed the battle.[49] Although the death of Rama Raya led to Sadasiva's immediate release from captivity, the dynasty did not survive the king's own death several years later. In 1570 Rama Raya's brother Tirumala was crowned the first king of Vijayanagara's last dynasty, the Aravidu, which for another century maintained a tenuous hold over fragments of the kingdom's earlier realm from successive capitals that migrated ever southward – first to Penukonda, then to Chandragiri, finally to Vellore.

Whether Talikota also caused a civilizational rupture, as often maintained, is however another matter. During the two centuries prior to 1565, states on both sides of the Krishna River had assimilated so much Persian culture, and had experienced so much cultural interaction, that their mutual struggles were practically reduced to the usual rivalries over territory and forts, and not over matters of "civilization," whether Hindu or Islamic. Architectural historians of metropolitan Vijayanagara have noted the spatial separation between the city's Sacred Center and Royal Center. In reality, this separation reflects a conceptual compartmentalization of the kingdom's "sacred" and "royal" domains – typical of the sultanate form of government – which enabled rulers to assimilate exogenous culture in the royal domain without affecting the sacred domain.

For example, most of the political culture of both Vijayanagara and its northern neighbors was Persian, whether elements of that culture had originated in Iran itself or had been transmitted through Iran en route to India. Consider the adoption of the title "sultan" by Vijayanagara's monarchs, as in the formula "Sultan among Indian kings." Meaning "all-powerful ruler" in Arabic, the term entered Persian, was carried to India by ethnic Turks, was then assimilated into Sanskrit as "*suratrana*," and in the Deccan became naturalized in Telugu and Kannada, among other vernaculars. This migrant orphan, which Phillip Wagoner has analyzed as part of a wide range of Vijayanagara's cultural

---

[49] It was customary for military victors in premodern India to desecrate the principal temple of a defeated enemy, in this way detaching the latter from the most visible representation of his state deity. By 1565 Vitthala, not Virupaksha, had become the deity before whom important documents were witnessed and authenticated. This seems to be why, of all the monuments in Vijayanagara, the Vitthala temple suffered the most damage when the city was sacked, whereas the Virupaksha escaped desecration. See Verghese, *Archaeology, Art and Religion*, 108. See also Pierre-Sylvian Filliozat and Vasundhara Filliozat, *Hampi-Vijayanagar: the Temple of Vithala* (New Delhi, 1988), 29.

borrowing from the Persian world, presents a classic instance of an idea, and a term, that resisted appropriation by any single language or ethnic group.[50] Virtually every ruler at Vijayanagara included "sultan" among his other titles. And while most were content with "Sultan among Indian kings," Rama Raya went further and styled himself "Sultan of the World" (*gola suratrana*), a title even more inflated than "Chalukya Emperor" (*Calukya-cakravarti*).[51]

As for the visual arts, metropolitan Vijayanagara, especially the Royal Center, is saturated with Persian architectural elements: domes, vaulted arches, parapets of merlons, corner finials, fine plasterwork, and so forth (see Plate 7).[52] The same holds for the city's layout. As Wagoner has further noted, Vijayanagara's citadel does not appear in the center of a concentric *mandala* pattern, as is prescribed in classical Indian texts, and is actually seen in the Kakatiya capital of Warangal. Rather, it appears off to one side, a design that finds antecedents in Indo-Persian citadels as in Daulatabad (1326–27), or a few years earlier in Tughluqabad (1320–23). Similarly, whereas Vijayanagara's north-facing throne hall has no known precedent in classical Indian courts, it does find antecedents in most Persian or Persian-inspired courts – as at Bidar, Sultanpur (i.e., Tughluq Warangal), Tughluqabad, and Samarqand – extending clearly back to Persepolis, capital of the ancient Persian Empire. To that famous site, too, can be traced the widespread tradition of royal halls with forty columns, 100 columns, or even 1,000 columns. These are found in courts throughout the Iranian plateau and South Asia, as in Delhi's "Hazar Sutun" (1343) built by Muhammad bin Tughluq. Moreover, Vijayanagara's multi-columned "House of Victory" and "Great Platform" find striking correspondences to the throne hall and Apadana of Persepolis. As on the Apadana, sculptural reliefs carved at the base of Vijayanagara's Great Platform depict processions of figures bearing tribute to the enthroned king.[53]

Further linking Vijayanagara with the wider Persian world were the thousands of Iranian or Deccani Muslim mercenaries who took up service with

---

[50] Phillip B. Wagoner, "'Sultan among Hindu Kings': Dress, Titles, and the Islamicization of Hindu Culture at Vijayanagara," *Journal of Asian Studies* 55, no. 4 (November 1996): 851–80.

[51] Konerunatha Kavi, *Padya Balabhagavatamu* (1543), in Krishnaswami Aiyangar, ed., *Sources of Vijayanagar History*, 204.

[52] George Michell, "Royal Architecture and Imperial Style at Vijayanagara," in *The Powers of Art: Patronage in Indian Culture*, ed. Barbara S. Miller (New Delhi, 1992), 175. See also Catherine B. Asher, "Islamic Influence and the Architecture of Vijayanagara," in *Vijayanagara – City and Empire: New Currents of Research*, ed. Anna Dallapiccola (Stuttgart, 1985), 188–95.

[53] Phillip B. Wagoner, "The Islamicate Contribution to the City Plan of Vijayanagara," Paper delievered at a symposium on "Hindu and Muslim in Precolonial South Asia," University of Texas, Austin (November 13, 1998).

the court and were accommodated in a large quarter of the capital – such as the 10,000 "Turks" hired by Deva Raya II in 1430, or the 3,000 Westerners that Rama Raya himself employed when they had been dismissed by the sultan of Bijapur. To these may be added the many Arab or Persian long-distance merchants, especially those involved in the international horse-import trade, memorialized in bas-relief sculptures along the base and exterior walls of numerous Vijayanagara monuments, sacred and secular. As a result of such contacts, a wide spectrum of Arabo-Persian words infiltrated spoken Telugu and Kannada, while courtly dress increasingly conformed to fashions set in the Middle East and Central Asia.[54]

In sum, the quickening pace of peninsular India's commercial and cultural interaction with the Iranian plateau in the fifteenth and sixteenth centuries had the effect of drawing the *whole* Deccan into the orbit of Persian culture. After all, that culture was widely perceived as prestigious, cosmopolitan, and most importantly, readily portable across ethnic frontiers. In 1443, just ten years before Mahmud Gawan first entered the heavily Persianized Bahmani court of Bidar, 'Abd al-Razzaq Samarqandi, a Timurid ambassador from Central Asia, visited Vijayanagara. There he found a court just as steeped in Persian culture as the one that Gawan would encounter a few years later nearly 200 miles to the north. Wearing a green satin robe, Deva Raya II was seated on a magnificent golden throne set in a north-facing throne hall that 'Abd al-Razzaq called a *chihil sutun* ("forty columns"). The ambassador's use of that Persian term suggests that he recognized in Vijayanagara the same sort of multi-columned hall already familiar to him from Middle Eastern courts. And during his interview with the king, 'Abd al-Razzaq was closely questioned about his own sovereign's nobles, army, warhorses, and cities such as Samarqand, Herat, and Shiraz – all indicating Deva Raya II's awareness of, and avid interest in the Timurid court.[55] In fact, the ambassador's experience illustrates Marshall Hodgson's remark that by the sixteenth century Vijayanagara had found itself "more or less enclaved" in what he called an "Islamicate" world, that is, a domain characterized not by religious identity but by standards of taste long established in the Middle East.[56]

---

[54] Wagoner, "'Sultan among Hindu Kings,'" 851–80. "They have breeches after the order of the Turkes," remarked Cesare Federici, who visited Vijayanagara in 1567. Federici, "Extracts," x:99.

[55] W. M. Thackston, trans., *A Century of Princes: Sources on Timurid History and Art* (Cambridge MA, 1989), 310–14.

[56] Marshall Hodgson, "The Role of Islam in World History," *International Journal of Middle East Studies* 1, no. 2 (April 1970): 118.

SUMMARY

In his own day, Rama Raya was understood in many ways. To his subjects he was son-in-law of Krishna Raya, powerful general, godfather of a sprawling patrimonial state, savior of that state from civil war, and patron of Telugu literature and of the Venkateśwara temple at Tirupati. The sultans of the northern Deccan viewed him either as a powerful ally or as a feared adversary, depending on whether they were allied with him or against him.[57] Rama Raya appears to have seen himself as, among other things, "lord" of Kalyana – simultaneously conqueror of that city and heir to the Chalukya imperial tradition. No evidence, however, suggests that his contemporaries saw him as a defender of Hindu dharma or the Deccan itself as a region permanently divided between a Muslim north and Hindu south. Like other soldiers, Rama Raya served rulers on both sides of the Krishna River; and like other rulers, he employed soldiers from both sides of that river. In a word, his career exemplified the remarkable extent of élite mobility that in the fifteenth and sixteenth centuries was occurring throughout the Deccan plateau, enabled in part by the diffusion of a common, Persian culture in the whole region.

Yet Sewell's idea of Vijayanagara as a "Hindu bulwark against Muhammadan conquests" persisted throughout the twentieth century and continues in the twenty-first.[58] Noting the many books on south Indian history whose titles include the phrase "to the fall of Vijayanagara," Burton Stein has drawn attention to the sense of total break that the debacle at Talikota came to mean for modern historians. Implicit in the phrase is the notion that before Talikota the Vijayanagara era had been a Hindu "golden age," and that after that battle it became a *lost* golden age. Such thinking, argues Stein, lies in "the attribution of a spurious nationalism to the Vijayanagara state."[59] In other words, the history of the early modern Deccan is to some extent a prisoner of modern politics.

[57] The only contemporary description of the Battle of Talikota was composed by Aftabi, a court poet of Sultan Husain Nizam Shah. Aftabi refers to Rama Raya, the enemy of his patron, as a "useless infidel" (*kafir-i nabakar*). But when describing the battle scene, Aftabi resorts to stock poetic tropes appropriate for any powerful and respected adversary: "Ram Raja was Rao of Bijanagar; He was with tied waist and wore a crown. When he arranged his army of swordsmen and archers, Its lightning-like flash reached the clouds. Because of movement of iron shoes of animals, the swords and the tent poles, The earth was shaken up from its very foundations. Due to the loud cries coming from ambush, The sky appeared to be thrown down on the earth." Kulkarni and Mate, *Tarif-i-Husain Shah*, 173, 183.

[58] A world history time-line published in 2001 characterized fifteenth-century peninsular India in the following words: "The Hindu kingdom of Vijayanagar becomes the independent center for resistance to Islam." Andreas Nothiger, *World History Chart* (Vancouver, 2001).

[59] Burton Stein, "Vijayanagara and the Transition to Patrimonial Systems," in *Vijayanagara*, ed. Dallapiccola, 73, 74.

One way to overcome such modernist or "nationalistic" readings of Vijayanagara history, and of Deccan history generally, might be to take very seriously
the lexical categories that were used by contemporary actors, instead of projecting backwards onto them "our" own, modern categories. A case in point
is a mosque in metropolitan Vijayanagara built by one Ahmad Khan in 1439.
Our understanding of the monument has been greatly distorted by imposing on it modern presuppositions of what a proper mosque ought to be and
how it ought to appear. For one thing, its dedicatory inscription, composed in
Kannada, does not state that Ahmad Khan built the structure for the glory of
God, but rather for the merit of the king, Deva Raya II. Second, the inscription refers to the structure not by the Arabic *masjid* ("mosque"), but by the
Sanskrit *dharma-sala* ("hall of religion"). And third, the structure lacks domes
and arches – to modern sensibilities emblematic features of Islamic architecture – and instead takes the form of a pillared hall (*mandapa*) typical of temple
architecture of its own day. But because twentieth-century scholars imposed
their own rigidly bipolar categories of meaning on the structure, for many years
it was not identified as a mosque at all, but as a "rest house." It was not until
the 1980s that its true identity as a mosque was finally recognized.[60]

Modern categories hinder our understanding of the premodern Deccan in
still other ways. The many references to "Turks" one finds in contemporary
records – as in Deva Raya II's reference to the 10,000 cavalry he had recruited
to his service – are routinely glossed by modern historians as "Muslims." But
the habitual substitution of "our" religious category for "their" ethnic category
can be very distorting, as it reads into the past a concern with religion that is
not warranted by original sources. In the end, such transpositions probably say
more about our own preoccupation with communalism than they do about
the peoples and cultures we are trying to understand.

---

[60] Phillip B. Wagoner, "Fortuitous Convergences and Essential Ambiguities: Transcultural Political
Élites in the Medieval Deccan," *International Journal of Hindu Studies* 3, no. 3 (December 1999):
241–64.

CHAPTER 5

MALIK AMBAR (1548–1626): THE RISE AND FALL OF MILITARY SLAVERY

The slaves of this kingdom [Damot, in Ethiopia] are much esteemed by the Moors, and they do not let them go at any price; all the country of Arabia, Persia, India, Egypt, and Greece, are full of slaves from this country, and they say they make very good Moors and great warriors.[1]

Father Francisco Alvares (1523)

FROM "CHAPU" TO "MALIK AMBAR"

An Ethiopian slave known to history as "Malik Ambar" was already seventeen years old in 1565, the year of the Battle of Talikota. If that date signaled the beginning of a slide into near-oblivion for the city of Vijayanagara, for the Ethiopian it heralded the dawn of an extraordinary career. His original name was not, of course, Malik Ambar, for *malik* means "king," conceptually quite distant from a slave. In his native land he was known as "Chapu," a name that suggests an origin in the Kambata region of southern Ethiopia.

Born in 1548, Chapu as a youth had fallen into the hands of slave dealers operating between the Ethiopian highlands and the coasts of eastern Africa. He might have been captured in war, or he might have been sold into slavery by his impoverished parents. In any event, he joined streams of other Ethiopians – known in the Arab world as "Habshis"[2] – who turned up in slave markets in the Middle East, there to enter élite households as servants or, as in Chapu's case, to be re-exported to the Deccan plateau to meet that region's insatiable demand for military labor. Chapu thus appears to have been sold and resold several times after his initial entry into slavery. A contemporary European source relates that he was sold in the Red Sea port of Mocha for the sum of eighty

---

[1] Francisco Alvares, *The Prester John of the Indies: a True Relation of the Lands of the Prester John, being the Narrative of the Portuguese Embassy to Ethiopia in 1520,* trans. Lord Stanley of Alderley, rev. and ed. C. F. Beckingham and G. W. B. Huntingford (Cambridge, 1961), 1:455.

[2] A note on terminology: "Ethiopia" is the ancient Greek term for Abyssinia. I am using "Ethiopian" and "Habshi" to refer to members of various ethnic communities from the Abyssinian highlands and the immediately surrounding regions. Contemporary Indo-Persian accounts refer to Ethiopians in the Deccan by the term "Habshi," while sixteenth-century Portuguese accounts called them Abyssinians. In Dutch records of the seventeenth century they were known by the term *caffer,* which referred more generally to blacks from Africa.

Dutch guilders.[3] A near-contemporary Persian chronicle reports that he was taken to Baghdad and sold to a prominent merchant who, recognizing Chapu's superior intellectual qualities, raised and educated the youth, converted him to Islam, and gave him the name "Ambar" (Ar. 'anbar: "ambergris").[4] From Baghdad he was taken to the Deccan and purchased by Chengiz Khan, who held the office of peshwa, or chief minister, of the Nizam Shahi sultanate of Ahmadnagar. This kingdom, the westernmost of the five successor-states to the Bahmani Sultanate, was then ruled by the son of Sultan Husain Nizam Shah, one of the victors at Talikota.[5]

Although a black African, Ambar would hardly have stood out amidst the mosaic of ethnic groups then inhabiting the western Deccan (see Plate 8). In the first place, he was one of a thousand other Habshi slaves purchased by Chengiz Khan, himself a Habshi and a former slave.[6] In turn, Chengiz Khan was only one of many high-ranking state servants in the five Deccan sultanates who had been systematically recruiting Habshis as military slaves in the sixteenth century, as Bahmani officials had done in the fifteenth. Of the five successor-states to the Bahmanis, however, Ahmadnagar and Bijapur probably had the greatest number of Habshi slaves in their service. Controlling the seaports along the Konkan coast, both states had ready access to slave markets in the Middle East, as it took Arab dhows only several weeks to reach India's western ports sailing down from the Red Sea or the Persian Gulf.

Modern histories typically narrate Malik Ambar's career in heroic terms, as though Shakespeare's Othello had been somehow transposed from Venice to India. We thus read stirring stories of this Ethiopian ex-slave who rescued the kingdom of Ahmadnagar from annexation by the imperial Mughals, or at least postponed that outcome. Some historians even construe Ambar as a proto-nationalist figure.[7] Yet Malik Ambar's career can also provide a window onto a range of other issues pertaining to the social history of the Deccan – issues of race, class, or gender, and especially issues related to the institution of slavery. What explains the rise and disappearance of military slavery in the Deccan between the fifteenth and seventeenth centuries? Why was Ethiopia

---

[3] W. Ph. Coolhaas, ed., Pieter Van den Broecke in Azië (Hague, 1962), 1:148.

[4] Hashim Beg Astarabadi, Futuhat-i 'Adil Shahi (London: British Library, Add. 26, 234), cited in D. R. Seth, "The Life and Times of Malik Ambar," Islamic Culture 31 (1957): 142.

[5] Radhey Shyam, Life and Times of Malik Ambar (New Delhi, 1968), 35.

[6] Jadunath Sarkar, House of Shivaji (Studies and Documents on Maratha History, Royal Period), 3rd edn. (Calcutta, 1955), 6.

[7] Prominent biographies include: Jogindra Nath Chowdhuri, Malik Ambar: a Biography Based on Original Sources (Calcutta, c. 1933); D. R. Seth, "Life and Times," 142–55; Shyam, Life and Times of Malik Ambar; and B. G. Tamaskar, The Life and Work of Malik Ambar (Delhi, 1978).

the major source for India's military slaves at that time? How did these slaves become assimilated into the society into which they had been introduced, over time evolving from slaves, to clients, to patrons, and in some cases to slave-holders themselves? And, what role did Habshis play in the old struggle between Deccanis and Westerners?

ETHIOPIAN SUPPLY, DECCANI DEMAND

To answer these questions we need first to step back into the land of Malik Ambar's birth – the remote highlands of sixteenth-century Ethiopia. Ever since the seventh century when the rise of Islam cut if off from the Mediterranean world, the ancient Christian kingdom of Ethiopia evolved along its own distinctive path, creating a remarkable synthesis of Semitic and northeast African (i.e., Cushitic) cultures. Presiding over a predominantly agricultural society were nobles, patriarchs, priests, monks, and a dynasty of sacred kings believed to have been descended from the biblical Solomon. Although Jesuits of the seventeenth century would denigrate the Ethiopian Church as a Jewish–pagan corruption of "true," that is, Latin, Christianity,[8] earlier European assessments were far more favorable. Based on sketchy reports drifting in from points east, from the twelfth century on rumors circulated through European capitals of a mighty Christian monarch named "Prester John" whose kingdom was thought to lie somewhere beyond the Muslim world, in "the Indies." By the end of the fifteenth century, after concluding that the long-sought Christian king was not to be found in Asia, Europeans had identified the Solomonic kingdom of Ethiopia with that of Prester John.[9]

Once Portuguese navigators had found an all-sea route into the Indian Ocean, the Roman Church and Catholic monarchs, hoping to forge an anti-Muslim strategic alliance with this Prester John, eagerly sought news about Ethiopia and its Christian tradition. "They all have woolly hair," noted the Portuguese traveler and official Tomé Pires in 1516, adding, "and instead of being baptized they are branded on the forehead. They have priests, patriarchs and other monks. They go on pilgrimages to Jerusalem and Mount Sinai every year."[10] In addition to this promising, if fragmentary, news about the

---

[8] Mordechai Abir, *Ethiopia and the Red Sea* (London, 1980), 215.

[9] See Manuel João Ramos, "Ethiopia in the Geographical Representations of Mediaeval and Renaissance Europe," in *Cultures of the Indian Ocean*, ed. Jessica Hallet and C. Amaral (Lisbon, 1998), 44–54.

[10] Tomé Pires, *The Suma Oriental of Tomé Pires: an Account of the East, from the Red Sea to Japan, Written in Malacca and India in 1512–1515*, trans. Armando Cortesão (London, 1944; repr. New Delhi, 1990), 1:8.

religion of Ethiopia, Pires also identified this region as the principal source of the slaves then known to be taken from eastern Africa to Arabia and points east. The Arabs, Pires wrote, "make raids on horseback, in the course of which they capture large numbers of Abyssinians [i.e., Ethiopians] whom they sell to the people of Asia."[11] Some slaves were obtained directly by raiding parties coming from outside, in the manner that Pires described; others were captured in internal wars between local communities and then bartered to long-distance merchants; still others were sold into slavery by impoverished parents.

Between the fourteenth and seventeenth centuries both Muslims and Christians obtained most of their slaves from amongst pagan communities that lay along the western and southern fringes of the Christian kingdom, in regions such as Damot, Kambata, or Hadya.[12] In 1520 Father Francisco Alvares, a member of the first Portuguese mission to reach the Ethiopian highlands, kept a journal in which he sketched the broad contours of Ethiopia's slave-extraction system. As he approached the southern perimeters of the Christian kingdom, he encountered semi-independent pagan states that paid tribute to the Solomonic dynasty. With reference to Damot, one of these kingdoms, Alvares wrote:

> The slaves of this kingdom are much esteemed by the Moors, and they do not let them go at any price; all the country of Arabia, Persia, India, Egypt, and Greece, are full of slaves from this country, and they say they make very good Moors and great warriors. These are pagans, and among them in this kingdom are many Christians.[13]

That is to say, although some Christians were to be found in this non-Christian kingdom – a tributary satellite of the Ethiopian state – those enslaved in Damot were pagans who were converted to Islam and sent to serve as warriors in lands far beyond Arabia. Kambata, the region from which Malik Ambar appears to have come, lay directly south of Damot. "Cumbala Hill," a quarter in modern Mumbai whose name is probably derived from "Kambata," attests to the importance of the slave trade between this part of East Africa and the Deccan plateau.

International commerce, though less conspicuous to foreign observers than Arab slave-raiding, formed a more important element in Ethiopia's slave-extraction system. In one town in the northeastern highlands, Father Alvares found "merchants of all nations," including "Moors of India," and noted that

---

[11] *Ibid.*, 1:14.
[12] By the 1640s and '50s, the Ethiopian state was engaging in slave-raiding expeditions on its western frontier with Sudan. Non-Christian slaves were integrated into the Ethiopian state apparatus as palace guards or cavalrymen. Richard Pankhurst, *A Social History of Ethiopia: the Northern and Central Highlands from Early Medieval Times to the Rise of Emperor Tewodros II* (Trenton NJ, 1992), 111–12.
[13] Alvares, *Prester John*, 1:455.

Ethiopian priests wore white cloaks made of Indian cotton. The Ethiopian emperor himself ("Prester John") presented Alvares and five other Europeans with fine Indian cloths. Alvares also noted the enormous quantities of Indian silks and brocades consumed by the Ethiopian court, acquired both by gifting and by purchase.[14] Writing a century later of a small pagan state in southwestern Ethiopia, the Jesuit priest Manuel de Almeida observed that whenever the king of that state bought foreign cloth from merchants, the price would be fixed in slaves, which the king would then procure and use to settle the transaction.[15]

Clearly, Indian textiles were reaching the Ethiopian highlands in exchange for Ethiopian exports, which included gold and ivory in addition to slaves. In the fifteenth and sixteenth centuries, as the Ethiopian highlands became more tightly integrated into Indian Ocean trading networks, huge caravans of long-distance merchants, most of them Muslims, pushed ever deeper into the hinterland, exchanging goods brought from the coasts for goods extracted from the interior. The outflow of Ethiopian slaves was thus responding to forces of supply and demand that spanned the larger Indian Ocean trading world. African demand for Indian textiles, however, appears to have been the principal engine behind Ethiopia's slave-extraction process, in this respect anticipating by several centuries the much better known slave trade from West Africa to the Americas. At its height in the eighteenth century, this trade was likewise driven mainly by African demand for Indian textiles.[16]

Facilitating Ethiopia's slave export system were the mutually supportive ties between the Solomonic dynasty and the long-distance Muslim merchants that connected the Christian kingdom with the outside world. Ethiopia's "Law of the Kings" (*Fethä Nägäst*), a law code dating to the thirteenth century, permitted the enslavement of non-Christian war captives and the ownership of children of slaves by their parents' owners, basing such principles on Hebrew scripture (i.e., Leviticus xxv:44–46). It also prohibited Ethiopians from selling Christian slaves to non-Christians, although they were not in principle prevented from capturing and selling pagans to others to enslave. Taken together, these legal traditions had the effect of leaving Ethiopia's entire export slave trade in non-Christian, that is, Muslim, hands.[17]

[14] *Ibid.*, 1:187, 270; 11:359, 429, 434, 447–48.

[15] C. F. Beckingham and G. W. B. Huntingford, trans. and ed., *Some Records of Ethiopia, 1593–1646: being Extracts from* The History of High Ethiopia or Abassia *by Manoel de Albeida* (London, 1954), 162.

[16] Herbert S. Klein, "Economic Aspects of the Eighteenth-century Atlantic Slave Trade," in *The Rise of Merchant Empires: Long-distance Trade in the Early Modern World, 1350–1750*, ed. James D. Tracy (Cambridge, 1990), 290–93.

[17] Pankhurst, *Social History*, 64.

In fact, the Christian kingdom collaborated with long-distance Muslim traders in exporting slaves to the wider world. Ever since the fourteenth century the Ethiopian state, jealously claiming sovereignty over the trade routes that connected the interior with the sea, imposed taxes on all Muslim commercial activity in its domain.[18] Court officials therefore protected an activity from which they benefited financially. A Jesuit account dated 1556 records that owing to the taboo against enslaving Christians, the Solomonic kingdom actually refrained from baptizing neighboring pagan communities so that it could capture and send such peoples down to the coasts, there to be sold to Arab brokers and shippers, evidently in exchange for Indian textiles. In this way, from 10,000 to 12,000 slaves annually left Ethiopia, according to this account.[19]

Of course, the extraction of slaves from the Ethiopian highlands forms only part of the story; the other was the demand for slaves in the various hinterlands behind the ports that rimmed the Arabian Sea. The Habshis drawn into the Indian Ocean trading world were not intended to serve their masters as menial laborers, but, as Tomé Pires correctly observed already in 1516, as élite, military slaves – "knights," as he put it.[20] As in other forms of slavery, military slaves were severed from their natal kin group, rendering them dependent upon their owners. But unlike domestic or plantation slaves, military slaves performed the purely political task of maintaining the stability of state systems, since in most cases their masters were themselves high-ranking state servants. Dating from ninth-century Iraq, the institution of military slavery was predicated on the assumption that political systems can be corrupted when faction-prone webs of kinship take root within their ruling class. A perceived solution to this problem was to recruit into state service soldiers who were not only detached from their own kin, but also were total outsiders to the state and the society it governed. Such measures, it was assumed, would guarantee the slave's continued loyalty to the state. As the Seljuk minister Nizam al-Mulk (d. 1092) put it, "One obedient slave is better than three hundred sons; for the latter desire their father's death, the former his master's glory."[21]

Although military slavery is often identified as an "Islamic" institution, it never occurred throughout the Muslim world. In fact, it was more the exception

---

[18] Taddesse Tamrat, *Church and State in Ethiopia, 1270–1527* (Cambridge, 1972), 85–88; Harold G. Marcus, *History of Ethiopia* (Berkeley, 1994), 19.

[19] Richard Pankhurst, *The Ethiopian Borderlands: Essays in Regional History from Ancient Times to the End of the 18th Century* (Lawrence NJ, 1997), 252–53.

[20] Pires, *Suma Oriental*, 1:8.

[21] Nizam al-Mulk, *The Book of Government, or Rules for Kings: the Siyar al-muluk, or Siyasat-nama of Nizam al-Mulk*, trans. Hubert Darke, 2nd edn. (London, 1978), 117.

than the rule. Historian André Wink has proposed that "élite slavery was and always remained a frontier phenomenon."[22] It would be more accurate to say that the institution thrived in politically unstable and socially fluid contexts in which hereditary authority was weak, as is often the case with frontiers. Such was certainly the case in the northern Deccan from the fifteenth through seventeenth centuries, where the deadly struggle between the region's two dominant power groups, the Deccanis and the Westerners, produced chronic instability. With neither faction able to achieve permanent dominance over the other, state officials sought stability by recruiting to their service slave soldiers whose loyalty lay in principle with the state, but in practice with their legal owners.

On either side of the Arabian Sea, then, two very different kinds of markets – one commercial, the other political – were driving the slave trade. On the Ethiopian side, African manpower was extracted and exported in exchange mainly for Indian textiles consumed by clerical or ruling élites in the Christian kingdom. In the Deccan, a chronically unstable environment caused by mutually antagonistic factions, the Deccanis and the Westerners, created a market for culturally alien military labor.

Once these men entered slavery, their lives took a dramatic turn from what they had known in Africa. Their buyers fed them, housed them, taught them in the ways of household life and duties, and in all respects protected them, receiving in return an absolute and unswerving loyalty. This intimate relation between African slave and Indian master was both asymmetrical and complementary: the Africans possessed power but lacked kin and inherited authority, whereas the Indians possessed kin and inherited authority, but lacked sufficient power. Such an interdependent relationship engendered lasting bonds of mutual trust, which explains why court officials, administrators, or high-ranking army commanders were willing to entrust the most delicate and important official duties to their Habshi slaves, and to them alone. Thus, already in Bahmani times Habshis in the court of Sultan Firuz (1397–1422) served as personal attendants, bodyguards, and guards of the harem. Sultan Ahmad Bahmani II (1436–58) also assigned to Habshi slaves his most trusted posts, such as key governorships and keeper of the royal seal. Similarly, Mahmud Gawan appointed a Habshi as his personal seal-bearer and entrusted the governorship of the politically sensitive Kolhapur region to an Ethiopian slave.[23]

---

[22] André Wink, *al-Hind: the Making of the Indo-Islamic World*. vol. 2: *The Slave Kings and the Islamic Conquest, 11th-13th Centuries* (Leiden, 1997), 181.

[23] Richard Pankhurst, "The Ethiopian Diaspora to India: the Role of Habshis and Sidis from Medieval Times to the End of the Eighteenth Century," in *The African Diaspora in the Indian Ocean*, ed. Shihan de Silva Jayasuriya and Richard Pankhurst (Trenton NJ, 2003), 195.

And in 1481, when Gawan was executed, it was a Habshi – one of the sultan's slaves – who wielded the sword.

The status of Habshi slaves in Deccan society was not, however, fixed or permanent. On the death of their masters, Habshi slaves generally became freemen, continuing their military careers as free lancers in the service of powerful commanders. In this way they exchanged a master–slave relationship for a new patron–client one. The humbler sorts sought out and served commanders as paid troopers; the more talented managed to attract their own troopers (frequently other ex-slaves), obtain land assignments, and enter the official hierarchy as ranked commanders (*amirs*).

As this happened, Habshi ex-slaves generally allied themselves both culturally and politically with the Deccani class. This was because the institution of slavery had permanently severed their ties with Africa. Unlike the Westerners, who after several generations of living in the Deccan continued to cultivate the Persian language and to nourish close family or commercial ties with the Middle East, Habshis had no option of returning to Ethiopia. The Deccan being their only home, they readily assimilated into Deccan society, embracing its regional culture and its vernacular languages.

MUGHAL IMPERIALISM AND DECCANI REGIONAL IDENTITY

The emergence of a distinct Deccani regional identity, already visible in the mid-fourteenth century as both cause and consequence of the Bahmanis' successful revolution against north Indian Tughluq rule, gained force in the sixteenth century. Once again, driving the process was pressure from powerful and alien northerners, this time the imperial Mughals. Still a fragile kingdom occupying the Delhi plain in the days of Babur (1526–30), the Mughals by the late sixteenth century had swollen into a vast imperial formation whose appetite for annexing ever more territory seemed insatiable. Sooner or later, every state of the Deccan had to deal with this colossus of the north, and of these, Ahmadnagar, occupying the northwestern corner of the Deccan plateau, was the first. To make matters worse, the same internal ferment and instability that had been drawing military labor from Africa into Ahmadnagar also invited interference from the aggressive and expanding Mughals, then under the rule of Jalal al-Din Akbar (d. 1605), one of the most expansive emperors in Indian history.

In 1595, when Sultan Burhan Nizam Shah II of Ahmadnagar died and disputes over his succession revived the deadly factional struggle between

Westerners and Deccanis, one of the two parties committed the blunder of inviting Akbar's son, Prince Murad, to march south and intervene on its behalf. Possessing the very excuse they wanted, Prince Murad and his generals arrived at Ahmadnagar and promptly laid siege to the fort. The Mughal conquest of the Deccan might well have begun then and there, were it not for the gallant and spirited defense of the citadel led by Chand Bibi, the sister of the late sultan.

In March 1596, with the military situation at Ahmadnagar's fort stalemated, representatives of the two sides met just beyond the city walls to discuss a settlement. Here, in those negotiations, we can glimpse something of the vast chasm separating the culture of the Mughal ruling class from that of the various groups then ruling Ahmadnagar. The meeting opened with Ahmadnagar's diplomat, Afzal Khan, challenging the Mughals' right to make demands on Deccani territory. Whereupon one of the Mughal generals, with Prince Murad at his side, exploded in rage:

> What nonsense is this? You, like a eunuch, are keeping a woman [i.e., Chand Bibi] in the fort in the hope that she will come to your aid . . . This man [i.e., Prince Murad] is the son of his Majesty the Emperor, Jalal al-Din Muhammad Akbar, at whose court many kings do service. Do you imagine that the crows and kites of the Deccan, who squat like ants or locusts over a few spiders, can cope with the descendant of Timur and his famous *amirs* – the Khan-i Khanan and Shahbaz Khan, for example – each of whom has conquered countries ten times as large as the Deccan? . . . You, who are men of the same race as ourselves, should not throw yourselves away for no purpose.

First, the haughty general challenged Afzal Khan's manliness. Second, he contrasted the lofty dignity of Akbar and his illustrious ancestor Timur with the mere insects of the Deccan. Third and most importantly, he played the race card, reminding the Ahmadnagar diplomats that, in the end, all the assembled negotiators for both sides of the conflict were Westerners. That is, they all were of the same, proud Persian stock, in contrast to the assortment of Marathas, Habshis, and Indo-Turks – contemptuously dismissed by the Mughal as "the crows and kites of the Deccan" – then defending Ahmadnagar's fort against the advancing tide from the north.

But Afzal Khan, yielding no ground to his arrogant counterpart, replied,

> For forty years I have eaten the salt of the sultans of the Deccan . . . There is no better way to die than to be slain for one's benefactor, thereby obtaining an everlasting good name . . . Moreover, it should be evident to you that the people of this country are hostile toward Westerners. I myself am a Westerner and a well-wisher of the emperor [Akbar], and

I consider it to be in his interest to withdraw the Prince's great *amir*s from the neighborhood of this fort.[24]

By invoking the ancient metaphor of "salt," the Ahmadnagar envoy articulated a conception of socio-political solidarity very different from his counterpart's baser appeal to a common, Iranian ethnicity. "Eating the salt" or "fidelity to salt" refers to the oath that binds a patron and client through mutual obligations of protection and loyalty – an idea that, owing to Britain's former connection with India, survives in English to this day (e.g., to be "true to the salt").[25]

The confrontation between Prince Murad and Afzal Khan reveals a face-off between two distinctly different political structures. For their part, the Mughals present a posture of racial arrogance, a sense of pedigree, and a strong sense of hereditary aristocracy. In north India, military slavery as an actual institution had long since disappeared, surviving only in a vestigial, rhetorical form: high-born Mughal officials, all of them free men, customarily swore political loyalty to the emperor by styling themselves "slaves of the court" (*bandagan-i dargah*). On the Deccan side, by contrast, military slavery as an actual institution still existed. But among Ahmadnagar's fighting men there were also large numbers of Habshi ex-slaves whose African background gave them no purchase on political power, and to whom appeals to Iranian racial solidarity would have had no meaning. On the other hand, oaths of loyalty based on the ethnically neutral notion of salt, and specifically on "eating the salt" of a political superior, expressed the new ethically based patron–client relation into which former slaves had entered, replacing the earlier, legally based master–slave relation they had known since childhood.

---

[24] The phrase "You, who are men of the same race as ourselves" reads in the original: *shuma mardum ki ibna-yi jins-i ma'id.* See 'Ali Tabataba, *Burhan-i ma'athir* (Delhi, 1936), 629–30. Extracts trans. T. Wolseley Haig, "The History of the Nizam Shahi Kings of Ahmadnagar," *Indian Antiquary* 52 (Nov. 1923): 343–45. I have modernized the language of Haig's English translation.

[25] In the ancient Mesopotamian world, the Akkadian phrase meaning "to eat the salt of (a person)" expressed the act of making a covenant with a person or of permitting a reconciliation with another individual. See Daniel Potts, "On Salt and Salt Gathering in Ancient Mesopotamia," *Journal of The Economic and Social History of the Orient* 27, no. 3 (October 1984): 228. The phrase "not worth his salt" is traceable to Petronius Arbiter (*Satyricon*, first century AD), but the political sense of an oath of salt entered modern English through the British Raj, as in Rudyard Kipling's

> I have eaten your bread and salt,
> I have drunk your water and wine;
> The deaths ye died I have watched beside,
> and the lives ye led were mine.

(*Departmental Ditties* [1886], Prelude, st. 1). Persian usages include *namak khurdan* and *namak-shinas,* contrasted with *namak shikastan* and *namak-nashinas.*

COLOR PLATES

Plate 1. Warangal fort: east gate of stone wall from the outside, showing steps to parapet.

Plate 2. Warangal: earthen wall west of fort, looking south.

Plate 3. Warangal fort: interior of Tughluq audience hall (*c.* 1323–35).

Plate 4. Bidar: southern gate to fort (1432).

Plate 5. Bidar: *madrasa* of Mahmud Gawan (1472).

Plate 6. Rama Raya beheaded at the Battle of Talikota (1565). Miniature painting in the contemporary text, *Tarif-i Husayn Shahi*. Courtesy: American Council for South Asian Art, University of Michigan, Ann Arbor, MI, and Bharata Itihasa Samshodaka Mandala, Pune, India. ACSAA slide 1795.

Plate 7. Vijayanagara: domed gateway, southeast of royal center.

Plate 8. Portrait of Malik Ambar, signed by Hashem (*c.* 1624–25). Courtesy: V&A Images/Victoria and Albert Museum, No. IM-21-1925.

Plate 9. Painting of Jahangir shooting the head of Malik Ambar, signed by
Abu'l-Hasan (*c.* 1616). Courtesy: The Trustees of the Chester Beatty Library, Dublin,
CBL In.07A.15.

Plate 10. Statue of Tukaram. Bhandara Hill, near Dehu.

Plate 11. Indrayani River where Tukaram submerged his books.

Plate 12. Portrait of Papadu by an anonymous artist (*c.* 1750–80). Courtesy: V&A Images/Victoria and Albert Museum, No. IS-205-1953.

Plate 13. Shahpur: walls and watchtower of fort, looking northeast.

Plate 14. Equestrian statue of Tarabai in Kavala Naka Square, Kolhapur. Erected in 1981 from donations of people of Kolhapur district. Sculptor: Ravindra Misra.

Plate 15. Pratapgarh: exterior walls and bastion, looking south.

Plate 16. Panhala: northern granary, looking west.

MALIK AMBAR AND THE MUGHALS

It was during the tumultuous period 1595–1600 that the Ethiopian slave born as "Chapu," and later renowned as "Malik Ambar," rose to prominence. During his involuntary travels from Ethiopia to Baghdad to India, Ambar had been sold and resold several times before finally entering Ahmadnagar's service in the early 1570s as a slave of Chengiz Khan, the *peshwa* (chief minister) of Ahmadnagar. In 1574–75, his life took a critical turn when his master and patron, Chengiz Khan, died. Freed by the widow of his former master,[26] Ambar now became a free lancer. He also acquired a wife. Abandoning Ahmadnagar, for some time he served the sultan of neighboring Bijapur, who placed him in charge of a small contingent of troops and gave him the title "Malik." But in 1595, complaining of insufficient support, he quit Bijapur and, with his corps of 150 loyal cavalrymen, returned to Ahmadnagar where he entered the service of another Habshi commander, Abhang Khan. This was just the moment when armies of the imperial Mughals were besieging the capital with a view to annexing the entire kingdom to Akbar's vast and still-expanding empire. Within the fort, meanwhile, four rival power-players vied for control of the floundering state, each one promoting his or her own candidate for sultan.

On the night of December 21, 1595, Malik Ambar and his troops managed to break through Mughal lines, but they could not cope with the besiegers' far superior force. As Nizam Shahi nobles and disbanded troopers dispersed into the countryside, so did Malik Ambar. Such unstable conditions provided an opportune moment for men with natural leadership ability, and Ambar, owing to his success in harassing Mughal supply lines, soon attracted a following of 3,000 disciplined cavalrymen. But in August 1600, Ahmadnagar's fort finally fell to the determined and heavily armed Mughals, who carried into captivity the state's reigning sultan. Nonetheless, Mughal authority extended no further than the immediate hinterland of Ahmadnagar's fort; the countryside still teemed with troops formerly employed by the now-crippled Nizam Shahi state.

With Ahmadnagar's fate truly up for grabs, and with his own forces having grown to 7,000 cavalry, Malik Ambar now joined the fray over the kingdom's destiny.[27] Finding a twenty-year-old scion of Ahmadnagar's royal family in neighboring Bijapur, he promoted the cause of this youth as future ruler of a reconstituted Nizam Shahi state. To bind his royal candidate more closely to him, Ambar offered him his own daughter in marriage, and in 1600 the two

---

[26] Coolhaas, *Pieter Van den Broecke*, 1:148.   [27] Sarkar, *House of Shivaji*, 6–7.

Chart 3   Nizam Shahi dynasty and its patrons (abbreviated)

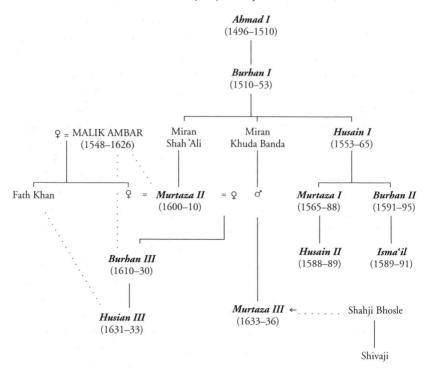

[Note: dots indicate patronage]

were married at Malik Ambar's headquarters at Parenda, a fort located seventy-five miles southeast of Mughal-occupied Ahmadnagar (see Map 5).[28] When the wedding ceremonies were concluded, Ambar presided over the installation of his son-in-law as Sultan Murtaza Nizam Shah II.[29] Content to be the new sultan's regent, Malik Ambar now devoted himself to preserving the stricken Nizam Shahi state, whose defense against northern aggression became a rallying point for many communities of the western Deccan.

Yet Malik Ambar was not the only would-be leader of that cause, as he was soon challenged in this capacity by a rival named Raju Dakhni. Though never a slave himself, Raju Dakhni was a personal servant of the commander Sa'adat

[28] For an excellent description and account of the fort, see G. Yazdani, "Parenda: an Historical Fort," *Annual Report of the Archaeological Department of His Exalted Highness the Nizam's Dominions* (1921–24): 17–36.
[29] Shyam, *Malik Ambar*, 38–39.

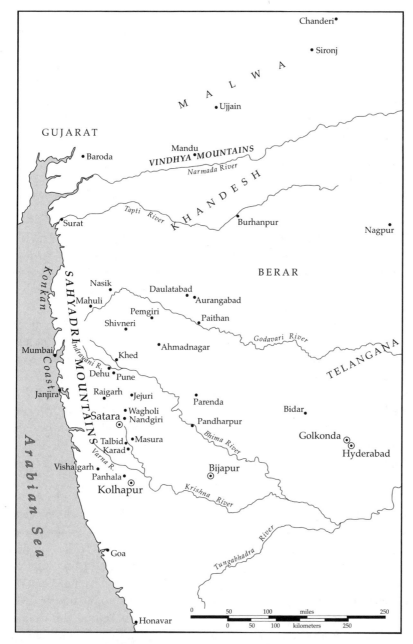

Map 5. Western Deccan in the time of Aurangzeb, 1636–1707.

Khan, who had been a slave of Sultan Burhan II. When the latter died in 1595, Sa'adat Khan, now a freedman, retained Raju Dakhni as his servant. Somewhat later, when the Mughals were besieging Ahmadnagar's fort and bribing Nizam Shahi officers over to their side, Sa'adat Khan was one of those who defected, together with his 3,000 troops. But Raju Dakhni hesitated over whether to follow his patron to the Mughal camp. Sensing his indecision, the Habshi commander Abhang Khan appealed to Raju Dakhni to remain loyal to the Nizam Shahi cause, arguing,

> Fortune has made you a great man . . . Sa'adat Khan was (only) a slave of [Burhan] Nizam Shah. As he has turned traitor to Nizam Shah and gone over to the Mughals, do you act bravely, because the reward of fidelity to salt is greatness. Guard carefully the territory and forts now in your hands, and try to increase them.[30]

Once again, we find "fidelity to salt" being invoked as the highest possible claim on one's political and social allegiance. Detached from race, religion, territory, or ethnicity, the ideology of "salt" provided the ideal basis for solidarity amongst disparate groups living in a culturally mixed society – especially among those who, like Abhang Khan, were former slaves.

For the next six years Malik Ambar and Raju Dakhni, picking up the pieces of the shattered Nizam Shahi kingdom, resisted the Mughal occupation. Although both men acknowledged Sultan Murtaza II – the prince that Ambar had crowned in 1600 and to whom he had married his daughter – the two rivals mounted separate military operations from separate bases. While the Mughals held the capital city of Ahmadnagar, Raju controlled the Nizam Shahi territory to the north and west of that city and Ambar controlled that to its south and east. The rivalry continued until 1606, when Ambar defeated Raju in battle and imprisoned him in the old Bahmani fort of Junnar (north of Pune), which Ambar now made his capital and court.

But Mughal armies would not quit the Deccan. To the contrary, after Akbar's death in 1605, a new emperor, Jahangir, came to the Peacock Throne determined to consolidate Mughal authority over territory the northern imperialists regarded as already conquered. General after general was dispatched south to do away with Ambar and his puppet sultan, but not one of them could capture or neutralize the adroit and charismatic Ethiopian. The more times he defeated superior Mughal armies, the more men rallied to his side; in 1610, he even managed to expel the Mughals from Ahmadnagar fort. This triumph emboldened Ambar to transfer the court from Junnar to the former Tughluq

---

[30] Sarkar, *House of Shivaji*, 7–8.

capital of Daulatabad, whose northerly location provided a better defense against Mughal attacks. The move could also have stoked regional pride among Marathi-speakers, since Daulatabad had been built on the site of Devagiri, capital of Maharashtra's Yadava dynasty (1185–1317).

Despite these impressive gains on the geo-political front, Malik Ambar now found himself beset by knotty domestic problems. For one thing Sultan Murtaza II, by this time a mature thirty years of age, refused to play the role of docile puppet and had begun meddling in affairs of state that Ambar, as *peshwa*, regarded his own. What is more, high up in Daulatabad's lofty royal palace, a family quarrel broke out in 1610 between the sultan's senior and junior wives. A contemporary Dutch traveler records that a fair-skinned "Persian" wife ("een witte Parsianse vrouwe") from an earlier marriage reproached her younger co-wife, who was Malik Ambar's own daughter, slandering the latter as a concubine and even "a mere slave girl" ("maer een cafferinne"). Issues of both race and slave-status appear involved here. What is more, in the heat of the outburst, the sultan's senior wife defamed Malik Ambar himself, calling him a former state rebel. When the daughter informed her father of the altercation, Ambar, swollen with anger, ordered his secretary to poison both his meddlesome sultan and his quarrelsome senior wife.[31] In the former ruler's place, Ambar enthroned Murtaza II's five-year-old son by his "Persian" wife.[32] Crowned as Sultan Burhan III, the youth now became the second Nizam Shahi prince installed by Malik Ambar as his puppet sultan.

Rather suddenly, the revitalized Nizam Shahi kingdom had acquired a distinctly African character. As *peshwa*, Malik Ambar himself held undisputed control over Ahmadnagar's military and civil affairs, while his daughter had been assimilated into the Nizam Shahi royal household for twenty years. His family had also merged with the ruling class of neighboring Bijapur. In 1609, with a view to shoring up relations with this powerful sultanate to the south while taking on the Mughals in the north, Ambar married off his son, Fath Khan, to the daughter of Yaqut Khan, a free Habshi and one of Bijapur's most powerful nobles.[33] Here we see networks of free Ethiopians engaging in interstate marital relations at a level immediately below that of the dynastic

---

[31] Coolhaas, *Pieter Van den Broecke*, 1:149.

[32] Pieter Gielis van Ravesteijn, "Journal, May 1615 to Feb. 1616," in Heert Terpstra, *De opkomst der Westerkwartieren van de Oost-Indische Compagnie (Suratte, Arabië, Perzië)* (The Hague, 1918), 176–77. The earliest text of the journal is in Leiden, National Archives, "Journal of Pieter Gillisz van Ravesteijn on his Journey from Masulipatam to Surat and Back, 8.5–29.10.1615," VOC 1061, f. 239v. I am indebted to Gijs Kruijtzer for his assistance in interpreting the texts of both van Ravesteijn and Van den Broecke.

[33] Radhey Shyam, *The Kingdom of Ahmadnagar* (Delhi, 1966), 257–58.

houses, and mimicking the pattern of inter-dynastic marriages practiced by those houses.

By this time, too, entire armies of Habshi warriors were fighting for the revitalized kingdom of Ahmadnagar. The English merchant William Finch, who happened to be in the region in February 1610, reported that Malik Ambar's army consisted of 10,000 men "of his own caste," in addition to 40,000 Deccanis.[34] In an engagement with the Mughals six years later, Malik Ambar is said to have brought to the field 10,000 Habshi youths (*bachigan*), aged seventeen or eighteen, mounted on Persian horses. The chronicler of this event also mentioned that many of those killed by the Mughals had been "slaves" of Ambar.[35] This suggests a pattern of Ethiopians entering India in considerable numbers as military slaves, with some of them, on becoming freedmen, subsequently purchasing large numbers of their own Habshi slaves. Malik Ambar had himself arrived in the Deccan as one of a thousand slaves belonging to Chengiz Khan, then *peshwa* of Ahmadnagar. And before that, Chengiz Khan had in turn been brought to the Deccan as a Habshi slave. One sees, then, a diachronic process of movement from slave, to free lancer, to commander, to slave-owning commander – a remarkable pattern of upward mobility.

For one person to advance clear from slave to *peshwa* as Ambar did, however, was exceptional. But then, he was an exceptional person. To this day he is respectfully remembered for having surveyed much of the rural western Deccan and for placing the region's revenue administration on a firm and just basis. We also have the testimony of contemporary observers. The Mughal ambassador Asad Beg, who met him in 1604, was impressed that "he offered his prayers along with the common people" and that "his charities are beyond description."[36] The Dutchman Pieter Gielis van Ravesteijn, who met him while traveling across the plateau in June 1615, commented on the orderliness of Ambar's camp in contrast to those of other Deccani sovereigns he had seen. He was also struck by the large number of Africans ("caffer") in the camp of Ambar, whom the Dutchman described as substantial in body and limb, of more than average height, and "black as a Moor."[37]

In 1617 another Dutchman, Pieter Van den Broecke, described Ambar as tall and strong, with a stern, "Roman" face and white glazed eyes, adding that

---

[34] William Foster, ed., *Early Travels in India, 1583–1619* (New Delhi, 1968), 138.

[35] Fuzuni Astarabadi, *Futuhat-i ʿAdil Shahi*, composed 1640–43 (British Library, Persian MSS. Add 27, 251), fol. 278b, cited in Sarkar, *House of Shivaji*, 17.

[36] Banarasi Prasad Saksena, "A Few Unnoticed Facts about the Early Life of Malik Amber," *Proceedings, Indian History Congress* 5 (1941): 603.

[37] van Ravesteijn, "Journal," 177.

"he is very much loved and respected by everyone and keeps good government." A traveler himself, the Dutchman admired Malik Ambar's policy of severely punishing highway robbers, noting that "one may travel through his country with gold." But he also detected a rigid, puritanical streak in the Habshi's character: Ambar would not allow anybody, on pain of corporal punishment, to bring alcoholic drinks to the army camp, or even to travel through the country with such beverages. Molten lead, wrote Van den Broecke, was poured down the throat of anybody who drank to inebriation.[38]

Malik Ambar's severest critic, however, was his bitter enemy, the Mughal emperor Jahangir, whose reign (1605–27) coincided with the height of the Ethiopian's career as *peshwa* of the revived Ahmadnagar sultanate. Jahangir was simply obsessed with Ambar, whose outstanding military skills he understood but could not bring himself to acknowledge, given his own exalted position as ruler of one of the world's mightiest empires. Instead, the emperor spewed imprecations on his African adversary. In his memoir for the year 1612, Jahangir calls him "'Ambar, the black-faced"; in 1616, he is "the ill-starred 'Ambar" and "the rebel 'Ambar"; in 1617, "'Ambar of dark fate" and "that disastrous man"; in 1620, "'Ambar, the black-fated one," while his men are "the rebels of black-fortune"; in 1621, he is "the ill-starred one" and "the crafty 'Ambar."[39] One notes how darkness, specifically the color black, dominates Jahangir's thinking about Malik Ambar.

The Mughal emperor's obsession with Ambar is most tellingly revealed in an extraordinary portrait of the two men commissioned by Jahangir and painted around 1616 by the renowned Mughal artist Abu'l-Hasan (see Plate 9). In this painting Jahangir stands atop the globe – as befits a man whose name means "world-conqueror" – and, holding a bow and arrow, takes aim at the severed head of Malik Ambar, which is impaled on the tip of a spear. Rich in symbolism, the painting repeatedly associates the emperor with light and justice, whereas the head of Malik Ambar, surrounded with owls both dead and alive, is associated with night, darkness, and usurpation. Persian captions on the painting also play on Ambar's dark color. Both words and images point beyond the Mughal–Deccan conflict to a deeper tension between light-skinned Westerners – personified by Jahangir himself – and dark-skinned Deccanis, especially Habshis, personified by Malik Ambar. Most of all, the portrait reveals the emperor's profound frustration with his failure ever to

---

[38] Coolhaas, *Pieter Van den Broecke*, 1:146–47, 150.
[39] Jahangir, *The Tuzuk-i-Jahangiri, or Memoirs of Jahangir*, trans. Alexander Rogers, ed. Henry Beveridge (1909–14; repr. Delhi, 1968), 1:220, 312, 313, 368, 373, 2:155, 156, 207, 208.

vanquish Ambar: he fantasized in art what he could not accomplish on the battlefield.[40]

HABSHI DOMINANCE, MARATHA DOMINANCE

It is instructive to contrast Jahangir's assessments of his Ethiopian adversary with those of Mu'tamad Khan, who completed the emperor's memoirs when his patron fell too ill to continue writing them. In 1626, only a year before the emperor's death, news reached north India that Malik Ambar, the Mughals' long-term nemesis, had died, evidently of natural causes. "This 'Ambar was a slave," records the Mughal chronicler, "but an able man."

In warfare, in command, in sound judgment, and in administration, he had no rival or equal. He well understood that predatory (*kazzaki*) warfare, which in the language of the Dakhin is called *bargi-giri*. He kept down the turbulent spirits of that country, and maintained his exalted position to the end of his life, and closed his career in honour. History records no other instance of an Abyssinian slave arriving at such eminence.[41]

Notable in this extraordinary tribute is the acknowledgment of Malik Ambar's mastery of guerrilla warfare. Refusing to engage in pitched battles against the Mughals' imposing façade of artillery, infantry, and heavy cavalry, Ambar had deployed surprise night attacks, harassed enemy supply lines, and drawn Mughal forces into wooded hills and rugged ravines where they could be hacked to pieces by his light cavalry.

It is also revealing that the Mughal term for guerrilla warfare, *bargi-giri*, referred to units of Marathas – indigenous Marathi-speaking warriors – who were trained by the state and paid directly out of the state's central treasury. Light and swift, Maratha cavalrymen in Malik Ambar's service wielded deadly effect on the Mughals' cumbersome armies; on occasion they pursued Mughal troopers clear up to their regional headquarters at Burhanpur.[42] Although Ahmadnagar was not the first Deccani sultanate to make use of Maratha cavalrymen – they had also served Bahmani sultans in the late fifteenth century – the Nizam Shahi state under Malik Ambar's leadership made more extensive use of them than did any other Deccani kingdom. Under him, the units

---

[40] Linda York Leach, *Mughal and Other Indian Paintings from the Chester Beatty Library* (London, 1995), I:401–05. The painting's captions include: "The head of the night-coloured usurper became the house of the owl," and "Thine enemy-smiting arrow has driven from the world [Malik] 'Anbar, the owl which fled the light."

[41] Mu'tamad Khan, *Iqbal-nama-yi Jahangiri*, in *History of India as Told by its Own Historians*, ed. and trans. Henry M. Elliot and John Dowson (Allahabad, 1964), VI:428–29.

[42] Shyam, *Malik Ambar*, 96–98.

of Maratha cavalry in Ahmadnagar's service grew from 10,000 in 1609 to 50,000 in 1624.[43] The different quarters of Khirki, the town near Daulatabad that Ambar had founded and which was later renamed Aurangabad, were named after prominent Maratha chiefs – i.e., Malpura, Khelpura, Paraspura, Vithapura.[44]

In fact, the Ahmadnagar sultanate under Ambar's direction had effectively become a joint Habshi–Maratha enterprise. In the late sixteenth century, both Westerners and Deccan-born Muslims had receded in relative importance in the state's political system, due largely to their long history of mutual antagonism, even civil war. Steadily filling the power vacuum created by this discord were slave and free Ethiopians.[45] But theirs was a brief moment of prominence. When Malik Ambar died in 1626, his son Fath Khan succeeded him as Ahmadnagar's *peshwa*. Before long, another Habshi ex-slave, Hamid Khan, bribed Sultan Burhan III for that position. In revenge, Fath Khan in early 1632 poisoned the sultan and, upon recovering his former position of *peshwa*, placed the murdered sultan's seven-year-old son on the throne as Husain III. Lacking his father's many skills, however, Fath Khan buckled before a renewed siege of Daulatabad by the Mughals, to whom he surrendered the Nizam Shahi capital in June 1633. The Mughals then carried off both him and his puppet sultan to north India. Fath Khan was retired on a pension; the boy-sultan was imprisoned for life.

If the most notable Habshi in Ahmadnagar had been Malik Ambar himself, the most notable Maratha chieftain was certainly Shahji Bhosle, whose father Maloji had been Malik Ambar's right-hand man, and whose son Shivaji would found the Maratha state (see chapter 8). When Maloji died in 1620, Shahji inherited his father's position and land assignment (*jagir*), which included the Pune region.[46] And at the critical moment in 1633 when the Mughals captured Daulatabad, together with Fath Khan and his puppet sultan, Shahji boldly took up the cause of preserving the Nizam Shahi state. Finding yet another royal prince, an eleven-year-old youth, Shahji crowned him as Sultan Murtaza III

---

[43] *Ibid.*, 147. In 1610, when William Finch described Malik Ambar's army as composed of 10,000 Habshis and 40,000 Deccanis, it is likely that the latter figure actually referred to the 40,000 Marathas that he had by this time recruited and trained. Foster, *Early Travels*, 138.

[44] Promod B. Gadre, *Cultural Archaeology of Ahmadnagar during Nizam Shahi Period (1494–1632)* (Delhi, 1986), 182.

[45] Some of the more important Maratha chiefs in Ambar's service were Shahji, Sharofji, Maloji, Parsoji, Mambaji, Nagoji, Trimbakji, Hambir Rao, Chavan, Madhji, Nar Singh Raj, Ballela Tripul, Vithal Raj, Kavata, Dattaji, Naganath, Nar Singh Pingle, and Sunder Jagdev. See Shyam, *Kingdom*, 277.

[46] Govind Sakharam Sardesai, *New History of the Marathas* (Bombay, 1971), 1:59–60.

and installed the puppet sultan in successive courts at Pemgiri and Shivneri, hill-forts in the Sahyadri Range. During the next three years Shahji negotiated with Maratha and Habshi commanders for support, recovered forts in the old Nizam Shahi territory, and collected troops, which numbered at most about 12,000. But it was a lost cause. Like vultures, both Bijapur to the south and the Mughals to the north coveted Ahmadnagar's territory and used their greater resources to bribe Nizam Shahi officers to their respective causes. Cornered in the fort of Mahuli near modern Mumbai, Shahji watched helplessly as supporters melted away either to Bijapur or to the Mughals. Finally, in 1636 these two powers concluded a treaty that formally dissolved the Nizam Shahi state, whose territory they divided between themselves. Shahji was permitted to join Bijapur's service, while Ahmadnagar's last boy-sultan was marched off to the Mughal prison at Gwalior, there to join for life two of his royal predecessors, captured respectively in 1600 and 1633.

THE FATE OF THE HABSHIS

Paradoxically, even while Maratha clans and chieftains were gaining in social and political prominence in the early seventeenth century, military slavery as an institution had begun to decline. By the eighteenth century, Habshis had nearly disappeared as a distinct Deccani group and military caste.[47] For

---

[47] The scattered communities of so-called "Siddis" that survive in western India today appear to be descended not from élite Habshi slaves of the fifteenth through seventeenth centuries, but from male and female domestic slaves brought from East Africa by European or Arab dealers in the eighteenth and nineteenth centuries. On the African diaspora eastward, see Shanti Sadiq Ali, *African Dispersal in the Deccan* (New Delhi, 1996); Edward A. Alpers, "Recollecting Africa: Diasporic Memory in the Indian Ocean World," *African Studies Review* 43, no. 1 (April 2000): 83–99; Rudy Bauss, "The Portuguese Slave Trade from Mozambique to Portuguese India and Macau and Comments on Timor, 1750–1850: New Evidence from the Archives," in *Camoes Center Quarterly* 6 and 7, nos. 1 and 2 (1997): 21–26; Helene Basu, *Habshi-Sklaven, Sidi-Fakire: muslimische Heiligenverehrung in westlichen Indien* (Berlin: Das Arab Buch, 1995); Helene Basu, "The Siddi and the Cult of Bava Gor in Gujarat," in *Journal of the Indian Anthropological Society* 28 (1993): 289–300; D. K. Bhattacharya, "Indians of African Origin," *Cahiers d'Études Africaines* 10, no. 40 (1970): 579–82; Jyotirmay Chakraborty and S. B. Nandi, "The Siddis of Junagadh: Some Aspects of their Religious Life," *Human Science* 33, no. 2 (1984): 130–37; R. R. S. Chauhan, *Africans in India: from Slavery to Royalty* (Delhi, 1995); Joseph E. Harris, *The African Presence in Asia: Consequences of the East African Slave Trade* (Evanston, 1971); Jayasuriya and Pankhurst, eds., *African Diaspora*; Cyrus H. Lobo, S. J., *Siddis in Karnataka* (Bangalore, 1980); T. B. Naik and G. P. Pandya, *The Sidis of Gujarat: a Socio-Economic Study and Development Plan* (Ahmadabad, 1981); J. C. Palakshappa, *The Siddis of North Kanara* (New Delhi, 1978); Jeanette Pinto, *Slavery in Portuguese India (1510–1842)* (Bombay, 1992); Kiran K. Prasad, "The Identity of Siddis in Karnataka," in *Relevance of Anthropology: the Indian Scenario*, ed. B. G. Halbar and C. G. Husain Khan (Jaipur, 1991); Vasant D. Rao, "The Habshis, India's Unknown Africans," *African Report* (Sept–Oct. 1973): 35–38; Markus Vink, "'The World's Oldest Trade': Dutch Slavery and Slave Trade in the Indian Ocean in the Seventeenth Century," *Journal of World History* 14, no. 2 (2003): 131–77.

one thing, few Ethiopian females were ever brought as slaves to the Deccan, meaning that Habshi men necessarily married local women, as did their male offspring. Consequently, unlike the Americas, where the introduction of both male and female African slaves created a self-reproducing and enduring black population, in the Deccan male Habshis and other Africans became mainly absorbed in the local society.

Moreover, the collapse of the Ahmadnagar sultanate ended the patronage system that was geared to recruiting military slaves from overseas. Replacing that sultanate, and soon thereafter replacing the other Deccani sultanates as well, were the imperial Mughals, who as a matter of policy did not recruit slaves into their armies.[48] Even if they had adopted such a policy, their Irano-Turkish racial bias – reflected in the remarks of Prince Murad's officers during the 1596 siege of Ahmadnagar, or in Jahangir's epithets for Malik Ambar – would hardly have inclined them to placing large numbers of black Africans in positions of power or responsibility. As a result, the demand for military slaves in Ahmadnagar abruptly ceased with the end of the kingdom itself, in 1636. The same would occur in Bijapur fifty years later, when it too was conquered and annexed by the Mughals.

A third factor in the Habshis' disappearance as a distinct community involved their transition from kinless aliens to native householders. This socio-historical process runs directly counter to characterizations of slavery as a permanent state of "social death."[49] Throughout the Middle East, the recruitment of slave soldiers from beyond the borders of the Muslim world was followed by their integration first into the central government and ultimately into their host society.[50] Referring to Ottoman history, Dror Ze'evi has drawn particular attention to the role of the master's household as an agent in the slave's socialization and as a springboard for his career. It was "meaningful integration into the household, as a special son of the master," writes Ze'evi, that "enabled the slave to complete the metamorphosis from slave to lord." Living in the same surroundings and eating the same food as their masters, such slaves not only

---

[48] Writes Jos Gommans, "Why have recourse to such an expensive and burdensome institution as slavery when there already existed a substantial flow of foreign military immigrants into India? Similar to slaves, these foreign warriors could also serve as an excellent deracinated elite without any local attachments. Decisive in this respect was the Mughal capacity to attract and to enlist these foreigners into their army, mainly through offering them substantial shares in Indian wealth, as ostentatiously epitomized in mansab." Jos Gommans, *Mughal Warfare: Indian Frontiers and High Roads to Empire, 1500–1700* (London and New York, 2002), 83.

[49] See Orlando Patterson, *Slavery and Social Death: a Comparative Study* (Cambridge MA, 1982).

[50] Miura Toru and John Edward Philips, eds., *Slave Elites in the Middle East and Africa: a Comparative Study* (London and New York, 2000), x.

became fictive kin of their masters, but they did so, Ze'evi argues, even *before* becoming manumitted.[51]

This suggests that the institution of military slavery was a self-terminating process, rather than an enduring condition. In Ahmadnagar, men who had begun their careers as culturally alien slaves without kin, over time became integrated into their host society, acquired kin, and embraced a Deccani regional identity.[52] Such a process could explain why we seldom hear of Habshi slaves in Nizam Shahi service ever being formally manumitted, for we know from the remarks of seventeenth-century foreign travelers that African slaves were tied to their Deccani masters by close and affectionate bonds.[53] The transition from a master–slave to a patron–client relationship was so smooth that, on the death of the patron, a former slave emerged as a de facto freedman, with or without a letter of formal manumission. This process seems to have been so common as not even to have warranted notice in contemporary Persian chronicles. In Malik Ambar's own case, it was only the Dutchman Van den Broecke, an outsider whose own culture drew a severe distinction between the categories of slave and free, who mentioned the Ethiopian's manumission by Chengiz Khan's widow. Persian chroniclers made no notice of Malik Ambar's manumission, nor of that of other Habshi slaves.

Although the transition from slave status to freedman passed unnoticed by contemporary chroniclers, the ethnic identity of Ahmadnagar's Habshis persisted throughout their own lifetimes, regardless of their legal status or their elevation to high rank in the kingdom's power élite. In the eyes of others, they were all still Africans. Contemporary chroniclers referred to free commanders of African origin not as "*amir*s," but as "Habshi *amir*s" (*umra-yi Habshi*), or as simply "the Habshis" (*Habush*).[54] Such usages point to the survival of an African identity well after the point that slaves had themselves become slave-holders. Indeed, Malik Ambar's own Ethiopian identity survived his many years in India. Whereas in official documents he referred to himself as "Malik Ambar," some outsiders continued to call him by his pre-slave, Ethiopian name – "Chapu." In 1610 William Finch referred to him as "Amber-champon," and

---

[51] Dror Ze'evi, "My Son, my Lord: Slavery, Family and State in the Islamic Middle East," in Toru and Philips, eds., *Slave Elites*, 74, 76.

[52] On the integration of slaves into their masters' households, see Paul G. Forand, "The Relation of the Slave and the Client to the Master or Patron in Medieval Islam," *International Journal of Middle East Studies* 2 (1971): 59–66. See also Indrani Chatterjee, "A Slave's Quest for Selfhood in Eighteenth-century Hindustan," *Indian Economic and Social History Review* 37, no. 1 (2000): 53–85.

[53] John Fryer, *A New Account of East India and Persia, being Nine Years' Travels, 1672–1681*, ed. William Crooke (London, 1912), II:52.

[54] See, for example, Tabataba, *Burhan*, 632. Trans. Haig, "History of Nizam Shahi Kings," 52: 346.

William Hawkins, another Englishman who was in India between 1608 and 1612, called him "Amberry Chapu."[55] Even if "Malik Ambar" was the name by which its owner wished to be publicly known, fully forty years after his arrival in the Deccan, an essential aspect of his African identity had survived in public consciousness.

SUMMARY

Like an incubator, the Ahmadnagar sultanate nurtured the growth of various social groups between its founding in 1496 and its collapse in 1636. Throughout this period a single house occupied the Nizam Shahi throne. Although powerful brokers periodically installed youthful princes as puppet sultans, no one outside the royal household usurped the throne for themselves or started a new dynasty. Just beneath the level of the dynastic house, however, competing groups struggled for power, often viciously. As in the late Bahmani period, the contest initially pitted Westerners against Deccan-born Muslims. But from the late sixteenth century on, as the Mughals exerted mounting pressure on the kingdom, new groups entered the arena.

The first were Habshis. Although for many years Ethiopians had fought in the service of Westerner or Deccani commanders, a new phase opened in 1600 when Malik Ambar became the first African to enthrone a Nizam Shahi prince and rule the country as regent and *peshwa*. During this period of Habshi ascendancy, thousands of Ethiopian warriors fought in Nizam Shahi service, both as freedmen and as slaves of other Habshis. In particular, the African *peshwa* appointed Habshis to staff and command strategic forts located throughout the plateau and along the Konkan seaboard, most famously at the impregnable island fortress of Janjira. Situated some fifty miles down the coast from modern Mumbai, this spectacular fortress remained in the hands of Habshis or their descendants until 1947.[56]

Malik Ambar also recruited into Nizam Shahi service numerous Maratha chieftains, together with their kinsmen and retainers. Like Bahmani sultans before them, the rulers of Ahmadnagar and Bijapur knew they could not govern the peoples of the Deccan by relying solely on the recruitment of African military slaves or the control of the many hill-forts that dot the plateau. In order to extend their reach down to the grassroots source of wealth – the surplus

---

[55] Foster, *Early Travels*, 100, 138.
[56] See A. Razzaq M. H. Peshimam, *Murud-Janjira, a Short History* (Murud-Janjira, Maharashtra, n.d.); A. A. Kadiri, "Inscriptions of the Sidi Chiefs of Janjira," *Epigraphia Indica, Arabic and Persian Supplement* (1966): 55–76.

grains produced by cultivating classes – they had to employ, and if necessary create, service groups from amongst the local population. Viewed from this perspective, the "rise of the Marathas," which occupies such a conspicuous place in Indian historiography, was hardly an accident. As Stewart Gordon notes, "military service was the principal form of entrepreneurial activity in premodern South Asia."[57] Indeed, Maratha warriors first emerged as a distinct social class in the context of just such activity. Like the other sultanates of the Deccan, Ahmadnagar possessed the wealth, derived from both international commerce and land revenue, to afford the patronage of new service classes. And the beneficiaries of this patronage, Maratha chiefs and their retainers, provided the sultanate with local knowledge and highly competent light cavalry. With their ties to the land, Marathas also connected the state to the kingdom's cultivating classes.

The Marathas' investment in the survival of the Ahmadnagar state is vividly seen in their eleventh-hour attempt to salvage the Nizam Shahi cause. Just when the imperial Mughals had captured Malik Ambar's son and were poised to swallow the kingdom whole, Shahji, a prominent Maratha chieftain with an illustrious career of service to several Deccan sultanates, came to its rescue. In raising yet another obscure Nizam Shahi prince to the throne, and in running the state as regent for that sovereign, Shahji played the same role in 1633 that Malik Ambar had played in 1600. By this time, however, the balance of power in the Deccan had shifted so far in favor of the Mughals that the kingdom had no chance of surviving.

Still, the Nizam Shahi sultanate had already performed a historically momentous function. It had served as the nursery in which Maratha power could grow, creating the political preconditions for the eventual emergence of an independent Maratha state. But that state would rest on more than Nizam Shahi political institutions. It would also be firmly grounded in social and religious roots that had been evolving during, and well before, the time that Malik Ambar and Shahji strove to stem the tide of Mughal imperialism in the Deccan. It is to those socio-religious roots that we now turn our attention.

---

[57] Stewart Gordon, "War, the Military, and the Environment: Central India, 1560–1820," in *Natural Enemy, Natural Ally: toward an Environmental History of Warfare*, ed. Richard P. Tucker and Edmund Russell (Corvallis OR, 2004), 51.

CHAPTER 6

TUKARAM (1608–1649): NON-BRAHMIN RELIGIOUS MOVEMENTS

> The *brahmin* who flies into a rage
> at the touch of a *mahar* [a low caste]
> – That's no *brahmin*.
> The only absolution for such a *brahmin*
> Is to die for his own sin.
> He who refuses to touch a *chandal* [a low caste]
> Has a polluted mind.
> Says Tuka, a man is only as chaste
> As his own belief.[1]
>
> Tukaram

TO THE BANKS OF THE INDRAYANI RIVER

The year 1608 saw Malik Ambar confidently moving about the western Deccan, his armies building on success after success. Just two years earlier, he had defeated his rival for leadership of the anti-Mughal resistance movement, Raju Dakhni, who now languished in a prison in the fort of Junnar, the temporary capital of the revived Nizam Shahi state. In 1608 Malik Ambar also negotiated an alliance with his neighbor to the south, Sultan Ibrahim II of Bijapur, so that he could concentrate all his forces on thwarting the gathering Mughal threat from the north. His efforts paid off, for just two years later, the Mughal garrison in Ahmadnagar would fall and the Habshi *peshwa* would be emboldened to move the Nizam Shahi court from Junnar further north, to Daulatabad.

While these events were taking place at the level of high politics, one of India's most revered poets was born in the village of Dehu, on the banks of the Indrayani River some forty miles south of Malik Ambar's capital at Junnar. This was Tukaram, whose life spanned the period 1608 to 1649 (see Plate 10). Familiar to millions of ordinary Marathi-speakers, Tukaram's verses, or *abhangs*, would enter the collective consciousness of a substantial portion of the Deccan's population. While historians have approached his career from many perspectives, we are most interested in the impact his life and work had

---

[1] Dilip Chitre, trans., *Says Tuka: Selected Poetry of Tukaram* (New Delhi, 1991), 115.

on the social history of the seventeenth-century Deccan. Two questions, in particular, guide the inquiry. First, as is hinted in this chapter's epigraph, what can his career tell us about caste relations in the Marathi-speaking portion of the Deccan? And second, how did his poetry contribute to a collective consciousness among Marathi-speakers, regardless of class or caste, that would in turn facilitate the evolution of the Marathas as a political community?

Tukaram was born into a merchant family of modest wealth and social importance. In the caste hierarchy, his family was *sudra*, a large category with many endogamous subdivisions, occupying a middle position between Brahmins and Untouchables. From the standpoint of contemporary Brahmins, who monopolized both religious and social power, Hindu society in Maharashtra was composed of only two classes: Brahmins and *sudras*. Moreover, the barriers between these classes, enforced by the Brahmins' control over Sanskrit education and access to sacred Hindu texts, were clearly defined and understood by all. It is certain that Tukaram, having been raised in a family of traders and grocers adept at keeping written accounts, would have acquired basic literacy in Marathi at an early age. But as a non-Brahmin with no direct access to Sanskrit scripture, he would also have been cut off from the entire corpus of textually validated norms and traditions that Brahmins jealously guarded. It follows, then, that Tukaram's writings about religion in vernacular Marathi transgressed the established socio-religious norms of his day. But did that make him in any sense a social revolutionary? We can search for answers in his life-story.

A series of calamities profoundly affected Tukaram's transition to early adulthood. In his seventeenth year, both of his parents died, placing on his shoulders the responsibility of running the family business. Then in 1629–30 his locality suffered a failed monsoon and a severe famine that claimed the lives of many. Among those was Tukaram's first wife, Rakhma, who starved to death as the young householder stood by, horrified and quite helpless. Next, his business failed, which plunged his family into bankruptcy and debt. He was then removed from the village council and fell out of favor with the village headman. In the face of all this, Tukaram sought and found solace in Vithoba, the form of the great god Vishnu that his family had worshiped for generations. He spent increasing amounts of time in prayer and devotion before the small shrine dedicated to Vithoba in his village of Dehu, chanting and singing the songs that earlier poets had composed in praise of the deity. These songs had been composed not in Sanskrit – the language of the gods, preserved by Brahmins – but in Marathi, the language of Maharashtra's common people.

He also wandered away from Dehu for long periods of time, meditating on nearby hills, absorbed in blissful solitude:

> Trees, creepers and the creatures of the forest
> Are my kith and kin,
> And birds that sweetly sing.
> This is bliss! How I love being alone!
> Here I am beyond good and evil;
> Commit no sin.
> The sky is my canopy, the earth my throne.
> My mind is free to dwell wherever it will.
> A piece of cloth, one all-purpose bowl
> Take care of all my bodily needs.
> The wind tells me the time.
> I feast on the cuisine of Hari's lore,
> A delighted connoisseur.
> Says Tuka, I talk to myself
> For argument's sake.[2]

Tukaram's extended retreats, however, were bitterly resented by his second wife, Jijabai, who carped, nagged, and complained of behavior she considered not only irresponsible in view of her husband's neglect of his householder duties and the failed family business, but actually mad.

Then came the catalyst. Once while meditating, Tukaram experienced a dream in which the Marathi poet-saint Namdev (d. 1350) appeared and instructed him to start writing verse. Specifically, he was to complete Namdev's own unfulfilled vow to write a billion poems in praise of Vithoba. To reinforce the point, by Namdev's side in the dream stood Vithoba himself, who, Tukaram writes, "gave the measure, did some teasing, and warned me with a gentle slap, that the number to be done [by Namdev] was one billion, the remainder is given to Tuka."[3] It is significant that, among the dozen or so major poet-saints who had sung Vithoba's praises during the previous four centuries, it was Namdev who appeared in the dream. Clearly, Tukaram identified with his predecessor in important ways, not least being that they both were *sudras* – Tukaram a grocer, and Namdev a tailor. Nonetheless, for a man who had never composed anything in his life, and who had no formal training in literary arts, he must have been awed at the assignment given him in his dream.

Undaunted, though, Tukaram took up the charge and put pen to paper, thereby taking his place in a succession of Marathi poet-saints that stretched

---

[2] *Ibid.*, 148.
[3] Gail Omvedt and Bharat Patankar, trans., *The Revolutionary Abhangs of Tukaram* (forthcoming), abhang no. 1320.

back to Namdev's senior contemporary Jnanadev (d. 1296), who had authored the first Marathi commentary on the great devotional work, *Bhagavad Gita*. After Jnanadev a succession of poets wrote in praise of Vithoba, whose main shrine stands in Pandharpur in southern Maharashtra. Ever since the time of Namdev, who is thought to have inaugurated the tradition, men and women known as "Varkaris" had been making the pilgrimage from all over the Marathi-speaking Deccan to this famous temple, along the way fervently singing the songs of their beloved poet-saints. Tukaram's own literary output, which comprised some 4,000 *abhangs*, thus merged with a major Maharashtra-wide tradition.

A salient feature of this tradition was its predominantly non-Brahmin, at times even anti-Brahmin, character. Jnanadev, himself the son of an outcaste Brahmin, is said to have once caused a buffalo to recite the Vedas, mocking the notion that only Brahmins had access to scripture.[4] The sixteenth-century poet-saint Eknath (d. 1599), though himself a Brahmin, was harshly criticized in his native Paithan, a bastion of Brahmanic orthodoxy, for teaching the *Bhagavata Purana* in vernacular Marathi.[5] And he flagrantly transgressed the norms of socio-ritual propriety by dining at the home of an Untouchable, and worse, by inviting Untouchables to a feast for Brahmins.[6] By contrast, Untouchable poets in the Varkari tradition were less openly transgressive of social norms. Such was the experience of Chokhamela, a fourteenth-century Untouchable whose caste, the Mahars, had for generations been denied access to village wells and were forced to live outside village precincts, removing filth and carcasses for landowners. Centuries of such social oppression had ingrained a degree of resignation among communities like the Mahars. Thus Chokhamela, intimidated by the Brahmin priests who controlled access to the Vithoba temple in Pandharpur, is said to have worshiped the god from afar, until the night when Vithoba himself, out of love, came to his Mahar devotee, took him by the hand, and led him into the temple.[7]

Tukaram, by contrast, showed no such passivity in the face of Brahmin power. Disdaining caste pride of any kind, he felt honored to include among

---

[4] Narayan H. Kulkarnee, "Medieval Maharasthra and Muslim Saint-Poets," in *Medieval Bhakti Movements in India*, ed. N. N. Bhattacharyya (New Delhi, 1989), 205.

[5] S. G. Tulpule, "Eknath's Treatment of the *Ramayana* as a Socio-Political Metaphor," in *Ramayana and Ramayanas*, ed. Monika Thiel-Horstmann (Wiesbaden, 1991), 142.

[6] Eleanor Zelliot, "Four Radical Saints in Maharashtra," in *Religion and Society in Maharasthra*, ed. Milton Israel and N. K. Wagle (Toronto, 1987), 137.

[7] Charlotte Vaudeville, *Myths, Saints and Legends in Medieval India*, compiled by Vasudha Dalmia (Delhi, 1996), 227.

his spiritual predecessors Untouchables, Muslims, barbers, and artisans of all sorts. "Who is purified by pride of varna [caste]," he asks, "tell me if you know!"

> Untouchables are saved by hymns to Hari [i.e., Vithoba],
> legendary stories become their bards.
> Tuludhar Vaishya, the potmaker Gora,
> the leatherworker Rohidas.
> The momin Kabir, Latif the Muslim,
> the barber Sena are Vishnudas.
> Kanhopatra, Khodu, cotton-carder Dadu,
> sing hymns to Hari without discord.
> Banka, Chokhamela, by caste Mahar,
> have united with the Lord . . .
> Vishnu's servants have no caste,
> the Veda's science so decrees.
> Tuka says, which of your books
> have saved the fallen? I know of none.[8]

Declaring that the devotees of Vishnu (i.e., Vithoba) "have no caste," Tukaram was in effect looking beyond the caste system itself. And in professing ignorance of any books that could lead to one's spiritual emancipation, he cavalierly rejected the salvational value of the entire Sanskritic scriptural tradition. Such statements amounted to a two-front challenge to Brahmins, guardians both of the normative social hierarchy – that is, caste – and of access to texts prescribing the way to spiritual "release."

When situating himself in the social order, on the other hand, Tukaram could not break free of thinking in terms of caste. Rather than claim that he had no caste – a practical impossibility in his day – he affirmed his identity as a Kunbi, Maharashtra's dominant agrarian community (within the *sudra* category). In one of his many dialogues with Vithoba, he cries,

> Good you made me a Kunbi,
> else I'd have died of hypocrisy.
> You've done well, O God,
> Tuka dances and falls at your feet.
> If I had any learning
> I would have fallen into evil . . .
> Tuka says, pride and greatness go to hell.[9]

---

[8] Omvedt and Patankar, *Revolutionary Abhangs*, abhang no. 4299.
[9] *Ibid*, abhang no. 320.

Elsewhere, Tukaram associates learning with hypocrisy and pride, and all three with Brahmins. In one poem he compared Brahmins to donkeys, beasts of burden who carried the dead-weight of erudition,[10] and in another he protested, "I am no wretched pundit splitting Vedantic hairs."[11]

The Brahmins to whom Tukaram refers in such negative terms included not only religious specialists – i.e., family priests, functionaries of temples, or vessels and transmitters of Sanskritic scriptural learning – but also prominent figures in civil society such as judges, commercial inspectors, or servants of political overlords. As he writes,

> Dropouts from society,
>   Brahmins lie and steal.
> They have wiped off the sacred mark on the forehead
>   And they now wear trousers and leather things.
> They occupy seats of power
>   And mete out injustice to the poor.
> They write inventories of the pantry
>   Thinking of ghee, oil, and soap.
> They become the hired servants of the corrupt
>   And take a beating whenever they err.[12]

Notwithstanding these critiques of the Brahmins' non-religious roles, it was their claim to monopolize religious knowledge that Tukaram challenged most severely and consistently. Holding that fervent and selfless devotion to God sufficed for attaining spiritual emancipation – indeed was the only possible means to it – Tukaram dismissed the several paths to such emancipation as expounded in classical Hindu thought. As the poet succinctly says in one poem addressed to Vithoba, "Yoga cannot grasp You, sacrificial rites cannot get You, You do not yield to penance, the senses cannot touch You, Knowledge cannot discover You."[13] Just as audacious were his lines:

> We alone know the meaning of the Vedas,
>   Others carry them as dead weight.
> The taste of food can be known only by those who have eaten,
>   Not by those who merely watch.[14]

What led to Tukaram's dramatic confrontation with Brahmin power was not just that he held such deviant views. It was, rather, his act of committing those

---

[10] Jayant Lele, "Jnanesvar and Tukaram: an Exercise in Critical Hermeneutics," in Israel and Wagle, *Religion and Society*, 127.

[11] Chitre, *Says Tuka*, 120.   [12] *Ibid.*, 121.   [13] *Ibid.*, 71.

[14] Lele, "Jnanesvar and Tukaram," 125.

views to writing, thereby violating the principle that only Brahmins should or could write texts on religious matters. Moreover, the poet was certainly aware of this, for he confesses, "I have no right to read and write; In all ways poor – Tuka says, my caste is low."[15] In short, Tukaram had set himself on a collision course with the Brahmin community, a course narrated both by the poet himself and, with some elaborations, by his first biographer, Mahipati. Tukaram simply records that he had been inspired by Vithoba himself to write poetry, and that for this he was later denounced and assailed. So he drowned all his manuscripts in a river, appealing to Vithoba to restore them if he were a true devotee.[16]

Mahipati provides more detail. On the basis of local traditions collected in 1774, the biographer records that in the town of Wagholi, some fifty miles south of Dehu, there lived a Brahmin named Rameshvar Bhatt who had grown envious of Tukaram's fame. Charging that "Tuka was of the *Shudra* caste, and yet was publicly preaching the substance of the *Vedas*," Bhatt induced the chief official of Pune to have Dehu's headman expel Tukaram from the village. When Tukaram personally appealed to the Brahmin for clemency, Bhatt responded by demanding that the poet sink all his books of poetry in a river. Yielding to overwhelming social pressure, the poet took his manuscripts to a deep pool of the Indrayani River, which flowed by his native Dehu (see Plate 11). There he released his books, which he had wrapped in cloth and weighted with a heavy stone, and watched helplessly as his precious work slipped beneath the waves.[17]

The distraught poet now threw himself before the village shrine to Vithoba, tearfully imploring the deity for the restoration of his literary work. He also underwent rigorous austerities, determined to fast even unto death. But then, on the morning of the thirteenth day after he had sunk them in the water, Tukaram's manuscripts miraculously appeared floating on the surface of the river, completely dry. The villagers who witnessed the sight, who were among the throngs of people attracted to Tukaram's poetic recitations and his message of devotional service to Vithoba, rushed to the temple where their spiritual guide had been fasting and joyfully related to him what they had seen.[18]

The reappearance of the manuscripts in the Indrayani River represented perhaps the central event in Tukaram's life as narrated by subsequent

[15] Omvedt and Patankar, *Revolutionary Abhangs*, abhang no. 2766.
[16] Chitre, *Says Tuka*, 204.
[17] Justin E. Abbott, trans., *Life of Tukaram: Translation from Mahipati's* Bhaktalilamrita, *Chapter 25 to 40* (1930; repr. Delhi, 2000), 203–05.
[18] Abbott, *Life of Tukaram*, 203–05, 213–14.

generations of Marathi-speakers, and a major event in the remembered history of Maharashtra.[19] "The story of the dry manuscripts in the water," relates Mahipati, "spread from country to country. Pious people came from a distance to see Tuka." These included Rameshvar Bhatt, the Brahmin who had earlier persecuted Tukaram but was now overcome with contrition for what he had done.

> Repentant at heart, he came and fell prostrate before Tuka. His eyes filled with tears, and he exclaimed, "Blessed is the glory of the saints. I have read all the Upanishads and the Vedanta, but there is no power in me that could preserve paper dry in water. A *sadguru* [teacher] who can save one in this ocean of a worldly life, such is Tuka."[20]

The capitulation of the learned Rameshvar Bhatt – expert in the four systems of philosophy, the four *shastras*, the Upanishads, and the Vedanta – signaled that even Brahmins could be awakened to the validity and truth of Tukaram's message.

More basically, the episode at the Indrayani River vindicated Tukaram's endeavor to produce a written text – available to all castes and classes and in the ordinary language of the people – which would propagate a means of attaining spiritual emancipation, bypassing the norms prescribed by the Brahmin establishment. It is true that other Marathi poets had for centuries been delivering much the same message. But the miracle of the dry manuscripts validated the dissemination of non-Brahmin religious writing in a far more dramatic manner than had been the case with previous poets.

Finally, by expressing in ordinary language the socio-religious aspirations of non-Brahmins of all sorts, Tukaram's life work helped transform what had been a tradition focused on a pilgrimage to Pandharpur into a broad-based social movement. This outcome was shaped by two factors: first, the socio-religious identity of those groups to whom the message of Tukaram and his literary predecessors appealed; and second, the manner in which a Marathi literary tradition had emerged.

---

[19] This narrative of the text and the river is not altogether unique in South Asian traditions. Commenting on Telugu folk epics having similar themes, V. Narayana Rao notes that the motif "of the text thrown into the river and later retrieved, accomplishes a number of symbolic functions. Sacred knowledge has to be lost and then regained. The Vedas, too, were stolen and brought back to Visnu from under the earth, where the demon Somaka had hidden them . . . The rivers into which the epic texts are thrown represent both the sacred waters and the flowing of oral tradition. The motif explains the fragmented nature of the available epics . . ." Velcheru Narayana Rao, "Epics and Ideologies: Six Telugu Folk Epics," in *Another Harmony: New Essays on the Folklore of India*, ed. Stuart H. Blackburn and A. K. Ramanujan (Berkeley, 1986), 154–55.

[20] Abbott, *Life of Tukaram*, 219.

PASTORAL TRIBES AND RELIGIONS OF THE DESH

The Indrayani River, which for thirteen days had claimed Tukaram's manuscripts, is one of several tributaries of the Bhima, the middle of three major river systems that flow in an east-southeasterly direction across the upper Deccan plateau (see Map 5). To its north lies the Godavari and to the south the Krishna, which as we have seen formed until 1565 the historic frontier between Vijayanagara and the northern sultanates. All three rivers flow out of the Sahyadri Mountains, which rise abruptly some thirty miles inland from the seacoast. By trapping much of the rain carried by the monsoons off the Arabian Sea, this range sharply divides the low, moist Konkan coast from the dry uplands to the east, that is, the Marathi-speaking portion of the Deccan plateau known as the Desh. The mountains also divide two different ecological worlds – the Konkan, a lush coastal terrain whose wet-rice economy supports a dense population linked commercially to markets across the Arabian Sea; and the Desh, an arid plateau whose sparser population is supported primarily by the cultivation of millet and by cattle pastoralism.

Günther-Dietz Sontheimer, who carefully studied the historical sociology of the Desh, writes of the long-term "layering" of this region's peoples. The earliest inhabitants were tribals such as the Kolis, followed first by Gavli pastoralists, then by Dhangar pastoralists, and finally by Kunbi and Mali farmers.[21] Although such a diachronic movement from tribal to pastoral to agrarian societies is found in many parts of South Asia, pastoralists of the Desh have played an especially prominent role in shaping Marathi society and culture. Throughout the Desh, for example, one finds many undated "hero stones," most of which depict the heads of cattle bent over a hero who had died defending them in cattle-raids. Such stones, which are especially abundant in the Bhima watershed where pastoralism continued until modern times, allude to conflicts both among pastoral groups and between pastoralists and intruding farming communities.[22]

Whereas cities along the Konkan arose from maritime commerce dating to Roman times, the earliest settlements on the plateau, which lie along a north–south axis just east of the mountains (e.g., Nasik, Paithan, Pune, Satara, Karad, Kolhapur), appeared somewhat later. From the eighth century on, farming communities slowly but steadily migrated eastward and settled along the great

---

[21] Günther-Dietz Sontheimer, *Pastoral Deities in Western India*, trans. Anne Feldhaus (Delhi, 1993), 179.

[22] Gunther D. Sontheimer, "Hero and Sati-Stones of Maharasthra," in *Memorial Stones: a Study of their Origin, Significance, and Variety*, ed. S. Settar and Günther-Dietz Sontheimer (Dharwad, 1982), 262–63.

river valleys of the Desh. This colonizing movement is especially associated with the growth of Yadava state power in the twelfth and thirteenth centuries, which synchronized with the diffusion of Telugu farming communities in the eastern Deccan under Kakatiya rule (see chapter 1). At this time, too, millet cultivation and the construction of temples – especially those dedicated to Śiva and to Devi (the Goddess) – expanded throughout the Desh. In or near these temples are often found stones depicting a slain hero and the cattle he had rescued or defended, suggesting conflicts between pastoralists and cultivators. From the early fourteenth century, when the region came under the authority of the Delhi Sultanate, down to the time of Tukaram and even beyond, cultivating communities continued to extend their territorial reach, pushing out from the lower valleys onto the intervening plains of the Desh, displacing, incorporating, or simply coexisting with pastoral communities.[23]

The millennium-long transformation of the Desh from a predominantly pastoral to a predominantly agrarian economy was accompanied by changing patterns of religious culture, seen in both iconography and theology. The pastoral deities Biroba, Mhaskoba, and Khandoba, which were originally represented by unhewn stone, and later by representations of their "vehicles" (*vahana*), finally appeared as carved, figural images. As the iconography of the gods evolved over time, so did the way they were conceived, a change that appears to have arisen from encounters between pastoral and agrarian societies. Contact with more Hinduized farming groups seems to have led pastoralists like the Dhangars to think of Biroba not only as an individual god, but also as a local manifestation of the great deity Śiva.[24] In the same way, the pastoralists' deity Mhaskoba was thought to be married not only to a woman who had come from the underworld of the snakes, but also to a "pure" woman of high caste who was ultimately identified with Durga/Parvati, the consort of Śiva.[25] Mhaskoba's upgrading and assimilation into the India-wide pantheon illustrates an important phase in the historical evolution of this pastoral god, for once these identifications became securely established, Mhaskoba was finally adopted by all the castes of settled farming communities.[26] Given the long-term presence of pastoralism on the Desh, the early assimilation of pastoral deities to Śaiva theology would seem to explain the largely Śaiva substrate that has endured into modern times in the religious culture of the bulk of the region's pastoral and cultivating castes.

---

[23] Sontheimer, *Pastoral Deities*, 19–20, 151–52, 155–77.
[24] *Ibid.*, 205.
[25] *Ibid.*, 184.   [26] *Ibid.*, ix.

The cult of Vithoba, which would play such a vital role in the religious culture of Maharashtra, also evolved from pastoral origins. The cult's geographic focus, Pandharpur, lies squarely in the Desh's former pastoral domain; as early as AD 616 the town is mentioned as "Pandarangapalli," with *palli* meaning "settlement of wild tribes."[27] And the arms-akimbo stance of the image of Vithoba in Pandharpur, which is ascribed to the sixth century, resembles the image of Bir Kuar, the cattle-god of the Ahirs of western Bihar.[28] Most explicitly, a thirteenth-century Marathi text mentions a hero named "Vitthala" (i.e., Vithoba) who had died while protecting the cows of Pandharpur, adding that a stone there had been erected in his memory. Even today, Dhangar pastoralists identify Vithoba's wife as Padubai, a forest goddess understood as a protectress not only of people but especially of cattle.[29]

Although poets like Namdev, Eknath, or Tukaram saw Vithoba as a form of Vishnu, the deity's earliest contact with "high" Hindu culture was not with Vaishnava theology. As with other pastoral deities, Vithoba was assimilated first with Śaiva religion and thought, a process that was completed well before the thirteenth century, by which time the popularity of the cult had spread widely throughout the Desh. There is evidence pointing to this earlier, Śaiva, association. Pandharpur's oldest temple, that of Pundalik, is Śaiva. The headgear of the Vithoba image in Pandharpur is in the form of a Śiva-linga. And in the late thirteenth century, Pandharpur was known, among other names, as the city of Pandurang, which means "the white god," a name for Rudra-Śiva.[30]

From the thirteenth century on, however, the cult's sectarian identity gradually shifted from a Śaiva to Vaishnava orientation, a consequence of the increasing social prominence of Vaishnava Brahmins in the region's agrarian society. For Brahmins not only gave semantic order and ideological leadership to socially stratified agrarian societies; they also gave order to the divine world. "The Brahman's task," as Sontheimer puts it, is

to recognize the god and to identify him. He does not impose any new system, but interprets the same phenomenon in a loftier and more prestigious way . . . the Brahman is necessary for the identification of the [tribal] god, an event typical of the introduction of 'Hindu' deities among the tribes.[31]

In this way, whereas Vithoba had earlier been conceived as a form of Śiva, by the fourteenth century the god was becoming understood as an original form (*swarup*) of Vishnu.

---

[27] *Ibid.*, 70.   [28] Vaudeville, *Myths, Saints and Legends*, 212–13.
[29] Sontheimer, *Pastoral Deities*, 47–49.
[30] Vaudeville, *Myths, Saints and Legends*, 203, 213, 250–51.
[31] Sontheimer, *Pastoral Deities*, 147.

This final identification of Vithoba also coincided with the slow but steady advance of agrarian communities in the pastoral Desh. Because such communities are by nature more socially differentiated and stratified than are pastoral societies, those parts of the Desh that had been exposed the earliest and longest to agriculture tended to be especially preoccupied with the kind of social categories, distinctions, and hierarchies that characterize the caste system. The advance of agrarian society in the Desh therefore implied a growth in the caste system in the region, and of ideas of social categories and graded hierarchies presided over by Brahmins.

Yet the cult of Vithoba never lost touch with its pastoral origins. For one thing, Vithoba's identity with Vishnu would remain weakest among pastoral communities and strongest among agricultural castes such as the Kunbi, the community to which Tukaram belonged.[32] Moreover, the open, egalitarian ethos characteristic of pastoral culture shaped notions of devotion (*bhakti*) to a personal deity who was accessible and available to all people, regardless of kin group. This ethos effectively transcended, in fact predated, a fully elaborated caste system in the Desh. As noted by Vijaya Ramaswamy, the Varkaris' notion of the devotee's relation to Vithoba was typically one of equality and camaraderie.[33] When Tukaram speaks of the interface between deity and devotee, he emphasizes not the individual's encounter with God, but that of the collective, the community of devotees. One is struck by his use of plural pronouns:

> God ignores our hierarchies,
>> Showing loyalty only to devotion.
>> *   *   *   *   *   *   *
> They've organized a game on the river sands,
>> The Vaishnavas are dancing, ho!
> Pride and wrath they trample underneath their feet,
>> At one another's feet they're falling, ho!
>> *   *   *   *   *   *   *
> We servants of Vishnu are softer than wax,
>> But hard enough to shatter a thunderbolt.
> Dead but alive, awake while asleep,
>> Whatever is asked of us we go on giving.[34]

---

[32] Writes Sontheimer, "the nomadic Dhangars are more inclined toward Śaiva deities; even Vithoba of Pandharpur is not (yet) Visnu for them." *Ibid.*, 147.

[33] Vijaya Ramaswamy, "Women 'In', Women 'Out': Women within the Mahanubhava, Warkari, and Ramdas Panths," in *Organizational and Institutional Aspects of Indian Religious Movements*, ed. Joseph T. O'Connell (Shimla, 1999), 253.

[34] Omvedt and Patankar, *Revolutionary Abhangs*, abhangs nos. 2820, 189, 987.

In a sense, then, Tukaram, like his poet-predecessors, gave voice to a deep-rooted collective identity among Marathi-speakers, and particularly among non-Brahmins of Maharashtra. Understanding the power of vernacular Marathi, these poets, writes Dilip Chitre, "made language a form of shared religion and religion a shared language. It is they who helped to bind the Marathas together against the Mughals on the basis not of any religious ideology but of a territorial cultural identity."[35]

LANGUAGE COMMUNITIES AND VERNACULARS OF THE DECCAN

Dilip Chitre's remark about language and territorial cultural identity raises the question of how this identity might have evolved. Was it, as Chitre implies, the product of a three centuries' tradition of poet-saints writing Marathi poems in praise of the immensely popular deity Vithoba? And if so, to what extent can the emergence of Marathi vernacular literature itself be attributed to the rise of this or other devotional traditions of Maharashtra? Recently, Sheldon Pollock has raised the broader question of how and why India's vernacular languages achieved literary status between the tenth and sixteenth centuries, questioning the role that devotional religious cults might have played in the process.[36] In this context it might be useful to consider how other vernacular languages of the Deccan achieved literary form, what historical forces facilitated their appearance, and what social classes underlay them. Table 3 presents a highly schematic chart intended not to cover all possibilities of this complex issue, but merely to suggest some of the different ways that written languages – both vernacular and classical – were used in the Deccan during the sixteenth and seventeenth centuries.

One way the sultanates of Ahmadnagar, Bijapur, Golkonda, and Bidar affirmed sovereign authority was by issuing coins and inscriptions recorded not in any Indian vernacular, but in the classical languages of Islam. Coins were inscribed mainly in Arabic, following formulaic conventions inherited from centuries of Islamic numismatic tradition. On the other hand, inscriptions, being more informative than formulaic, were generally recorded in the prestige court language, Persian, excepting those on mosques or Muslim shrines,

---

[35] Chitre, *Says Tuka*, xvii.
[36] Sheldon Pollock, "India in the Vernacular Millennium: Literary Culture and Polity, 1000–1500," *Daedalus* 127, no. 3 (1998): 41–74; Sheldon Pollock, "The Cosmopolitan Vernacular," *Journal of Asian Studies* 57, no. 1 (February 1998), 6–37. For Pollock's reservations about the role played by religious devotionalism in the rise of vernacular literatures, see p. 29 of the second article.

Table 3 *Language usage in the Deccan sultanates, 1500–1687*

Function	Authors	Medium	Language
State authority	court officials	coins, inscriptions	Arabic, Persian
Aesthetic cultivation	court literati	texts	Telugu, Dakani, Persian
Revenue and judicial administration	Niyogi Brahmins, Parasnavis	documents	Telugu, Marathi, Kannada, Persian
Popular devotion (related to a religious institution)	poet-saints, Sufi shaikhs	texts	Marathi, Dakani

which normally appeared in Arabic. Only a handful of bilingual inscriptions were recorded in Persian and one of the local vernaculars.[37]

At the same time, the courts of the Deccan did patronize the production of vernacular literature, though in varying degrees as one moves from west to east across the plateau. In the west, the Nizam Shahi court of Ahmadnagar is not known to have patronized any vernacular literature. More centrally located Bijapur patronized literature in Dakani but not in Kannada or Marathi. In the east, by contrast, the Qutb Shahi rulers of Golkonda patronized so much Telugu literature that, writes one authority, they "virtually became Telugu Sultans."[38] For his part, Sultan Ibrahim Qutb Shah (1550–80) was moved by genuine love of the language. In 1543, as a prince seeking to escape the deadly intrigues of the Golkonda court, he had fled to Vijayanagara where he was warmly received by Rama Raya. Although the latter's capital lay in the Kannada-speaking sector of the plateau, Telugu was at that time the principal language at the Vijayanagara court, which lavishly patronized Telugu literature. Prince Ibrahim spent fully seven years at this court before returning to Golkonda where he was crowned sultan in 1550. But by this time "Ibharama cakravarti," as he was called in Telugu sources, had become so thoroughly steeped in Telugu aesthetics that he would sit, "floating on waves of bliss," as one court poet put

---

[37] See Stan Goron and J. P. Goenka, *The Coins of the Indian Sultanates* (New Delhi, 2001), 312–42; Ziyaud-Din A. Desai, *A Topographical List of Arabic, Persian and Urdu Inscriptions of South India* (New Delhi, 1989); Ziyaud-Din A. Desai, *Arabic, Persian and Urdu Inscriptions of West India, a Topographical List* (New Delhi, 1999).

[38] K. Lakshmi Ranjanam, "Telugu," in *History of Medieval Deccan (1295–1724)*, ed. H. K. Sherwani and P. M. Joshi (Hyderabad, 1974), ii:147.

it, listening to the *Mahabharata* recited to him not in Sanskrit, but in the Telugu translation begun in the eleventh century by the poet Nannaya.[39] Not only did Ibrahim himself patronize works of Telugu poetry; so did his Muslim noble Amin Khan, and more importantly his son and successor, Muhammad Quli Qutb Shah (1580–1612). In doing so, these men were following a time-honored tradition in Andhra, where local élites had patronized the production of Telugu poetry ever since the time of the Kakatiya monarchs.[40]

A very different pattern is seen in the case of Dakani, the vernacular tongue of Deccani Muslims. Traceable to the speech of northern immigrants who had settled the upper Deccan in the early fourteenth century, Dakani had no literary history prior to the fifteenth century. When it did appear, it was initially called "Hindvi" or "Hindi," owing to its remembered association with the Delhi Sultanate's colonial connection with the Deccan, and with immigrants who had come down from the north ("Hind"). The language's high level of Punjabi vocabulary alone points to this northern connection. By the seventeenth century, however, authors referred to the language as "Dakani," a term reflecting the new point of geographical reference, and the new spirit of cultural independence, of the language's native speakers – the Deccani class. For the growing antagonism between Deccanis and Westerners found its linguistic and literary counterpart in the appearance, and patronage, of Dakani literature. By the sixteenth and especially the seventeenth century, as Shamsur Rahman Faruqi observes, poets confidently composed in their own language without seeking ratification from outside authority, without feeling the need to "genuflect before the ancients, Sanskrit and Perso-Arabic." Writing in the 1640s, the poet San'ati Bijapuri summed it up: "Dakhani comes easy to one who doesn't have Persian. For it has the content of Sanskrit, but with a flavor of ease."[41]

Dakani poets like San'ati or Nusrati Bijapuri (d. 1674) were patronized by enlightened royal patrons such as Sultan Muhammad Quli Qutb Shah of Golkonda and Sultan Ibrahim 'Adil Shah II (1580–1618) of Bijapur, both of whom invested themselves deeply in both classical Indian and local cultures.

---

[39] Phillip B. Wagoner, "Emperor Ibharama and the Telugu World of Qutb Shahi Hyderabad" (Paper delivered at the Institute of Fine Arts, New York University, March 10, 2004).

[40] Lakshmi Ranjanam, "Telugu," II:147–61, 161–63.

[41] Shamsur Rahman Faruqi, "A Long History of Urdu Literary Culture, Part I: Naming and Placing a Literary Culture," in *Literary Cultures in History: Reconstructions from South Asia*, ed. Sheldon Pollock (Berkeley, 2003), 824, 831, 836, 837. Shamsur Rahman Faruqi, *Early Urdu Literary Culture and History* (New Delhi, 2001), 95–104. See also Simon Digby, "Before Timur Came: Provincialization of the Delhi Sultanate through the Fourteenth Century," *Journal of the Economic and Social History of the Orient* 47, no. 3 (April 2004), 333–36.

They also wrote Dakani verse themselves. Sultan Ibrahim's outstanding literary achievement was his *Kitab al-Nauras*, an essay on Indian aesthetics set to prescribed musical *ragas*. Sultan Muhammad, like other Dakani poets, even adopted the Indian trope – never found in Arabic or Persian poetics – in which the author speaks in the voice of a woman awaiting the favors of her male lover, as in the love of the cowherding woman Radha for Krishna.[42]

Apart from royal courts, Sufi shrines also emerged as centers of Dakani literary production. Like the temple of Vithoba in Pandharpur, such shrines provided an institutional base, or focus, for the production of devotional literature in the vernacular language. And, like Sufi shrines elsewhere in South Asia, those in the Deccan sought to preserve the remembered sayings and deeds of spiritually powerful shaikhs, which prompted disciples to record their biographies (*tazkirat*) and conversations (*malfuzat*). In addition, many shaikhs themselves wrote works on mystical subjects. In north India, where close ties with Persian-speaking Iran and Central Asia assured a high level of Persian usage and comprehension, shaikhs and disciples of this period continued to write in Persian. But in the Deccan, where Persian was far less widely used or understood, poets found it necessary to write in the vernacular, and so pioneered written forms of spoken Dakani.[43] In Bijapur, the innovators included Shah Miranji Shams al-'Ushshaq (d. 1499) and his son Burhan al-Din Janam (d. 1597), who used Dakani when writing verse for wider, commoner audiences. Prominent genres of this folk literature included the *chakki-nama* or *charkha-nama*, sung by village women while engaged in domestic chores like grinding meal or spinning thread. These songs used simple language and imagery to transpose abstract ideas about the Sufi's path to spiritual enlightenment into everyday guidelines for a pious life. By contrast, these authors used Persian when writing expository prose with technical vocabulary, intended for fellow Sufis.[44]

If the sultanates affirmed their Deccani identity by patronizing Dakani literature, and their sovereignty by issuing coins and inscriptions in classical Islamic languages, for conducting the routine business of government – collecting revenue and administering justice – they used the vernacular tongues of the masses. Rulers found that the most efficient way of managing their judicial

---

[42] D. J. Matthews, "Eighty Years of Dakani Scholarship," *Annual of Urdu Studies* 8 (1993): 104; Carla Petievich, "The Feminine and Cultural Syncretism in Early Dakani Poetry," in *The Annual of Urdu Studies* 8 (Madison, 1993), 120–21.

[43] Faruqi, "Long History of Urdu," 838–39; Matthews, "Eighty Years of Dakani Scholarship," 92.

[44] Richard M. Eaton, *Sufis of Bijapur, 1300–1700: Social Roles of Sufis in Medieval India* (Princeton, 1978), 136–42, 155–64.

and revenue bureaucracies, both of which came into regular contact with village communities, was to employ those same classes of skilled, literate administrators – mostly Brahmins – that for centuries had served ruling authorities. In Golkonda, for example, royal edicts were initially issued in Persian only; but by the early seventeenth century they were often bilingual, in Persian and Telugu. At local levels, meanwhile, revenue papers were prepared largely in Telugu by Niyogi Brahmins, that is, Brahmins expert in clerical and administrative skills. By the end of the seventeenth century, even royal edicts were issued in Telugu, with Persian summaries appearing only on their reverse sides.[45]

In Bijapur, the switch to the use of Marathi and Kannada in the revenue administration came in 1535 with the accession of Ibrahim 'Adil Shah I, who effected a top-down revolution that aimed to indigenize his regime. At court he replaced Shi'i rites with Sunni rites; he forbade the wearing of hats in the style of the Iranian court; he expelled from his nobility all but 400 Westerners, replacing them with Deccanis and Habshis. And he ordered that all public revenue accounts, formerly recorded in Persian, be kept in Marathi or Kannada and placed under Brahmin management. It is hardly surprising that, as a result of these reforms, Brahmins acquired great influence in his government.[46]

NARASOJI VS. BAPAJI, 1611

The sultanates' judicial systems were also maintained in the Deccan's vernacular languages, and in these systems, too, Brahmins played prominent roles. Inasmuch as the litigation of disputes in nearly any literate society tends to churn up evidence and leave "paper trails," an examination of contemporary court testimony and the processes of adjudication can reveal a great deal about social relations at the lowest level of local societies. Such evidence is also suggestive of the formation of language communities.

We see these themes in a case litigated in 1611 in the Marathi-speaking portion of the sultanate of Bijapur.[47] The case, whose roots extended back several

---

[45] Muzaffar Alam, "The Culture and Politics of Persian in Precolonial Hindustan," in Pollock, ed., *Literary Cultures in History*, 157.

[46] John Briggs, trans., *History of the Rise of the Mahomedan Power in India* (1829, repr. Calcutta, 1966), III:47–48. Text: "*daftar-i Farsi bar taraf sakhta Hindawi kard, wa Bahamana-ra sahib-i dakhl gardanida, jami'-i davabit-i Ibrahim 'Adil Shah-ra bar ham zad.*" Muhammad Qasim Firishta, *Tarikh-i Firishta* (Lucknow, 1864–65), II:27. Firishta called the new languages "Hindvi," the term Westerners used in referring to any Indian vernacular.

[47] See Graham Smith and J. Duncan M. Derrett, "Hindu Judicial Administration in Pre-British Times and its Lesson for Today," *Journal of the American Oriental Society* 95, no. 3 (July–September 1975): 417–23. The original Marathi document is cited in V. K. Rajwade, *Marathyameya Itihasacim Sadhane* 15 (Bombay, 1912), 22–28 (no. 6).

generations, involved a dispute between two kin-groups: a family of hereditary village headmen (*patil*), represented in court by the plaintiff Narasoji; and a family of Muslim merchants and money-lenders represented by the defendant Bapaji. In the background was an ancient shrine of a local Sufi saint, Pir Jalal al-Din, and its own family of hereditary attendants (*mujawirs*). The dispute began over the use of offerings made to this shrine, it evolved into a murder case, and it ended in a bitter struggle over which family should rightfully hold the office of headman of Masura, a village in modern Satara District. Each step of the dispute yields information on social, political, and communal relations at the village level, as well as on villagers' relations with the wider world. Most importantly, the case reveals the evolution of a larger community that defined itself not by caste, class, or religion, but by a shared language, a shared history, and a shared conception of civil society.

The dispute began sometime in the mid- to late-1500s over the disposition of offerings made to the tomb of Pir Jalal al-Din in Masura, a shrine venerated by both Muslims and Hindus. By ancient custom, Hindus placed offerings for Hindu mendicants on one side of the tomb, and Muslims put offerings for Muslim holymen on the other. But local Muslims persuaded servants of the shrine to discontinue the practice, evidently in a manner that would channel all offerings to themselves. When Narasoji's grandfather, who was village headman, ordered a return to the earlier practice, he and one of his sons were murdered by servants of the shrine. Later, another of his sons, who was Narasoji's father and had succeeded as village headman, avenged this act by killing three servants at the shrine.

At this point a prosperous trader and money-lender in the village, who was also the brother-in-law of one of the three murdered victims, sought justice by going to the district headquarters in nearby Karad. There he had an interview with the region's deputy governor (*na'ib*), 'Abd Allah Husain, who governed the district for Sultan Ibrahim 'Adil Shah II of Bijapur. Inasmuch as the two men were related – 'Abd Allah's son was married to the money-lender's daughter – the meeting was no doubt congenial. Its upshot was that the governor issued a warrant against Narasoji's father, the village headman. When the latter failed to answer the warrant, 'Abd Allah imposed harsh sanctions on him. Charging Narasoji's father with murdering the three shrine attendants, the governor fined him 4,500 *hun*s and ordered him kept in custody for three years. The man's home was also looted, with the governor's apparent connivance.

Narasoji's father paid part of the fine imposed on him, but then absconded without paying the balance. When the governor learned this – and here we reach the crux of the matter – he transferred the rights of village headman from Narasoji's father to his own in-law, the same prosperous trader and money-lender who had brought the complaint to him in Karad. As a money-lender, however, this man had enemies, including Narasoji's father, who had criticized his practice of compelling debtors to repay loans during the lean season when resources were scarce. In fact, threats against him were so severe that he was driven from the village altogether; at this point the office of headman passed to his son, Bapaji.

During his lifetime Narasoji's father, a known murderer, absconder, and enemy of the governor, was in no position to recover his ancestral office of village headman. But when he died, his son Narasoji appealed directly to Sultan Ibrahim 'Adil Shah II to have the office restored to his family, that is, to himself. To resolve the dispute, the sultan assigned to the case one Ambar Khan, who ordered Narasoji to pay the unpaid portion of the fine that had been levied on his father, upon doing which he would receive the office of village headman.

Before these measures could be implemented, however, some Muslims in the sultan's service harassed Narasoji, as a result of which the case was referred to an assembly of arbiters in Karad. They, too, ruled that the office of headman should be transferred from Bapaji to Narasoji. But Bapaji, complaining that the Karad arbiters were biased against him, arranged to have the case referred for final arbitration to a *dharma-sabha*, or an assembly of learned Brahmins, in "a distant place." This was Paithan, some 200 miles north of Karad. Bapaji had requested the change of venue since the *dharma-sabha* there was renowned for its fairness. When they reached Paithan, the contending parties were taken to the local *dharma-cauthara*, a holy place intended for such assemblies, where Narasoji and Bapaji presented their cases before a council of *dharmadhikaris*, Brahmin judges learned in Hindu law (*dharma-śastras*).

The judges first scrutinized all the documents sent up from earlier litigation: the deputy governor's orders, Ambar Khan's ruling, and the findings of the Karad arbiters, together with some royal edicts related to the case. The trial began with Bapaji observing that Pir Jalal al-Din, from whom he was descended, was originally a Hindu – an argument possibly intended to ingratiate himself with the panel of Brahmin judges he faced. Then he continued:

Bapaji: Since I am descended from Pir Jalal al-Din, I myself should hold the office of shrine attendant. Yet my relatives were killed.

Narasoji to judges: Ask Bapaji why the shrine attendants killed my grandfather and one of his sons.

Judges to Bapaji:	Why did the attendants kill them?
Bapaji:	They killed only two of Narasoji's relatives, whereas Narasoji's father killed three of my relatives. I am therefore entitled to compensation for one murder. Narasoji should also pay the amount owed my father by his debtors. And if he refuses, he should perform an ordeal.
Judges to Bapaji:	Did your father make these loans after consulting with Narasoji's father? If so, and if you can document it, we would order such payment.
Bapaji:	When Narasoji's father was in custody, he made a written commitment to repay me the money owed by my father's debtors.
Narasoji:	Any such agreement would have been made under duress. If Bapaji would give compensation for the looting of my [family's] house, which happened with the governor's connivance, then I will pay Bapaji the remaining balance.
Bapaji to Narasoji:	I call on you to perform an ordeal, and if you succeed, you owe me nothing and I owe you nothing.
Judges to Bapaji:	We doubt that anybody should be required to perform an ordeal when reliable witnesses and documents are available.

[The judges now cited the *Mitaksara*, a Sanskrit legal text written by the eleventh-century jurist Vijñaneśvara, to the effect that anybody who demands an ordeal when reliable testimony is available should be executed].

We conclude that you have caused much trouble to Narasoji and his family, and should be executed. But since you are Muslim, and the present government is a Muslim government, you will be pardoned.

However, we find that you have no valid claim to the position of village headman. And you have no right to recover money owed by your father's debtors. Nor do you have any right to receive compensation for the murder of your relatives.

On January 14, 1611 a document attested by witnesses, called a *mahzar*, was drawn up in Marathi, duly signed, and handed to Narasoji. It pronounced that Bapaji had no valid claims to the village headship, which was now finally transferred to the plaintiff, Narasoji.

What can we make of this case? In the first place, it reveals the depth to which the authority and symbolic presence of the sultan extended in the Deccan's rural society. Even a lowly village headman – or in this case, a man who made claim to the office – could lodge a complaint directly with the supreme authority of the realm. Conversely, by appealing to Ibrahim 'Adil Shah II for judicial redress, Narasoji tacitly acknowledged the sultan's ultimate sovereignty over his village. And to this appeal the sultan did indeed respond, through his representative Ambar Khan, whose ruling would have restored the headship to Narasoji. The case also reveals the prerogative of the state, in the person of the sultan's deputy governor, to make or unmake village headmen, even though by custom this position was hereditary and not appointed. All of these considerations point to the reach of state authority in village affairs and challenge the view of the Deccan sultanates as remote superstructures that sat uneasily atop village society.

But in the end, and this is the second major point arising from the case, it was a council of learned Brahmins, the *dharma-sabha*, that, at the request of the Muslim defendant, was called upon to adjudicate the matter, and whose judgment was deemed to be final. This occurred only after the dispute had been heard and ruled upon by several different authorities or arenas: the sultan's deputy governor (*na' ib*), the sultan's personal representative, and the district council (*pargana sabha*) at Karad. It is also significant that the *dharma-sabha* of Paithan settled the matter on the basis of Hindu law (*dharma-śastras*), to which all parties including the Muslim Bapaji consented. The only part of its judgment on which the council did not have jurisdiction was in the matter of capital punishment: as Bapaji was a Muslim living under a Muslim government, his execution would have required sanction under both Islamic Law and the *dharma-śastras*. Otherwise, the judges' finding on the central issue of the village headship served to confirm the judgments of all the earlier levels of adjudication. In effect, then, the offices of the deputy governor and district council functioned as de facto lower courts, inasmuch as their decisions could be, and were, appealed to the council of Brahmins whose judgments were considered final on all matters excepting capital punishment for a Muslim.

Finally, one must consider the longer-term effects of cases such as that of Narasoji and Bapaji. Involved here were repeated face-to-face disputations, in which a single case might be taken from court to court, from locale to locale across the Desh, and from level to level along the socio-political spectrum, in each instance involving diverse peoples of various castes, classes, and religions.[48] The very process of engaging in public disputation served to connect villagers with each other, even when they were gripped in bitter contention, and to reinforce a consensus on how conflicts should be resolved. This process had

---

[48] Noting that they combined both state officials and local officers and landholders, V. T. Gune concluded that Brahmin-led councils issuing *mahzar*s represented "an excellent mixture of the Muslim and indigenous institutions of local administration . . . All problems of local interest, whether administrative, social, or religious, were treated as a subject for Mahzar." V. T. Gune, *Judicial System of the Marathas* (Poona, 1953), 139.

the deeper effect of forging a larger, discursive community around vernacular Marathi both as spoken in the courts and as recorded by them. Moreover, by requiring appeals to a commonly shared past that was factual, credible, and anchored in "real-time," such public disputes, argues Sumit Guha, also generated among Marathi-speakers a collective historical consciousness, seen in the appearance of a new genre of written narrative, the Marathi *bakhar*.[49]

In short, Maharashtra's four centuries' tradition of devotional poetry praising Vithoba was not the only force that shaped a community of self-conscious Marathi speakers, or that promoted writing in that language. Hundreds of litigated cases like that of Narasoji and Bapaji had also contributed to those outcomes. Two factors, one political and one technological, had created the public space within which such disputations could legitimately occur and conflicts be adjudicated. One was the state, most immediately the sultanates of Bijapur and Ahmadnagar, but also their common Bahmani predecessor, all of which built the political and judicial framework for the resolution of conflicts. The other was the technology of paper-making, which Bahmani sultans had introduced to the Deccan in the fourteenth century and which diffused throughout the region in the succeeding centuries. The new technology facilitated the growth and reach of the sultanates' revenue and judicial bureaucracies, while enhancing the social prominence of those Brahmin writing communities that staffed them. Indeed, the ordinary words for "paper" and "pen" in the region's vernacular languages are derived from Perso-Arabic, suggesting not only the technology's path of transmission to the Deccan, but also the impact it had on the peoples of the plateau.

Owing, then, to state-created revenue and judicial bureaucracies, whose reach had been greatly expanded by the diffusion of paper-making technology, new public arenas slowly emerged in the fifteenth, sixteenth, and seventeenth centuries. Conducted and recorded in Marathi, the myriad face-to-face encounters that occurred in such arenas slowly knit together a discursive community, whose latent self-awareness could be awakened by a gifted poet like Tukaram.

---

[49] See Sumit Guha, "Speaking Historically: the Changing Voices of Historical Narrative in Western India, 1400–1900," *American Historical Review* 109, no. 4 (October 2004): 1092–96. What we know about Narasoji and Bapaji could be due to an accident of the preservation of Marathi documents; such documents in Telugu and Kannada have yet not turned up. But one may assume that, just as the sultan of Bijapur presided over an orderly system of dispute management operating in Marathi, the sultans of Golkonda, Bidar, and Berar would have managed similar institutions using the vernacular tongues of the lands they ruled. As a consequence, discursive communities of Telugu- and Kannada-speakers likely evolved along a similar path as occurred in the case of Marathi-speakers.

The surfacing of Tukaram's manuscripts, dry after being submerged for thirteen days in the Indrayani River, certainly vindicated the poet's project of writing on religious matters in the Marathi language. But the extraordinary event also contributed to the growth of a cult around Tukaram himself, an outcome the poet deeply deplored:

> The more these people admire me
> The more I am ashamed of myself,
> For I know there is nothing in me to be admired.
> Like a measure used over and over
> I am worn out now.
> This wasn't for any personal gain.[50]

Despite the poet's renown, his ultimate fate is cloaked in mystery. All that is certain is that sometime in 1649, at age forty-one, he disappeared. His own poetry suggests that, having bade farewell to his friends and fellow devotees, he simply left his village of Dehu with no intention of ever returning.[51] Perhaps he could not reconcile his sense of self-effacement before Vithoba with the public adulation he had achieved during his final years.

In any event, Tukaram's legacy would be enormous. Even during his life-time, the poet's work was seen as the culmination of Varkari devotionalism. In a well-known verse, the Brahmin poetess Bahina Bai (1628–99), who spent seven months in Dehu rapturously listening to Tukaram deliver his poetry and discourses,[52] describes the history of the Varkari tradition through the metaphor of a temple. The thirteenth-century poet Jnanadev, she writes, had laid the monument's foundation; Namdev built its walls, Eknath contributed its central pillar, and Tukaram added its crowning spire.[53] The metaphor con-veys an extraordinary sense of institutional self-awareness. Collapsing 400 years of development into a unified whole, contemporaries conceived the Varkari tradition as having had a beginning, a middle, and now a conclusion. Having added the spire, Tukaram had completed the edifice.

That edifice, in turn, has had two principal legacies – the rich corpus of devotional poetry stretching from Jnanadev to Tukaram, and the institutional-ized processions made by Varkari pilgrims to Pandharpur from points all across

---

[50] Chitre, *Says Tuka*, 158. [51] *Ibid*, xiv.
[52] Krishna P. Bahadur, trans., *Bahina Bai and her Abhangas* (New Delhi, 1998), 27, 30.
[53] Chitre, *Says Tuka*, xxvi. Another version of this metaphor appears in one of the editions of Tukaram's poetry, suggesting that Tukaram himself might originally have conceived it. See Omvedt and Patankar, tr., *Revolutionary Abhangs*, abhang no. 9.

Maharashtra. Although Tukaram himself had made informal pilgrimages to Vithoba's great temple at Pandharpur, it was his youngest son who, after his father's disappearance, inaugurated the tradition of a procession making its way from Dehu to Pandharpur, accompanied by a decorated cart carrying the poet's wooden sandals. In this way, Dehu joined other Maharashtrian villages or towns from which similar such processions, known as *palkhis*, made regular, simultaneous pilgrimages to Pandharpur. Each town from which a *palkhi* commenced was identified with a Marathi poet-saint whose wooden sandals, symbols of the saint's living presence, accompanied the pilgrims as they walked to Vithoba's temple at Pandharpur. The effect, suggests Charlotte Vaudeville, is "a form of mass communion in the exaltation of Vithoba's presence and the presence of his beloved saints."[54] As of Tukaram's day, enough *palkhis* had been established – beginning with that of Jnanadev – that the Varkaris' pilgrimage tradition had already come to embrace the entire Marathi-speaking Desh.[55]

This tradition doubtless helped knit together peoples of many different castes from points all across the Marathi-speaking Deccan, symbolizing the cultural unity of Maharashtra.[56] Nowhere else in the Deccan, or even in India, does one find an instance in which vernacular language, cultural space, and religious devotion reinforce one another so perfectly as in the Varkari tradition. In his monograph *The Cult of Vithoba*, G. A. Deleury maps the routes of the principal processions, showing how they converge on Pandharpur from every region of the far-flung Marathi zone, from Nagpur in the east, to the Tapti River in the north, to the Krishna in the south.[57] In 1949, having made the pilgrimage herself, the anthropologist Irawati Karve famously wrote, "I found a new definition of Maharashtra: the land whose people go to Pandharpur for pilgrimage."[58]

The pilgrimage tradition as described by twentieth-century observers,[59] however, had evolved considerably since its earliest beginnings in the thirteenth century, when it was celebrated by the poet Jnanadev. After Tukaram's day, processions became far more organized than before, being divided into

---

[54] Vaudeville, *Myths, Saints and Legends*, 216.

[55] G. A. Deleury, *The Cult of Vithoba* (Poona, 1960), 7, 18, 77–78. Since the seventeenth century, more *palkhis* were added. In fact, most of today's *palkhis* were established in the twentieth century.

[56] Anne Feldhaus, "Maharashtra as a Holy Land: a Sectarian Tradition," *Bulletin of the School of Oriental and African Studies* 49 (1986): 532.

[57] See Deleury, *Cult of Vithoba*, Plate 4: "Routes of the Palkhis," facing p. 76.

[58] Iravati Karve, "Vatcal," in *Paripurti* (Pune, 1949), trans. by D. D. Karve as "On the Road: a Maharashtrian Pilgrimage," *Journal of Asian Studies* 22, no. 1 (November 1962): 22.

[59] In addition to Irawati Karve's "On the Road," see Irina Glushkova, "A Study of the Term *ananda* in the Varkari Tradition," in *Tender Ironies: a Tribute to Lothar Lutze*, ed. Dilip Chitre, *et al.* (New Delhi, 1994), 220–30, and Deleury, *Cult of Vithoba*, 73–109.

units (*dindi*) that were differentiated by caste and ranked hierarchically, the more prestigious ones located closer to the cart carrying the poet-saint's sandals, and the poorer units lagging further behind. Some argue that such developments have undermined the radical, egalitarian foundations of the Varkari movement.[60] But from its beginnings that movement was concerned not with revolution – certainly not the overthrow of the caste system – but with reform, which in this context meant re-appropriating for non-Brahmins the religious ideas encompassed in classical texts like the *Bhagavad Gita*. "Both in theory and in practice," writes Jayant Lele, "the Varkari blueprint for a new and renewed society aimed at revolutionising orthodoxy without seeking to destroy tradition."[61]

What is more, from very early on Brahmins had integrated themselves with the Varkari movement, officiating at Pandharpur's temple to Vithoba ever since its founding in 1189, and serving as family priests for Varkari pilgrims. They had become an integral part of the social and ritual landscape. Even Tukaram never challenged the need for the Brahmin priesthood. To the contrary, the poet consistently displayed attitudes of generosity and humility toward Brahmins, even though these same qualities brought repeated hardship to him and bitter frustration to his wife. In the most dramatic confrontation of his life, when a Brahmin had him throw his life's work in the river, Tukaram complied without protest. Nor did he question the Brahmins' monopoly of ritual functions, or their claims of exclusive access to the Vedas; it was only their claim to monopolize the right to preach devotion to God and receive his grace that he challenged.[62]

Despite Tukaram's deference to Brahmins, his message concerning the irrelevance of caste for attaining spiritual goals did find a ready response among millions of Marathi-speaking non-Brahmins. Still vital for them was an egalitarian ideal that survived as an enduring legacy in the Desh. For, despite the steady advance of a Brahmin-ordered and hierarchically arranged agrarian society amidst pastoral communities, the egalitarian ethos associated with herdsmen never vanished, at least not in the western Deccan. Nor does one find there the enormous gap between prosperous town dwellers and poor peasants which, as Vijaya Ramaswamy has noted, is characteristic of state formations in both northern and southern India. "The peculiar geographical location of the Deccan plateau," she writes, "its rugged and harsh terrain, made impossible

---

[60] Ramaswamy, "Women 'In', Women 'Out'," 241–47. See also Deleury, *Cult of Vithoba*, 104–05.
[61] Lele, "Jnaneśvar and Tukaram," 124.
[62] David N. Lorenzen, "The Social Ideologies of Hagiography: Sankara, Tukaram, and Kabir," in Israel and Wagle, eds., *Religion and Society*, 105.

the growth of very stable and prosperous empires, or a sharply differentiated town–country landscape. Due to the dilution of sharp economic differentiations in Maharashtra, social inequalities also could not assume so markedly distinct forms."[63]

It is true that in the precolonial Desh, caste hierarchies were less complex and rigid, and caste boundaries more flexible and permeable, than was the case in the great geographic core zones in north or south India. Also, for many centuries the Marathi-speaking Desh between the Godavari and Krishna rivers had a weak tradition of stable or durable nuclear states. It is therefore striking that, just several decades after Tukaram's disappearance, a powerful state did indeed arise in what might seem the least likely place – the Sahyadri uplands straddling the divide between the Konkan and the Desh. Founded by families of chieftains that had risen to prominence by serving the sultanates of Ahmadnagar and Bijapur, this state explicitly championed the Marathi language, which was reflected in the dramatic drop in Persian vocabulary in bureaucratic Marathi during the seventeenth century.[64] The new state also absorbed non-Brahmin Marathi-speakers into a single collective, the "Marathas," a term that had initially referred only to Marathi-speaking warrior clans of the Desh.

These sweeping developments, which revolutionized the politics and society of the western Deccan in the seventeenth and eighteenth centuries, grew out of a number of pre-existing factors and forces. One of these was a model of state systems long planted in the Deccan by the sultanates. Another was increasing military pressure from Mughal imperialists, which elicited vigorous responses from peoples of the Desh. But perhaps most important was an ancient egalitarian ethos found among cattle-rearing pastoralists and dry-agricultural cultivators of the Desh. Nourished by state-sponsored revenue and juridical networks that brought Marathi-speakers in increasing touch with one another, this ethos was sustained by the Varkari pilgrimage tradition and catalyzed by vernacular poets – most immediately Tukaram. In this volume's final chapter, we shall consider in more detail the evolution of that state and its social base.

---

[63] Ramaswamy, "Women 'In', Women 'Out'," 253.

[64] Whereas in 1628 as much as 85 percent of the vocabulary in Marathi administrative documents was Persian, this figure dropped to only 37 percent in 1677, just several years after the Maratha state was established. See A. R. Kulkarni, "Social Relations in the Maratha Country in the Medieval Period," *Indian History Congress*, Proceedings of the 32nd Session, Jabalpur (1970): 235.

CHAPTER 7

PAPADU (FL. 1695–1710): SOCIAL BANDITRY IN MUGHAL TELANGANA

> Traveling alone, Papra [Papadu] appeared in Hasanabad, a village two marches away that he himself had settled. Coming across a toddy-seller, he said to the man, 'Bring me some good toddy.' But despite the fugitive's best efforts to disguise himself, the toddy-seller recognized his manner of speech. He scrutinized his face. He knew it was Papra.[1]
>
> Khafi Khan (d. *c*.1731)

The visitor to Shahpur, located some fifty miles northeast of Hyderabad near the main road to Warangal, cannot mistake its two most prominent landmarks – the hill-fort, and the bust prominently situated in the village square. The bust is of Sarvayi Papadu, Shahpur's most notorious native son. Commissioned in 1998 by the Telugu University, Warangal, this image of Papadu was sculpted on the basis of a portrait dating to 1750–80 (see Plate 12). In both the painting and the bust, the intense gaze in his eyes, his formidable moustache, and the falcon perched on his wrist all project a fearsome, swashbuckling demeanor.

Captured and executed by Mughal authorities in 1710 as a highwayman and bandit, Papadu would become celebrated in local memory as a hero who boldly defied imperial authority, indeed, most any authority. Shahpur's other prominent landmark, the fort, rests atop a hill immediately to the north of the village and consists of a square, stone-walled compound built around a cube-shaped watchtower (see Plate 13). Here, between *c*. 1701 and 1709 Mughal troops besieged Papadu and his men no fewer than four times.

Papadu's brief and turbulent career is of great interest from the standpoint of social history.[2] His stubborn resistance to various forms of authority, and his manifest success in garnering support for his cause, forced people of diverse

---

[1] Khafi Khan, *Muntakhab al-lubab* (Calcutta, 1874), 643.
[2] Two kinds of sources enable a reconstruction of Papadu's career: contemporary accounts recorded by his Mughal adversaries, and local legends subsequently recorded by folklorists. Despite their very different vantage points, the two sources converge on key aspects of his career, as is seen in J. F. Richards and V. Narayana Rao, "Banditry in Mughal India: Historical and Folk Perceptions," in *The Mughal State, 1526–1750*, ed. Muzaffar Alam and Sanjay Subrahmanyam (New Delhi, 1998), 491–519. First published in *Indian Economic and Social History Review* 17, no. 1 (1980): 95–120.

backgrounds to make crucial choices. Moreover, since he aroused considerable concern in official circles, which in turn attracted the attention of imperial news-writers, his recorded activities allow us to glimpse fault lines in the social order that would otherwise have remained concealed from view. In particular, an analysis of his supporters and opponents reveals much about the alignments of caste, class, and religious community in this part of India around the turn of the eighteenth century. Papadu's story is also instructive for its similarities, and contrasts, with other instances of "social banditry," a form of rebellion that Eric Hobsbawm finds in many pre-industrial peasant societies. In order to probe these issues, however, we must first sketch out the socio-economic and political context of Papadu's native Telangana – i.e., upland, northwestern Andhra – just before he emerged into the light of history.

FROM THE SULTANATE OF GOLKONDA TO MUGHAL HYDERABAD

When the Bahmani sultanate broke up into five regional kingdoms in the early sixteenth century, the kingdom whose borders most closely coincided with those of a pre-Bahmani state was the easternmost, the Qutb Shahi sultanate of Golkonda (c. 1518–1687). This kingdom mapped itself over nearly the same territory that formerly made up the Kakatiya kingdom, which had been extinguished in 1323 when Tughluq armies sacked its capital at Warangal and led its last *maharaja*, Pratapa Rudra, into exile (see chapter 1). As a result, the Qutb Shahi sultans of Golkonda inherited a culturally coherent territory with distinctive features that had evolved many centuries earlier. These included Telugu language and literature, castes of warrior-cultivators (Reddi and Valama), large-scale tank irrigation, Śaiva temples and monasteries, and *nayaka* chieftains who bore an ethic of courage and steadfast loyalty to their political overlords.[3]

Although it would be wrong to see the Golkonda sultanate simply as the Kakatiya kingdom reborn with a Perso-Islamic veneer, the Qutb Shahi kingdom certainly shared more continuities with pre-fourteenth-century Deccani society and culture than did any of the other Bahmani successor-states. This was especially true from the reign of Sultan Ibrahim Qutb Shah (r. 1550–80), who, as was noted in the previous chapter, had been steeped in the traditions of Andhra's regional culture. The sultan not only patronized Telugu literature, supported Brahmins and temples, and engaged in large-scale irrigation works

---

[3] J. F. Richards, *Mughal Administration in Golconda* (Oxford, 1975), 4–5.

in the style of a Kakatiya raja. He also assimilated into Qutb Shahi service many *nayaka* chieftains who proudly claimed descent from warrior-servants of the Kakatiya house, especially those serving its last dynast, Pratapa Rudra. Taking care to recognize their prior claims, Ibrahim allowed these men considerable autonomy in the agrarian sphere while also integrating them into the state's central system. One way he did this was by entrusting them with the command of the eastern Deccan's great forts. He also played down the state's Islamic and Persian character vis-à-vis the *nayaka*s, presenting himself, as John Richards notes, "as an indigenous king, ruling insofar as possible in the idiom and style of a Kakatiya, a Valama, or Reddi monarch."[4]

By 1589, the Qutb Shahi house felt sufficiently secure in its position that Ibrahim's successor, Muhammad Quli Qutb Shah, planned and laid out a new, unwalled city, Hyderabad, which was built across the Musi River just several miles from Golkonda fort. The new city's graceful centerpiece monument, Charminar (1592), would in time become perhaps the most renowned symbol of Deccani culture. What is more, the old fort of Golkonda and the adjacent new city of Hyderabad now became great magnets for wealth in the eastern Deccan. For one thing, the kingdom's monopoly on diamond production from mines located in its southern districts made Golkonda the world's most important market for large diamonds. In Europe and America the very name "Golkonda" became synonymous with fabulous wealth.[5] The reigns of sultans Ibrahim and Muhammad Quli also saw the rise to commercial prominence of the coastal city of Masulipatnam as the Qutb Shahis' principal seaport. By the close of the sixteenth century, textiles produced in the Godavari delta passed through Masulipatnam to markets throughout the Indian Ocean, attracting in exchange precious metals that flowed along the Masulipatnam–Hyderabad road to Golkonda's treasury. With its political and administrative activities concentrated on the interior plateau and its commercial activities focused on the coast, the kingdom reached its peak of prosperity in the 1620s and 1630s.[6]

But it was also in the 1630s that the dark clouds of Mughal imperialism began to gather over Golkonda's northern horizons, just as they had in Ahmadnagar four decades earlier. In 1636, the same year that the Nizam Shahi house was finally extinguished, its former territory divided between the Mughals and

---

[4] *Ibid.*, 10.
[5] The founding fathers of Golconda, Illinois, hoping no doubt for the prosperity of their new town, certainly made this association.
[6] Sanjay Subrahmanyam, "The Port City of Masulipatnam, 1550–1750: a Bird's Eye View," in *Craftsmen and Merchants: Essays in South Indian Urbanism*, ed. Narayani Gupta (Chandigarh, 1993), 47, 52, 54.

Bijapur, Golkonda was compelled to sign a "Deed of Submission." By the terms of this "agreement," the Qutb Shahi sultan was required to remit to Delhi an annual tribute of 200,000 gold *hun*s, and in his kingdom's mosques the Friday sermon was to be read in the name of Shah Jahan, the Mughal emperor. To enforce the growing Mughal pressure on Golkonda, and also on neighboring Bijapur, Shah Jahan dispatched his eldest son, Aurangzeb, to serve as his viceroy for the Deccan. From 1636 until his death in 1707, first as viceroy and after 1658 as emperor, Aurangzeb would spend a total of forty years in the Deccan, which he was obsessed with subduing and annexing to the empire. He realized a major component of this grand plan when Golkonda finally fell to his armies in 1687, just a year after Bijapur had suffered the same fate. The Deccan's last independent sultanate now snuffed out, a Mughal governor was installed in Hyderabad while a small cavalry unit escorted Abu'l-Hasan Qutb Shah, Golkonda's last ruler, to the imperial prison in Daulatabad fort.

In their endeavor to bring the new province in line with the rest of the empire, the Mughals introduced many changes in the former Qutb Shahi realm. They collected revenue in cash and not in kind; they bureaucratized the revenue-extraction procedure by regularly rotating local officers; and they changed the monetary system from gold to silver, conforming to north Indian usage. Brahmin officials, who had occupied the highest levels of Golkonda's government during the several decades prior to the conquest, were dismissed outright. And, not surprisingly given their pro-Turko-Iranian racial bias, the Mughals appointed many more Westerners than Deccanis to prominent administrative and military positions. All of the province's fort commanders and most of its military governors, or *faujdar*s, were Westerners.[7] Perhaps most importantly, the Mughals practically reversed the Qutb Shahs' policy respecting the employment of Telugu *nayaka*s. Whereas the erstwhile sultans had integrated these chiefs into their central political system, the Mughals classified them as *zamindar*s, which in the imperial lexicon denoted untrustworthy chiefs inherently hostile to Mughal interests.[8] Accordingly, the new rulers kept Telugu *nayaka*s at arm's length, allowing few of them admission into the imperial service as ranked nobles, or *mansabdar*s. The government was, however, willing to engage with those Valama or Reddi *nayaka*s who controlled only small patches of territory, treating them not as high-ranking nobles but as hybrid local officials

---

[7] Richards, *Mughal Administration*, 64, 87, 91, 98.

[8] Abu'l-fazl, the Mughals' principal theorist, thought of the empire as a lovely garden, and *zamindar*s as "weeds and rubbish of opposition." Abu'l-fazl 'Allami, *Akbar-nama*, trans. Henry Beveridge (repr., New Delhi, 1979), III:143, 169, 376.

who were allowed to keep part of the assessed taxes in return for cooperating with the system.[9]

In addition to these political changes, the imposition of Mughal authority also brought economic dislocations to the people of the eastern Deccan. The conquest itself was accompanied by widespread crop failures, together with famine, cholera epidemics, falling agricultural production, and finally, depopulation.[10] All this was made worse by Aurangzeb's policy of treating the province as a milch-cow for financing the empire's wider projects. And by century's end, the port of Masulipatnam had dried up as a source of wealth for the eastern Deccan. Within five years of the Mughal conquest, a Dutchman who had resided in the city for some time, Daniel Havart, published a book in which he blamed the port's decline mainly on the Mughal invasion and conquest of Golkonda. Recent research, however, suggests that the port was already in decline by the early 1680s, just before the Mughal conquest. The Brahmin ministers who ran Golkonda's government had replaced the Iranian faction at court with clerical (Niyogi) Brahmins, as a result of which the great Iranian ship-owners who had underwritten much of Golkonda's long-distance trade simply withdrew from commercial activities in the kingdom. As this happened, the focus of Dutch and English trade gradually shifted from Masulipatnam to other ports around the Bay of Bengal.[11]

A clear indicator of the eastern Deccan's economic malaise after the conquest is seen in the diminishing number of trade caravans that traveled the province's roads and safely reached their destinations. Obviously, the unhindered movement of such caravans was vital for the regional economy. But during the years 1702–04 *no* merchant caravans managed to reach Hyderabad, which for much of the previous century had been the Deccan's principal trade entrepôt.[12] Although this represented only one link in a chain of adverse factors that led ultimately to the final dissolution of Mughal authority in the Deccan, the failure of trade caravans to reach the provincial capital posed a major problem, to say the least. And one of the most immediate causes for this failure was highway banditry.

Here Papadu enters the picture. Though hardly the only highwayman working the roads of Mughal Hyderabad, Papadu attracted far more attention than did any of the others, both in official circles and in the collective memory of Telangana's villagers.

[9] Richards, *Mughal Administration*, 132–33, 173.
[10] *Ibid.*, 69.   [11] Subrahmanyam, "Port City," 59–61.
[12] Richards, *Mughal Administration*, 221.

Papadu seems to have grown up in the village of Tarikonda, some twenty-five miles southwest of Warangal (see Map 6). There he belonged to the toddy-tapper (Gavandla, or Gamalla) community, a low caste that made their living extracting sap from palm trees, fermenting it, and selling the liquor product. According to a folk ballad collected in the early 1870s, Papadu's first acts of defiance were directed as much at issues of caste propriety as they were at civil authority: he refused to follow the occupation of the caste into which he was born. When his own mother objected to his intention to abandon his proper caste-occupation, he replied,

> Mother! to fix and drive the share,
> the filthy household-pot to bear,
> Are not for me. My arm shall fall
> upon Golkonda's castle wall.[13]

A version of the ballad published in the early twentieth century clarifies the connection between abandoning one's caste-occupation and taking on "Golkonda's castle wall." Papadu is said to have reasoned that toddy-tappers were ideally suited for positions of leadership, and even power, since their work required them to mobilize and coordinate the skills of a number of different caste communities:

> When a toddy-tapper taps a toddy tree,
> He has a liquor-seller make the toddy.
> A basket-maker makes the knife basket,
> And a potter makes the pots.
> Doesn't such a man know how to be a ringleader?[14]

Such motives should be read with caution, as they were attributed to Papadu by later balladeers who perhaps read into his life a logic that made perfect sense to them, but which cannot be corroborated by contemporary evidence. Moving to the basic events of Papadu's life, on the other hand, we have the extraordinary narrative of Khafi Khan, a contemporary Mughal chronicler who compiled his account on the basis of official reports recorded by imperial news-writers. He records as follows.

---

[13] J. A. Boyle, "Telugu Ballad Poetry," *Indian Antiquary* 3 (January 1874): 2.
[14] Pervaram Jagannatham, "Sardar Sarvayipapadu Janapada Sahityagathalu," in Pervaram Jagan-natham, *Sahityavalokanam: sahitya vyasa samputi* [*Looking at Literature: a Collection of Literary Essays*] (Warangal and Hyderabad, 1982), 74. I am grateful to Phillip Wagoner for his translation of this passage.

Map 6. Eastern Deccan in the time of Aurangzeb, 1636–1707.

Sometime in the late 1690s Papadu assaulted and robbed his sister, a wealthy widow. With her stolen money and ornaments he gathered together a group of followers, built a crude hill-fort in Tarikonda, and began to engage in highway robbery, raiding merchants on the nearby artery connecting Warangal and Hyderabad. The first people to take notice of Papadu's activities were local *faujdars* and *zamindars*, that is, military governors and hereditary Telugu landholder/chiefs. When these local notables drove him out of Tarikonda, Papadu fled clear to Kaulas, some 110 miles to the west, where he took up service as a troop-captain (*jama'a-dar*) with the *zamindar* of that place, Venkat Rao.[15]

Reverting to his old ways, however, Papadu was soon back on the roads robbing travelers and merchants. Venkat Rao imprisoned him when he learned of this, but after several months the *zamindar's* wife, believing that an act of compassion might cure her sick son, freed all the prisoners in her husband's jail, including Papadu. At this point the careers of Venkat Rao and Papadu veered in opposite directions. In 1701 Venkat Rao threw in his lot with the Mughals, offering to serve the deputy governor in Hyderabad with his 500 horsemen and 2,000 infantry. Receiving a rank and a command of 200 horsemen, he became one of the few Telugu chieftains to have made the transition from *zamindar* to *mansabdar*, that is, he moved out of the group of indigenous landholder/chiefs whom the Mughals viewed as politically suspect, and joined the charmed inner circle of élite administrators.[16]

Papadu, on the other hand, resumed his lawless ways. Returning to his native district, he soon established himself at Shahpur, just several miles from Tarikonda. Here he had no difficulty gathering together a large number of followers, including a fellow named Sarva. Together, they built a crude hill-fort that served as their base for more marauding operations, whose victims this time included both Muslim and Hindu women. Such outrages now drew the attention of Mughal authorities and local notables alike. Khafi Khan writes that a delegation of merchants and "respectable people of all communities and castes" went straight to the court of Aurangzeb to demand justice. The emperor ordered action from Hyderabad's deputy governor, who in turn dispatched the *faujdar* of Kulpak, a town about fifteen miles from Shahpur, to deal with Papadu. But the *faujdar*, an Afghan named Qasim Khan, was shot and killed by one of Papadu's men in a skirmish near Kulpak.

Soon thereafter, most likely in 1702, the deputy governor himself, Rustam Dil Khan, resolved to besiege Shahpur and root out the miscreant

---

[15] Khafi Khan, *Muntakhab*, 631. [16] Richards, *Mughal Administration*, 229.

toddy-tapper. But after a two-month siege, Papadu and Sarva escaped, whereupon Rustam Dil Khan blew up the fort and returned to Hyderabad. At this point Mughal authority in the area appears to have vanished, for Papadu and Sarva quickly returned to Shahpur, gathered up their following, and replaced the former crude fort, now largely demolished, with a stronger one built of stone and mortar – the structure that stands today – and outfitted it with fixed cannon. But Rustam Dil Khan was unaware of these activities. He was also unaware of the favorable reception that Papadu's name and activities were receiving in districts remote from Shahpur. Nor was he aware of how Papadu had consolidated his position within the insurgent movement. The rebel's two principal lieutenants, Sarva and one Purdil Khan, had just quarreled with each other and engaged in a duel. After both men succumbed from wounds sustained in the duel, Papadu emerged in sole command of the movement. At this point he and his men began conquering neighboring forts. Papadu now seemed well on his way to becoming a regional warlord. Moreover, his ascendance in central Telangana coincided in time with the two-year period, 1702–04, when no trade caravans were reaching Hyderabad. These two facts would not appear to be coincidental.[17]

Meanwhile, between May 1703 and December 1705, Rustam Dil Khan had been transferred to postings far from Hyderabad, possibly owing to his failure to deal effectively with the growing banditry then plaguing the province. But by early 1706 he was back in Hyderabad, determined to curry the emperor's favor. In May of that year Dutch observers noted that the deputy governor had approached Riza Khan, another notorious bandit operating in Telangana, about suppressing Papadu's growing insurrection. Khafi Khan reports that Rustam Dil Khan appointed a "brave soldier who was seeking work" to punish Papadu, and that this second attack on Papadu had also failed.[18] It would thus appear that Mughal authorities had resorted to using one bandit to suppress another, an action indicative both of the government's desperation and of the very low level of Hyderabad's internal security.

Just over a year later, in the summer of 1707, Rustam Dil Khan resolved again to personally lead imperial troops against Papadu. Marching out to Shahpur with an imposing cavalry, the deputy governor besieged Papadu and his men for two or three months. But in the end Papadu was able to carry the day, not by force of arms, but by large sacks of money. Once received by Rustam Dil Khan, Papadu's bribe achieved its aim of calming the deputy governor's zeal for

[17] Khafi Khan, *Muntakhab*, 632–33.
[18] Richards and Narayana Rao, "Banditry," 498; Khafi Khan, *Muntakhab*, 632.

military operations. The siege lifted, the Mughal cavalry units quietly retraced their steps to their barracks in Hyderabad.[19]

The deputy governor's ignoble retreat now emboldened Papadu and his men to plan their most daring heist yet – a raid set for April 1708 on Warangal itself. This was no minor village or even hill-fort. The former Kakatiya capital was still fortified with the moats, the forty-five bastions, and the two walls – one stone, the other earthen (see Plates 1 and 2) – that dated from Kakatiya times, plus the fortifications subsequently added by Bahmani and Qutb Shahi engineers. Probably the province's second largest city after Hyderabad, Warangal had by this time evolved from a political center to a major commercial and manufacturing hub, exporting its costly carpets and other textiles throughout India and even beyond. To Papadu, the city would have seemed ripe for the taking.

Two considerations informed the timing of his attack. The first was the distraction of authorities in Hyderabad, owing to both empire-wide and local politics. In February 1707 the aged Aurangzeb had finally died, throwing the whole empire into the turmoil that all parties knew would accompany the inevitable struggle for succession. In June the eldest of Aurangzeb's three sons, having defeated and killed one of his brothers, crowned himself Bahadur Shah. The new emperor now offered the governorship of Bijapur and Hyderabad to his other brother, Kam Bakhsh. But the latter, already the governor of Hyderabad, refused the offer and instead crowned himself "King of Golkonda" in January, 1708. This defiant (and oddly anachronistic) act set the stage for a final confrontation between the two brothers.[20] From his roost in Shahpur, Papadu watched and waited.

Also determining the timing of the bandit's raid on Warangal was the approaching Muslim holiday of Ashura, which commemorates the day in AD 680 when the Prophet's grandson, Husain, was slain in Kerbala, Iraq. Representing the greatest tragedy in the history of Shi'i Islam, Ashura has for centuries been observed by Shi'as with intense mourning, including self-flagellation. But until recent times, Muslims and non-Muslims in many parts of the non-Arab world commemorated the day with parades of horses, elephants, banners, and visual representations of the Kerbala story. Urban neighborhoods would compete with one another over which one could create the most spectacular display for the occasion. In Papadu's time, residents of Warangal celebrated Ashura by making representations of Husain's tomb in Kerbala. Since

---

[19] Richards and Narayana Rao, "Banditry," 498; Khafi Khan, *Muntakhab*, 633–34.
[20] Richards, *Mughal Administration*, 236.

both Hindus and Muslims celebrated the holiday, the city's entire population would be busy making their preparations on the eve of the holiday.[21] And, so Papadu calculated, nobody would be minding the city walls.

As Ashura fell on April 1, 1708, on the evening of March 31 Papadu's forces, comprising 2,000 or 3,000 infantry and 400 or 500 cavalry, approached Warangal's stone walls. One party blocked the roads while others hurled ropes with slip-knots onto the ramparts, by which they scaled and breached the walls. Once the gates were opened from the inside, Papadu's main forces poured into the city, as its unsuspecting residents were engaged in preparing for the next day's celebrations. For two or three days the intruders plundered the city's shops, seizing great quantities of cash and textiles. Carpets too bulky to haul away whole were simply cut into strips. But the principal prize was the thousands of upper-class residents who were abducted to Shahpur, where a special walled compound was built at the base of the fort for their detention. Among those taken were many women and children, including the wife and daughter of the city's chief judge. Presumably, Papadu seized these people in order to hold them for ransom, since seizing the city's poorer classes would have had no such value.[22]

The Warangal raid completely transformed the character and the fortunes of the former toddy-tapper. From part of his booty, Papadu purchased more military equipment, which included 700 double-barreled muskets, state-of-the-art weaponry likely acquired from Dutch or English merchants who still called at Masulipatnam. He also began comporting himself in the style of a *raja*. Élite bearers carried him about in a palanquin, and an élite guard accompanied him when mounted on a horse. If he acted like a king, he had actually become a parvenu landholder. For we hear that he raided passing Banjaras (itinerant grain carriers) and seized their cattle, which he put to work plowing his fields for him. Since he is said to have seized between 10,000 and 12,000 head of

---

[21] Khafi Khan, *Muntakhab*, 634. In 1832 Ja'far Sharif, a Deccani Muslim and native of Eluru on the Andhra coast, wrote an ethnography entitled *Qanun-i-Islam* in which he described Ashura as it was celebrated in his own day: "On the tenth day in Hyderabad all the standards and the cenotaphs, except those of Qasim, are carried on men's shoulders, attended by Faqirs, and they perform the night procession (*shabgasht*) with great pomp, the lower orders doing this in the evening, the higher at midnight. On that night the streets are illuminated and every kind of revelry goes on. One form of this is an exhibition of a kind of magic lantern, in which the shadows of the figures representing battle scenes are thrown on a white cloth and attract crowds. The whole town keeps awake that night and there is universal noise and confusion . . . Many Hindus have so much faith in these cenotaphs, standards, and the Buraq, that they erect them themselves and become Faqirs during the Muharram." Ja'far Sharif, *Islam in India, or the* Qanun-i-Islam: *the Customs of the Musalmans of India*, ed. William Crooke, trans. G. A. Herklots (repr. London, 1972), 163, 166.

[22] Khafi Khan, *Muntakhab*, 634.

cattle for this purpose, the agricultural operations he controlled must have been extensive.[23] It is not clear whether these tracts were arable lands seized from local landholders, or uncultivated lands – forest or wastelands – that he brought into agricultural production for the first time. As for the latter possibility, we know of at least one village, Hasanabad, that he founded and settled. In any event, the evidence suggests that Papadu used plundered cash and cattle to acquire at least the trappings of royal status and the economic substance of a great landholder, though of course he lacked the pedigree of a hereditary Telugu chieftain (*nayaka*).

Flushed with the success of his Warangal raid, Papadu began planning a similar raid on Bhongir, a famous fort standing on a huge, barren rock between Shahpur and Hyderabad, just thirty miles from the latter city. As with his attack on Warangal, he again chose a day when he knew the population would be distracted – the feast of the Prophet Muhammad's birthday, which fell on June 1, 1708. But this expedition was far less successful. Just before dawn his men hurled stones up to Bhongir's parapets carrying ropes with slip-knots. But one stone missed its mark and dropped onto the house of the gatemen, who sounded an alarm, creating a general disturbance. To escape the botched raid, Papadu ordered his men to burn stacks of hay so that they could flee through the smoke undetected by the fort's gunners. Despite this seeming fiasco, the attackers nonetheless managed to carry off many hostages, who again seem to have been seized for their ransom value. Papadu had promised silver coins to those of his men who captured females, and gold coins to those who took élite women.[24]

In Hyderabad, meanwhile, the complexities of imperial politics prevented Mughal authorities from taking action against Papadu. Within weeks of the outrage at Warangal, Kam Bakhsh, the "King of Golkonda," was in Gulbarga praying at the shrine of Gisu Daraz, presumably for help in his anticipated showdown with his older brother, Bahadur Shah. But his prayers would be of no avail. The emperor soon left Delhi and advanced to the Deccan to confront his younger brother, and in January 1709, the two armies clashed just outside Hyderabad. Shortly afterwards Kam Bakhsh died from wounds sustained in that battle.

The stage was now set for the highpoint of Papadu's career. While in Hyderabad in January, Bahadur Shah gave a public audience, or *darbar*, and we learn from an on-site Dutch report that among those present who had

[23] *Ibid.*, 635.   [24] *Ibid.*, 635–36.

been received by the emperor was *den rover servapaper*, or the "bandit Sarvayi Papadu." Craving imperial recognition as a legitimate tribute-paying chieftain, Papadu on this occasion presented Bahadur Shah with the extraordinary gift of 1,400,000 rupees, in addition to large amounts of foodstuffs and other provisions for the imperial army. In return, the emperor bestowed upon Papadu one of the most prized gifts one could receive from a sovereign, a robe of honor.[25]

It had been twenty-two years since Hyderabad witnessed a royal audience in which a sovereign received subordinate chiefs, for since 1687 the city had been ruled by a governor and not a monarch. Bahadur Shah's formal *darbar* would therefore have had special impact on an older generation who could remember the days when Golkonda's Qutb Shahi sultans honored Telugu *nayakas* in their *darbars*. In this light, for a low-caste toddy-tapper and notorious bandit to be given the dignity of a formal audience with the most powerful sovereign in India, and even to receive a robe of honor, surely galled the more respectable elements of Hyderabad's society. Especially offended were those whose family members had been abducted by Papadu, such as Shah 'Inayat, the most venerable elder of Telangana's Muslim society. Soon after the public audience, Shah 'Inayat led a delegation of high-born Muslims to lodge a complaint before the imperial court. While stating that he himself would not deal with a mere toddy-tapper – even though he had just honored him with a robe of honor! – Bahadur Shah instructed his newly appointed governor of Hyderabad, Yusuf Khan, to "eradicate" the man. The new governor in turn ordered a fellow Afghan, Dilawar Khan, to lead an expeditionary force against Papadu.[26]

Meanwhile, the receipt of a robe of honor from the Mughal emperor had not visibly affected Papadu's behavior. In June 1709, we find him besieging the fort of a neighboring landholder, in the course of which he learned of Dilawar Khan's expeditionary force advancing towards him. Preferring to confront the Mughals on his own ground, he lifted his siege and started back to Shahpur – not knowing, however, that at that very moment the captives he had imprisoned there were staging an uprising. Among their leaders was the local deputy *faujdar* (military governor), who happened to be the brother of Papadu's wife. Using files that his sister had smuggled into the prison, the deputy *faujdar* and his fellow prisoners cut their shackles, overpowered their guards, and seized control of the fort while Papadu and his main force were still absent.[27]

---

[25] Cited in Richards and Narayana Rao, "Banditry," 502n. See also Richards, *Mughal Administration*, 245. On the symbolism of robes of honor, see Gavin R. G. Hambly, "The Emperor's Clothes: Robing and 'Robes of Honour' in Mughal India," in *Robes of Honour: Khil'at in Pre-Colonial and Colonial India*, ed. Stewart Gordon (New Delhi, 2003), 31–49.
[26] Khafi Khan, *Muntakhab*, 638–39.   [27] *Ibid.*, 639–40.

Papadu thus reached Shahpur only to be greeted by cannonballs fired from his own artillery by his own former hostages. Enraged at this turn of events and determined to force his way inside, he ordered his men to set fire to the fort's wooden gates. When the gates were ablaze, his men donned the blood-soaked hides of buffaloes they had just killed, and using these wet skins as shields they attempted to rush through the burning gates. But the heat was too intense; in addition, fallen timbers and heavy debris blocked the way for Papadu's charging elephants. At this moment Dilawar Khan's expeditionary force arrived on the scene. Unable to enter his fort and unwilling to engage the Mughal cavalry in the open, Papadu and his men took refuge in the walled enclosure at the base of the fort where they had been holding their captured hostages.[28]

The situation seemed dire. By evening, with some of his more dispirited men having already scattered, Papadu abandoned Shahpur and took his army to his nearby fort at Tarikonda. When Yusuf Khan learned that Papadu was on the run, the governor sent 5,000 or 6,000 fresh cavalry to besiege Tarikonda, while Dilawar Khan remained behind in Shahpur collecting and inventory-ing Papadu's wealth and revenue accounts (*mal wa band-u-bast*). But then things bogged down. Papadu entrenched himself in the fort overlooking the town in which he had launched his career, while the besiegers failed to make any headway dislodging him. Months passed. Finally, Yusuf Khan resolved to attack Papadu in person, and so in March 1710 he marched out of Hyder-abad at the head of 5,000 or 6,000 cavalry. Joining him were a number of local landholders who, clearly seeing Papadu as a threat to their own interests, mobilized between 10,000 and 12,000 cavalry and 20,000 infantry for the cause.[29]

Despite the enormous host besieging him at Tarikonda, Papadu managed to hold out for several more months. Then in May, the governor offered Papadu's men double pay if they would defect. Exhausted and famished, many did. Finally, when Papadu ran out of gunpowder, he made his last, desperate move. To disguise his identity, he changed his clothing. Then, with a view to throwing pursuers off his trail, he placed his sandals and hookah by one gate of the fort while departing through another. For two days he traveled alone, incognito, with a bullet wound in one leg. Nobody knew where he was, not even his sons, who continued fighting in the fort.[30]

Finally, he appeared in the village of Hasanabad, where he came across the shop of a toddy-seller. Papadu had reason to feel safe here, since he himself had founded this village and was in the company of a man of the same caste into

[28] *Ibid.*, 640–41.   [29] *Ibid.*, 641–42.   [30] *Ibid.*, 642.

which he had been born. Nonetheless, to be safe, he maintained his disguise. Taking a seat in the shop, he asked the proprietor for a glass of his very best toddy. The proprietor closely studied his customer's face. It was his manner of speech, though, that gave him away. Realizing his customer's true identity, the toddy-seller asked him to remain seated while he left his shop to fetch his best toddy.

Soon thereafter, he returned with the deputy *faujdar* and 300 soldiers. The officer was his wife's brother, the same man whom Papadu had imprisoned in Shahpur and who had led the recent prison uprising. The men brought their quarry before the governor, Yusuf Khan, who spent several days questioning Papadu as to the whereabouts of his collected wealth. Then they hacked him to pieces. His head was sent to Bahadur Shah's court; his body was hung from the gates of Hyderabad, both as trophy and as cautionary warning.[31]

PAPADU AS A "SOCIAL BANDIT"

The story of Papadu's exploits raises a number of questions about the meteoric career of this Telangana toddy-tapper and the society in which he lived. Why did he appear when and where he did? Why was he betrayed by his wife and by a member of his own caste? In terms of class, caste, or religion, who were his supporters and who were his opponents? What was the economic basis of his movement, and what can his story tell us about the relationship between caste and wealth?

In his comparative studies of peasant rebellions, historian Eric Hobsbawm formulated the notion of the "social bandit," which he defines as "peasant outlaws whom the lord and state regard as criminals, but who remain within peasant society, and are considered by their people as heroes, as champions."[32] Crucially, the "social bandit" is embedded both socially and culturally in a community of peasants, from which he draws support and sustenance over and against his (and their) twin adversaries: the "lord" and the state. A rich literature in the form of folk legends or ballads often grows up around such figures – especially the subset Hobsbawm calls "noble robbers," such as Robin Hood – precisely because they are so firmly rooted in their respective societies. They are not lone criminals, no matter how much the lord or the state might imagine or wish them to be. Indeed, they are potentially more dangerous than lone criminals, precisely because under the right circumstances social bandits can spark peasant revolutions, as happened repeatedly in the history of China.

---

[31] *Ibid.*, 643.   [32] E. J. Hobsbawm, *Bandits* (London, 1969), 13.

Other aspects of Hobsbawm's "social bandit" thesis seem pertinent here. They flourish, he writes, "in remote and inaccessible areas such as mountains, trackless plains . . . and are attracted by trade-routes and major highways, where pre-industrial travel is naturally both slow and cumbrous." They are likely to appear in times of pauperization and economic crisis. However, while they are certainly activists, social bandits "are not ideologists or prophets, from whom novel visions or plans of social and political organization are to be expected . . . Insofar as bandits have a 'program,' it is the defense or restoration of the traditional order of things 'as it should be.' "[33] Hobsbawm further argues that whereas social bandits are part of peasant society, they are usually not peasants themselves. The latter, being immobile and rooted to the land, are typically victims of authority and coercion, whereas "the rural proletarian, unemployed for a large part of the year, is 'mobilizable' as the peasant is not." To find bandits, writes Hobsbawm, "we must look to the mobile margin of peasant society."[34]

In all these respects, Papadu would appear to have conformed to Hobsbawm's model. Ballads narrating his life and sung in rural settings attest both to his rootedness in peasant culture and to his celebration as a local hero. His inaccessible roost on Shahpur hillock, located near a major highway, helped facilitate his career as a brigand. The breakdown of Mughal Telangana's economy and internal security in the early 1700s would have shaped the timing of his emergence. Though certainly an activist, he seems to have had no coherent ideology or program. And finally, his caste as a toddy-tapper placed him in precisely the niche where Hobsbawm predicts social bandits will appear – on the "mobile margins" of peasant society.

But what, exactly, constituted Papadu's social base? Who supported him? One might seek clues to these questions by identifying the groups most concerned with preserving his memory. Here it seems significant that no single caste identifies the popular epic of Papadu, as told by balladeers, as their own.[35] This suggests that the movement never did define itself in terms of caste. Preserved and sung by generations of itinerant singers, the ballad appears to have been embraced by all castes of rural Telangana, if not, indeed, the greater part of the Telugu-speaking Deccan. In 1974, folklorist Gene Roghair recorded a ballad sung of Papadu in coastal Guntur district; exactly a century earlier, J. A. Boyle recorded another version of the same ballad in distant Bellary district, in eastern Karnataka.[36] Sites named in the ballad itself – i.e., those that

[33] Ibid., 16–17, 20–21, 24.   [34] Ibid., 25.
[35] Velcheru Narayana Rao, "Epics and Ideologies: Six Telugu Folk Epics," in Another Harmony: New Essays on the Folklore of India, ed. Stuart H. Blackburn and A. K. Ramanujan (Berkeley, 1986), 132.
[36] Richards and Narayana Rao, "Banditry," 505n.

Papadu intended to attack – include only one in Telangana (Golkonda), two in southern Andhra (Nellore, Cuddapah), and one each on the Andhra coast (Masulipatnam), in southern Karnataka (Mysore), and on the Malabar coast (Cannanore). It thus seems that the "remembered" Papadu drifted far to the south of Telangana, but not to the north or west (see Map 6).

Nor does Papadu's social base appear to have been defined by religious community. Historian and folklorist Velcheru Narayana Rao has noted that

> several highly educated literary people . . . show great interest in interpreting and re-creating the story in an effort to represent Sarvayi Papadu as a model Hindu warrior against the Muslim tyrants. If their view gains wider acceptance, it is possible that the story will acquire epic-like proportions and status as a 'true' story.[37]

Evidence both from Khafi Khan's narrative and from oral ballads, however, would argue against any characterization of Papadu as a "Hindu warrior." The Mughal historian states that Papadu's earliest roadside attacks targeted "wealthy women of the region, whether Hindu or Muslim," and that in response to these attacks "merchants and respectable people of all communities" (*har qaum*) complained to Aurangzeb. And while the Hyderabad government mounted repeated attempts to root out Papadu's movement, it was Hindu chieftains who first opposed him, and in the end, such chieftains would send many more cavalry and infantry against him than did the government.

Another way of addressing this question is to identify Papadu's closest supporters. Two printed versions of his ballad (1909 and 1931) and an oral version that was tape-recorded in 1974 give virtually identical lists of his earliest followers. These include: Hasan, Husain, Turka Himam, Dudekula Pir (cotton-carder), Kotwal Mir Sahib, Hanumanthu, Cakali Sarvanna (washerman), Mangali Mananna (barber), Kummari Govindu (potter), Medari Yenkanna (basket-weaver), Cittel (a Yerikela), Perumallu (a Jakkula), and Pasel (a Yenadi).[38] In terms of their cultural background, the first five are the names of Muslims, the second five those of caste Hindus, and the last three "are tribal groups of itinerant fortune-tellers, thieves, animal breeders, singers, and performers."[39] If these names are representative of Papadu's broader movement, it would certainly appear difficult to characterize it as a "Hindu" uprising against "Muslim" tyranny. Rather, the oral tradition suggests that his followers included Hindus, Muslims, and tribals in nearly equal proportions. This is

---

[37] Narayana Rao, "Epics and Ideologies," 133.
[38] See Jagannatham, "Sardar Sarvayipapadu," 74; Richards and Narayana Rao, "Banditry," 507, 512n.
[39] Richards and Narayana Rao, "Banditry," 512n.

confirmed by contemporary evidence, for we know from Khafi Khan that Papadu's closest lieutenants, Sarva and Purdil Khan, were a Hindu and a Muslim respectively.

It is more revealing to examine the same list from the standpoint of occupation. Among the Muslims mentioned in the ballad, three were of indeterminate occupation, one was a cotton-carder, and the other a police captain (*kotwal*). Four of the five Hindus belonged to the rural proletariat – a barber, a washerman, a potter, and a basket-maker – while the three tribal names suggest people at the outer margins, if not beyond the pale, of "respectable" society. In sum, most of Papadu's immediate supporters, though diverse in point of religious community, clearly belonged to the lower orders of Telangana's rural society.

A large category of supporters not mentioned in the ballad, but inferable from Khafi Khan's account, were landless peasants. The sheer number of draft animals that plowed Papadu's fields – between 10,000 and 12,000 head – suggests the presence of many agricultural laborers whom he could count on for support. When Papadu abandoned Shahpur for Tarikonda, Dilawar Khan spent three or four days assessing his account books (*band-u-bast*), which evidently refers to records of rent owed by peasants working his fields. And the speed and apparent ease with which he could mobilize thousands of armed men – and laborers to build his forts – suggests a depth of support that reached beyond the rural proletariat and into the region's sizable peasant population.

It is an easier matter to identify Papadu's opponents. The first delegation that complained to Aurangzeb of Papadu's highway banditry included merchants (*biyopari*) and respectable people (*shurafa'*) of all communities and castes. However, while merchants were Papadu's primary targets at Warangal, their community posed no military threat to him. Also opposing him were the military governors, or *faujdars*, whom Mughal authorities in Hyderabad had posted throughout the countryside with specified units of cavalry. But after 1700 the power and authority of *faujdars* in Telangana appears to have progressively diminished. In 1702, for example, the *faujdar* of Kulpak, only some sixteen miles from Shahpur, had been Papadu's principal adversary; by 1709 the *zamindar* of that place was filling that role.

It was, then, the Telugu landholder/chieftains – *zamindars*, in Mughal terminology – who mounted the most effective opposition to Papadu. They well understood the threat that he posed both to rural society and to themselves. With their own inherited lands and armed militias, these chieftains were deeply invested in preserving the established order, which involved, among other things, maintaining secure roads. Papadu's only known employer, the *zamindar* Venkat Rao, threw him into prison when he was found to be involved in highway banditry. This was after *zamindars* of his native Tarikonda had already driven him out of their region for committing the same offense. Their most decisive challenge to Papadu, however, came when Yusuf Khan finally resolved to root him out of Tarikonda with 6,000 Mughal cavalry. On this occasion local *zamindars* raised a cavalry twice that size, in addition to 20,000 infantry. Evidently, these chiefs were determined to eradicate a parvenu who publicly claimed *zamindar* status, yet who as a lowly toddy-tapper had inherited neither land nor chieftaincy. Papadu's receipt of an imperial robe of honor, which seemed to represent official acknowledgment of his status as a legitimate, tribute-paying *nayaka-zamindar*, provoked strong reaction. Landholders claiming descent from ancient *nayaka* families were simply incensed at such impudence.

Papadu's receipt of an imperial robe of honor also aroused resentment from Telangana's *sharif* community, that is, high-born, respectable, urban-dwelling Muslims who cultivated learning and piety. These included shaikhs or judges (*qazis*) whose female relatives had been abducted to Shahpur, and who demanded that the state exert itself to uphold a certain moral order. Shortly after Bahadur Shah's Hyderabad *darbar*, the most respected member of Telangana's *sharif* community, Shah 'Inayat, whose own daughter had been one of Papadu's victims, took his complaint to the emperor. The latter replied that he would not stoop to dealing with a mere toddy-tapper, a response that so disgraced the shaikh that on returning home he shunned all human contact, fell ill, and died of bitter sadness.[40] Nonetheless, the moral pressure he had brought to the court did bear fruit: the governor of Hyderabad, Yusuf Khan, was ordered to take decisive action against Papadu.

With such varied forms of opposition, how did Papadu hold out for nearly a decade? One answer perhaps lies in Hobsbawm's observation that whereas the state might see social bandits as lone criminals, they are in fact entrepreneurs whose activities necessarily involve them with local social and economic systems. That is, bandits must spend the money they rob, or sell their booty. "Since they normally possess far more cash than ordinary local peasantry," he writes,

their expenditures may form an important element in the modern sector of the local economy, being redistributed, through local shopkeepers, innkeepers and others, to the commercial middle strata of rural society; all the more effectively redistributed since bandits

---

[40] Khafi Khan, *Muntakhab*, 638.

(unlike the gentry) spend most of their cash locally . . . All this means that bandits need middlemen, who link them not only to the rest of the local economy but to the larger networks of commerce.[41]

Were it not for the market, what else would Papadu have done with all the carpets and textiles he plundered from Warangal? How else could he have acquired his 700 double-barreled muskets?

For nearly a decade, Papadu, operating with substantial income and expenditures, occupied the center of a wide redistribution network. His income would have derived from direct raiding of towns and trade caravans, ransom demanded for the return of élite hostages, rent from landless laborers working on fields under his control, and the sale of stolen goods through complicit middlemen. His expenditures would have included purchases of weapons and supplies to maintain his forts, payment to his armed men, bribes for enemy combatants, "tribute" to the state, and the largess necessarily dispensed to his lieutenants and numerous underlings, as would be appropriate for a man who was carried about in a palanquin and was escorted by an élite guard. Clearly, the idea of the lone criminal is inadequate for understanding the wide range of Papadu's operations.

That said, Papadu's career exhibited a fatal tension between the considerable fortunes that he amassed, and his low birth-ascribed ritual rank as a toddy-tapper, together with the poor standard of living that normally accompanied that work. This tension seems to have had deep roots. There are hints that, even before he commenced his career as a bandit, members of his family were connected to wealth or authority. According to an oral version of his ballad, Papadu's father had been a village headman (*patil*) and his brother a petty army commander (*sardar*).[42] His sister, too, had married into considerable wealth. Indeed, it was envy for his sister's money and ornaments, which he robbed, that had first stimulated his taste for banditry. It has been suggested that the disjuncture between the attained secular status of his family, and the low ritual status of his caste, might explain his flat rejection of his caste occupation.[43] The same disjuncture might also explain why Papadu married a woman who, as the sister of a *faujdar*, was almost certainly outside the toddy-tapper caste.

In time, however, as Papadu became more successful as a bandit-entrepreneur, the disjuncture between his attained secular status and his low ritual and occupational status grew more acute. It reached its apogee with his brazen attempt to purchase political legitimacy by presenting a "gift" of

[41] Hobsbawm, *Bandits*, 73. [42] Richards and Narayana Rao, "Banditry," 507.
[43] *Ibid.*, 512.

1.4 million rupees to the Mughal emperor. After taking that audacious step before the full gaze of a public audience, his career immediately crashed, as the governor, the *sharif* community, and especially the Telugu *zamindars* all moved to crush him. It is hardly surprising that the high and mighty would strike down a toddy-tapper for having strayed so very far from his "proper" station.

More interesting is evidence of his rejection by his own people, a product of the social bandit's fundamental ambiguity. As a poor man who refuses to accept the normal roles of poverty, and in Papadu's case, the normal roles of caste as well, the bandit seeks freedom by the only means available to him: courage, strength, cunning, determination. "This draws him close to the poor," notes Hobsbawm,

he is one of them. It sets him in opposition to the hierarchy of power, wealth and influence; he is not one of them . . . At the same time the bandit is, inevitably, drawn into the web of wealth and power, because, unlike other peasants, he acquires wealth and exerts power. He is 'one of us' who is constantly in the process of becoming associated with 'them'. The more successful he is as a bandit, the more he is *both* a representative and a champion of the poor *and* a part of the system of the rich.[44]

As viewed from Shahpur, in other words, Papadu's audience with the emperor could well have certified, at least for some, that their leader was "one of them." Six months after the Hyderabad *darbar*, his own wife betrayed him by supporting the revolt among Shahpur's imprisoned hostages. It is of course possible that in a stressed situation, her loyalty to her brother – the *faujdar* she set free – proved greater than her loyalty to Papadu. On the other hand, Papadu's betrayal by the toddy-seller in Hasanabad, which led directly to his execution, was a purely political act. There was no possibility of sibling loyalty being involved, as might have been the case with Papadu's wife and her brother.

Papadu's ambiguous and ultimately untenable position is suggested in the only surviving artifacts he left to posterity – the forts he built at Tarikonda and Shahpur. The ramparts of his square-shaped citadel in Shahpur have the same rounded, crenelated battlements that are found in Bahmani, Qutb Shahi, and Mughal military architecture (see Plate 13). And the imposing south entrance gate to that fort, its arched passageway measuring sixteen feet in width and twenty-eight feet in height, features a graceful pointed arch typical of the Perso-Islamic aesthetic vision. By Papadu's time, these architectural elements had become thoroughly identified with the projection of Mughal power and

[44] Hobsbawm, *Bandits*, 76.

authority. On the other hand, the cube-shaped stone watchtower that occupies the center of that fort's compound, with its steps projecting out from its northern and eastern sides, is quite anomalous, finding no parallel in any center of Mughal power. Its only analog is the watchtower near the northern gate of Warangal's fort, itself a post-Kakatiya structure randomly assembled from disparate blocks of stone.[45] It is as though, in his defiance of Mughal authority, Papadu planted in the middle of his main fort the least Mughal-like emblem that would have been familiar to him.

Shahpur fort thus projects Papadu's two sides: the would-be subimperial tributary lord comfortably integrated into the Mughal order and recognized by the emperor himself, and the rebellious Telugu son-of-the-land who defied any and all authority. In the society of his day, he could not have it both ways.

---

[45] See N. S. Ramachandra Murthy, *Forts of Andhra Pradesh* (Delhi, 1996), Warangal: Plate 8.

CHAPTER 8

TARABAI (1675–1761): THE RISE OF BRAHMINS IN POLITICS

[The Mughals felt] that it would not be difficult to overcome two young children and a helpless woman. They thought their enemy weak, contemptible and helpless; but Tara Bai, as the wife of Ram Raja [i.e., Rajaram] was called, showed great powers of command and government, and from day to day the war spread and the power of the Mahrattas increased.[1]

Khafi Khan (d. *c.* 1731)

People say that I am a quarrelsome woman.[2]

Tarabai (1748)

Between 1700 and 1710, just when Papadu was most active in Telangana, a powerful anti-Mughal resistance movement convulsed the Marathi-speaking western Deccan. Endeavoring to suppress this larger movement in the west, Aurangzeb siphoned off needed men and resources both from Hyderabad and from north India, hindering imperial efforts to pursue the Telangana bandit. More importantly, it was in the western Deccan that the octogenarian's dreams of a vast, Delhi-based all-India empire would be dashed to pieces, as had earlier happened to Sultan Muhammad bin Tughluq in the 1330s and 1340s (see chapter 2).

The movement was led by Tarabai, one of the most remarkable women in Indian history. Her life also coincided with significant developments in the eighteenth-century western Deccan: (a) the rise of powerful Brahmins in the central administration of the new Maratha state, (b) the eruption of Maratha warriors out of the Deccan and across the whole of north India from the Punjab to Bengal, and (c) changes in the social composition of the category "Maratha." Although Tarabai was by no means the cause of these developments, they can all be found woven into the fabric of her extraordinary career. In fact, her long life – which stretched nearly from the founding of the Maratha kingdom in 1674 through the disastrous Battle of Panipat in 1761 – spanned a momentous epoch of Indian as well as of Maratha history.

---

[1] Khafi Khan, *Muntakhab al-lubab*, in H. M. Elliot and John Dowson, ed. and trans., *History of India as Told by its Own Historians* (Allahabad, 1964), VII:367.
[2] Cited in Manohar Malgonkar, *Chhatrapatis of Kolhapur* (Bombay, 1971), 181.

Chart 4   Tarabai and the Bhosle family – Satara and Kolhapur branches

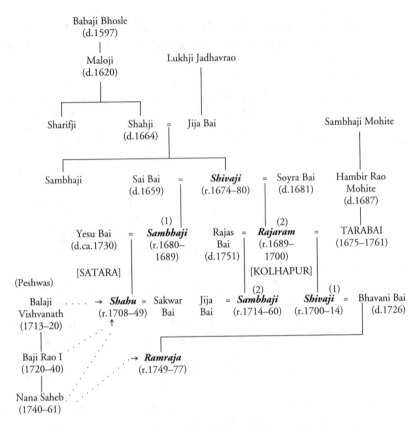

[Note: dots indicate service]

A "QUEEN OF THE MARATHAS" (1675–1714)

Born in 1675, just several months after Shivaji Bhosle had launched the new Maratha state, Tarabai was married at age eight to Shivaji's second son, Rajaram (see Chart 4). Since her father, Hambir Rao Mohite, had been Shivaji's commander-in-chief, the marriage cemented an alliance between two distinguished Maratha lineages, the Bhosle and the Mohite clans.

Much of her youth, however, was passed in great danger. The very year after Shivaji's death in 1680, Aurangzeb's son Prince Akbar fled south and found refuge in the new Maratha kingdom after unsuccessfully rebelling against his father. In response, the emperor pursued his rebel son to the Deccan, which he reached in early 1682. Although the prince would eventually flee to Iran,

Aurangzeb resolved to extinguish the Maratha kingdom for having given refuge to his son and for establishing a defiantly anti-Mughal state along the empire's southern frontier. He also aimed at snuffing out the plateau's two remaining sultanates, Bijapur and Golkonda, thereby completing a process of southward imperial expansion that his predecessors had begun nearly a century earlier. Aurangzeb would spend the next twenty-five years in the Deccan. He never returned to north India.

The emperor first concentrated on Bijapur and Golkonda, which he conquered and annexed in 1686 and 1687 respectively. Then he turned to the Marathas, whose principal hill-forts he sought to reduce, one by one. Perched atop the craggy peaks and ridges of the Sahyadri Mountains (see Plate 15), these forts, most of which long predated the rise of the Maratha kingdom, guarded the east–west trade routes that historically connected the western Deccan plateau with the maritime commerce of the Konkan coast.[3] Yet they also served as power-bases for ambitious chieftains seeking to intercept that trade. "The numerous steep but flat-topped mountains," writes Sumit Guha,

provided natural refuges for the lords whose power was based not only on the taxes of the peasantry but also on resources garnered by raiding and trading in the plains to the east and west. The size of their take may be gathered . . . from the amounts invested in building the scores of hill-forts that crown almost every suitable peak in the western mountains. The Sultans of the Dakhan found it convenient to term them *deshmukhs*, but in their own estimation they were rajas.[4]

The most successful of these rajas was doubtless Shivaji, who upon intercepting Bijapur's trade with the coast established a new kingdom based on hill-forts that he either appropriated from Bijapur or built anew. When his first son Sambhaji succeeded to the Maratha throne in 1680, Shivaji's principal fort of Raigarh remained the kingdom's capital. There, too, resided Sambhaji's younger half-brother Rajaram and the latter's several wives, including Tarabai. But with the fall of the last Deccan sultanate in 1687, the Marathas had to face the full brunt of Mughal power. In that year Tarabai's father, Hambir Rao, died in a battle with one of the emperor's generals. Then in February 1689 Sambhaji himself was captured, taken to Aurangzeb's camp, and brutally executed. In these desperate circumstances, Maratha leaders at Raigarh deemed it essential that Rajaram, now the Marathas' de facto king, not suffer his brother's fate. So they arranged that he and his three wives, including Tarabai, abandon Raigarh. Eluding Mughal patrols by moving furtively from fort to fort, in

---

[3] See M. S. Naravane, *Forts of Maharashtra* (New Delhi, 1995).
[4] Sumit Guha, *Environment and Ethnicity in India, 1200–1991* (Cambridge, 1999), 83.

August 1689 they finally reached the great stronghold of Panhala, one of the Deccan's mightiest forts (see Map 5).

Standing 275 feet above the Kolhapur uplands, themselves 2,772 feet above sea level, the immense complex at Panhala projects a commanding presence over the southern Sahyadri range. The fort measures four-and-a-half miles in circumference, half of which is protected by a steep scarp ranging from thirty to forty feet in height, and strengthened by a loopholed parapet wall. The other half consists of a strong stone wall ranging from fifteen to thirty feet thick at the top, pierced by numerous bastions with fixed cannon that peer out over the lower approaches. In Tarabai's day, the fort was reached from the tableland by long flights of stone steps leading to three magnificent double gateways. Although parts of Panhala date to the twelfth century, the sultans of Bijapur made extensive additions to it, their distinctive architectural style reflected in the fort's ramparts, gateways, and huge granaries (see Plate 16). It is for good reason that Bijapur's style is so prominent here. Until its capture by Shivaji in 1659, this fort had guarded the main routes that passed through the Sahyadri range between Bijapur and the seaports of the Konkan coast. It would be more closely associated with Tarabai's career than any other fortress in Maharashtra.

Even Panhala, though, was thought insufficiently secure to protect Rajaram from Aurangzeb's armies. So in September 1689, he and a small party slipped out of the fort and, under various disguises, made their way to Jinji (or Gingee), a stronghold deep in the Tamil country more than 400 miles southeast of Panhala (see Map 6). Just two months later Raigarh, the capital of the slain king Sambhaji, fell to Aurangzeb's armies, while the late monarch's wife and son were seized and taken to the emperor's camp. Rather than execute the son as he had the father, however, Aurangzeb chose a subtler course: he renamed the seven-year-old boy "Shahu" and held both him and his mother hostage for possible future use as pawns in the Mughal–Maratha struggle.

Meanwhile, Rajaram's three wives remained in Panhala for five more years. Then in 1694 the nineteen-year-old Tarabai and the other wives made the risky trip down through the mountain passes to the coast, from where they sailed south to the port of Honavar. From there they traveled overland to Jinji where they were reunited with Rajaram and the transplanted Maratha court. All these operations were fraught with danger, as Jinji, too, was then besieged by a huge Mughal army that Aurangzeb had sent to capture or kill Rajaram. But intrigues swirled around the camp of the obsessive emperor, and these served to help, if not indeed rescue, the Maratha cause. In late 1697, Mughal officers who anticipated the need to accommodate the Marathas once the aged

Aurangzeb had died, quietly allowed Rajaram to slip out of the fort and return to Maharashtra; his family followed shortly thereafter.[5]

When Tarabai returned to Maharashtra after her long journey from the south, she arrived with a two-year-old son born in Jinji's lofty fortress. Named Shivaji, doubtless after the kingdom's founder, this first son born to Rajaram by a legitimate wife would soon become a pivot in Maratha politics. Meanwhile Rajaram, who reached Maharasthra in early 1698, had taken over the reins of government and begun rebuilding the Maratha state, battered by more than a decade of Mughal assaults. After establishing a new capital at Satara in June 1699, he began counterattacking the Mughals throughout the upper Deccan. He even launched the kingdom's first ever raid north of the Narmada River into Mughal-administered terrain, although imperial troops easily pushed the raiding party back to the fastness of the Sahyadri Mountains.[6] Only several months later, however, in March 1700, the thirty-year-old Rajaram died a natural but untimely death, cutting short his budding attempts at restoring his father's kingdom.

On the solemn occasion of his funeral rites, one of Rajaram's three wives nobly committed *sati*, throwing herself onto her husband's burning pyre. But Tarabai and the other remaining wife, Rajas Bai, had other plans. Each was rearing a son by Rajaram. Within weeks of Rajaram's death, in fact, Tarabai declared her intention to have the sacred thread ceremony performed for her four-year-old son Shivaji. This news startled Ramchandra Nilkanth, the veteran administrator who had looked after the kingdom's governance during Rajaram's long absence in Jinji. For the thread ceremony would confirm the boy's ritual status as a member of the *kshatriya*, or warrior, rank, thereby qualifying him for kingship. Foreseeing a potential schism caused by two rival contenders for the Maratha throne – the eighteen-year-old Shahu, still a captive in Aurangzeb's camp, and Tarabai's four-year-old son Shivaji – Ramchandra advised against performing the ceremony. But the strong-willed Tarabai, not to be deterred, in early 1700 carried out her plans in the remote hill-fort of Vishalgarh, some thirty-five miles west of Panhala. There, seating the boy on a throne and adorning him with the symbols of royalty, her supporters declared the young Shivaji king and Tarabai his regent. As such, she would govern the kingdom during the boy's minority.

---

[5] André Wink, *Land and Sovereignty in India: Agrarian Society and Politics under the Eighteenth-century Maratha Svarajya* (Cambridge, 1986), 60–63.

[6] V. G. Khobrekar, ed., *Tarikh-i-Dilkasha (Memoirs of Bhimsen Relating to Aurangzib's Deccan Campaigns)*, trans. Jadunath Sarkar (Bombay, 1972), 216.

Now twenty-five years old, Tarabai had clearly revealed her driving ambition. But we should not suppose that she had achieved all this on her own. According to the contemporary Mughal chronicler Khafi Khan, she enjoyed powerful support:

The chiefs then made Tara Bai, the chief wife [and] the mother of one son [of Rajaram], regent. She was a clever intelligent woman, and had obtained a reputation during her husband's lifetime for her knowledge of civil and military matters.[7]

The reference is to the period 1689–1700, in particular the five years from 1689 to 1694 when Rajaram was besieged in remote Jinji and Tarabai remained in Panhala, where Ramchandra Nilkanth ran the kingdom's day-to-day government. There she spent her late teenage years acquiring administrative knowledge under Ramchandra's tutelage. The experience and skills gained at this time evidently infused her with considerable self-confidence. For in February 1699, after she and Rajaram had returned to Maharashtra from Jinji, it was Tarabai, not her husband, who resolved a dispute between the kingdom's commander-in-chief and another prominent chieftain. The issue turned on which man should rightfully receive the offerings made at a particular religious fair. Notably, the plucky young woman decided the dispute *against* her husband's powerful commander-in-chief, Dhanaji Jadhav.[8]

Contemporary observers corroborate the qualities of courage and independence revealed in that decision. Bhimsen, a Mughal officer then serving in the region, stated bluntly that Tarabai "was a stronger ruler than her husband." He also observed that after Rajaram's death Tarabai "became all in all and regulated things so well that not a single Maratha leader acted without her order."[9] And Khafi Khan: "She won the hearts of her officers, and for all the struggles and schemes, the campaigns and sieges of Aurangzeb up to the end of his reign, the power of the Mahrattas increased day by day."[10]

It is therefore hardly surprising that in 1701 Portuguese officials based in nearby Goa were already calling Tarabai the "Queen of the Marathas"[11] – an image dramatically conveyed by equestrian statues standing in Kolhapur today (see Plate 14). Such statues evoke images of the seven-year period, 1700–1707, when Tarabai single-handedly directed the Marathas' defense against the armies of Aurangzeb, at that time arguably the mightiest ruler in the world. Moving

---

[7] Khafi Khan, *Muntakhab*, in Elliot and Dowson, *History*, VII:367.
[8] Appasaheb Pawar, ed., *Tarabaikalina Kagadpatre*, 3 vols. (Kolhapur, 1969), I: no. 71.
[9] Khobrekar, *Tarikh-i-Dilkasha*, 232, 256.
[10] Khafi Khan, *Muntakhab*, in Elliot and Dowson, *History*, VII:374.
[11] Pawar, *Tarabaikalina*, I: no. 103.

tirelessly from fort to fort, she energized her commanders, mobilized resources, and coordinated attacks while at the same time mastering Aurangzeb's own game of offering bribes and counterbribes to commanders on both sides of the conflict.[12]

Tarabai's greatest strategic innovation, however, lay in her bold policy of sending large forces beyond the Marathi-speaking Deccan deep into Mughal domains to the north, even while major forts of her own were falling into Aurangzeb's hands. Building on the precedent of her husband's single raid beyond the Narmada, in 1700 Tarabai sent 50,000 troops as far north as the region west of Chanderi, in modern Guna district in northwestern Madhya Pradesh. In 1702 she invaded Maharashtra's northern and eastern borderlands (Khandesh, Berar, Telangana). In 1703, she attacked urban centers in Khandesh and Malwa (Ujjain, Burhanpur, Mandu, Sironj). And in 1706, her generals struck cities in Gujarat and Khandesh (Baroda, Burhanpur).[13] Notably, these were more than just raids. In an important passage in which he noted the Marathas' increasing audacity, Khafi Khan states:

they penetrated into the old territories of the Imperial throne, plundering and destroying wherever they went. In imitation of the Emperor, who with his army and enterprising *amirs* ["commanders"] was staying in those distant mountains, the *commanders of Tara Bai cast the anchor of permanence wherever they penetrated,* and having appointed *kamaish-dars* [revenue collectors], they passed the years and months to their satisfaction, with their wives and children, tents and elephants. Their daring went beyond all bounds. They divided all the districts [*parganas*] among themselves, and *following the practice of the Imperial rule,* they appointed their *subadars* [provincial governors], *kamaish-dars* [revenue collectors], and *rahdars* [toll-collectors].[14]

In short, with Tarabai we already see evidence of a policy usually associated with Maratha activities undertaken later in the eighteenth century – namely, a systematic attempt to "cast the anchor of permanence" in areas formerly under Mughal suzerainty. In such regions the Marathas established their own revenue collectors in direct imitation of Mughal practice. They even settled down with their families, governing as though they were imperial overseers. Maratha forces had never done this before.

---

[12] The following extract of a letter written in 1702 to one of her generals from the fort of Pratapgarh illustrates her style: "The Master [her son] is now at Pratapgarh, and it is vital to have a force close at hand sufficient for any emergency that may develop. Aurangzeb is full of cunning and unpredictable. Only by your strengthening this front, will he be kept out of mischief . . ." Cited in Malgonkar, *Chhatrapatis of Kolhapur*, 50.

[13] Brij Kishore, *Tara Bai and her Times* (Bombay, 1963), 68–93.

[14] Khafi Khan, *Muntakhab*, in Elliot and Dowson, *History*, VII:374. Emphasis mine.

Ironically, Tarabai's political fortunes soared so long as Aurangzeb's generals were besieging her hill-forts, but they collapsed once Mughal armies retired to north India following Aurangzeb's death in early 1707. Why was this so? For years, imperial nobles had been jockeying for position anticipating the succession struggle that everyone knew would follow Aurangzeb's death. Of the emperor's three surviving sons, Prince A'zam was the nearest to the emperor when he died. So A'zam, taking command of the late emperor's entourage, buried his father near Daulatabad and hastily prepared to move north to challenge his older brother for the Peacock Throne. Still in the late emperor's entourage, however, were the two Maratha hostages, Shahu and his mother, whom Aurangzeb had captured in 1689 and held for eighteen years as political pawns that he never used. With their fate now in A'zam's hands, the prince made a crucial decision. His advisers persuaded him that releasing the twenty-five-year-old Shahu and allowing him to return to Maharashtra would create a schism among the Marathas. After all, as the son of Sambhaji, Shivaji's oldest son and heir, Shahu could stake a claim to the Maratha throne that was at least as valid as that of Tarabai's son.

So in May 1707 A'zam, as he was crossing the Narmada River en route to north India, set Shahu free – thereby injecting the prince into the Maratha body politic. The fates of the two princes now diverged radically. Within a month Prince A'zam lay dead on a battlefield near Agra, killed by his older brother who now crowned himself Emperor Bahadur Shah. Soon the new emperor would depart for Hyderabad to dispatch his other brother, Kam Bakhsh. Shahu, on the other hand, embarked upon a long career that did indeed divide Maratha loyalties, just as the Mughals had hoped. On learning of his release and arrival in the Maratha realm, Tarabai first responded by declaring him an impostor. Then, after Shahu's true identity was confirmed, she deployed a number of arguments intended to prevent her supporters from defecting to this stranger-prince who had suddenly arrived in their midst. She pointed to his eighteen years spent in the Mughal camp, his fluency in Persian, his refined courtly manner – all suggesting that culturally the Maratha prince had "gone Mughal" and therefore was not to be trusted. She drew particular attention to Shahu's contention, in her view treasonous, that his claims to kingship had been approved by the new Mughal emperor, Bahadur Shah – as though the Mughals had the right to name the successors to Shivaji's throne! In fact, that August Shahu seemed to confirm Tarabai's charges when he made a pilgrimage to Aurangzeb's tomb by foot and paid his respects to the memory of the late emperor.

But despite her exhortations, many of Tarabai's men drifted toward Shahu's camp. In October 1707, supporters of the two sides finally resorted to an armed contest at Khed, on the Bhima River some twenty-two miles north of Pune. Shahu's forces not only carried the day, but went on to drive Tarabai out of Satara, since 1699 the Maratha capital, and to crown Shahu king in January 1708. Now there were two Maratha kings; soon there would be two Maratha kingdoms. When Tarabai fell back to Panhala, the fort where she had spent much of her youth, the political division among Marathas hardened into a lasting schism that was displaced onto territory: Shahu's strength lay in the north, with his capital at Satara, and Tarabai's lay in the south, based in Kolhapur and Panhala. Ironically, as feelings between the two houses grew more bitter, both sides looked to the Mughals to decide which rival Maratha king – Shahu, or Tarabai's son Shivaji – had the right to collect taxes in those parts of the Deccan that the Mughals theoretically governed, but were in fact too weak to collect.

Amidst this fierce competition for supporters, there emerged in Shahu's kingdom a new political institution, the Peshwa. At the same time, Brahmins began appearing in high levels of Shahu's government at Satara. The process evolved in stages. Among the many institutions that the Maratha state had carried over from its Bahmani, Nizam Shahi, and 'Adil Shahi predecessors was a prime minister called *peshwa*, Persian for "leader." As early as 1397 the Bahmanis had called their prime minister by that title, as did both Bijapur and Ahmednagar in the sixteenth and seventeenth centuries.[15] We have seen that the official in the sultanate of Ahmadnagar who purchased the slave Malik Ambar was that kingdom's *peshwa*, an office later held by Malik Ambar himself. Shivaji headed up his own "council of eight" with a *peshwa*, and the councils of Rajaram, Tarabai, and Shahu all included a *peshwa*.[16]

The institution of *peshwa*, then, was hardly new in Deccan history. Nor was there anything new about Brahmins serving the bureaucracies of the Deccan states. We have seen that in the course of the sixteenth and seventeenth centuries, Brahmins dominated the judicial and revenue bureaucracies of sultanates across the plateau (chapters 4, 6). What was new in eighteenth-century Maharashtra was the entry of Brahmins in political (as opposed to bureaucratic) life, the transformation of the *peshwa* from an appointed to a hereditary office, and the concentration of so much power in that office

---

[15] Haroon Khan Sherwani, *Mahmud Gawan, the Great Bahmani Wazir* (Allahabad, 1942), 48n.

[16] H. N. Sinha, *Rise of the Peshwas* (Allahabad, 1954), 10–11.

as to displace the authority of the king himself. In effect, *peshwas* evolved into Peshwas; that is, they became all-powerful, hereditary rulers, de facto sovereigns.

The process began in late 1713 with Shahu's efforts to win over Tarabai's most formidable supporter, Kanhoji Angria, the powerful lord of the Konkan coast whose navies dominated the shipping lanes between Mumbai and the Malabar coast. For this purpose Shahu engaged Balaji Vishvanath, a Chitpavan Brahmin from the Konkan coast with political and administrative connections in both the Konkan and the Desh. Starting out as a clerk in the coastal saltworks, Balaji had worked up to administrator for Pune and Daulatabad; he also served Shahu's commander-in-chief Dhanaji Jadhav, himself a defector from Tarabai's government.[17] When Shahu asked Balaji to go win over Kanhoji Angria, Balaji demanded that, in order to strengthen his negotiating hand, he must first be made the government's *peshwa*. Shahu agreed. Using both flattery and argument, and befriending Kanhoji as a fellow Konkani, Balaji managed to woo the coastal lord's allegiance away from Tarabai.[18]

While a victory for Shahu, Kanhoji's defection represented a stunning reversal for Tarabai. Moreover, it came at an unfortunate time, as it coincided with her son Shivaji's coming of age. Because powerful players in her court considered her son mentally unsound, or perhaps because Tarabai was unwilling to relinquish power to her son, sometime between July and October of 1714 both mother and son became targets of a palace coup. The movement seems to have been led by supporters of Tarabai's co-wife Rajas Bai, who had been quietly waiting in the wings, and who now promoted her own sixteen-year-old son, Sambhaji, to be the new king of the Kolhapur branch of Marathas.[19] By the end of October, this youth had been crowned king, while both Tarabai and her son Shivaji were unceremoniously thrown into Panhala's prison.

Tarabai would remain in that prison for sixteen years – her son would die there after the first twelve – until 1730, when Shahu defeated Sambhaji in a skirmish between the two Maratha houses. On this occasion Tarabai met her rival and nephew for the first time since the two had been youngsters in Raigarh forty-one years earlier. When Shahu offered his aunt the option of remaining in Panhala or of returning with him to Satara, Tarabai wearily replied, "Whether

---

[17] Wink, *Land and Sovereignty*, 69–71.   [18] Kishore, *Tara Bai*, 136–38.
[19] Shalini V. Patil, *Maharani Tarabai of Kolhapur (c. 1675–1761)* (New Delhi, 1987), 191. There is also evidence that Tarabai's veteran administrator Ramchandra Nilkanth had a hand in the coup. See A. G. Pawar, "Palace Revolution at Kolhapur, 1714," in *Studies in Indology and Medieval History*, ed. M. S. Mate and G. T. Kulkarni (Poona, 1974), 159–70.

I go back or stay, I shall have to spend my life in prison anyway; let me therefore stay with you."[20] For eighteen more years she was kept under house arrest in Satara's palace. Confined first by her co-wife and then by her nephew, this former "Queen of the Marathas," once so hyperactive, spent her next thirty-four years reduced to a political non-entity. Yet her story was not over.

SOCIETY AND STATE IN TARABAI'S TIMES

Let us for a moment leave Tarabai in Panhala's prison, step back, and consider some of the broader trends taking place in Maharashtrian society during her lifetime, especially between 1714 and 1748 when she was in confinement. Five themes stand out.

Of these the first and most basic was the increasing militarization of the western Deccan. Visible from the mid-seventeenth century on, this trend grew out of changing patterns of military recruitment in the region. These become clear when contrasted with the pattern found in north India. The Mughals, like the Delhi sultans before them, could easily recruit warhorses and cavalrymen from Central Asia and the Iranian plateau, owing to north India's proximity to these regions' ample labor markets and abundant pasture lands. But the Deccan sultanates, geographically cut off from inner Asia's labor markets and pastures, had no such option. Yet they had other choices. They could either import via the Arabian Sea military slaves from East Africa and warhorses from the Persian Gulf, or they could recruit both horses and cavalrymen from their own locality.

Actually, they did both. We have seen that Malik Ambar, himself a former slave recruited from Ethiopia, in turn recruited thousands of Maratha light cavalry into Nizam Shahi service; by 1624, 50,000 were in his pay. The sultans of Bijapur were no less successful in this respect. Sultan Ibrahim 'Adil Shah I (1534–58) hired 30,000 Maratha cavalry and introduced the practice of enlisting *bargirs*, or Maratha cavalrymen whose horses were supplied by the state.[21] Such reliance on local resources implied a rather thorough integration of indigenous land tenure systems with the political economies of the sultanates. As Stewart Gordon has shown, hereditary territorial chiefs of the western Deccan, or *deshmukhs*, not only collected revenue, adjudicated disputes, and provided ritual leadership in the lands they controlled. They also raised troops and made them available to the sultan, who in return gave them written *sanads*, or documents formalizing their rights to specified lands. "It was the sanad from the court," he writes, "which gave an individual authority over

---

[20] Cited in Malgonkar, *Chhatrapatis of Kolhapur*, 142.
[21] James Grant Duff, *History of the Mahrattas*, ed. J. P. Guha (New Delhi, 1971), I:36.

his own kinsmen and the state's backing if they opposed him, as they often did. The history of Maharashtra and the Maratha polity is, thus, the history of these deshmukh families."[22]

In this way many leading Maratha clans rose to prominence in tandem with the rise of the sultanates themselves.[23] The Shinde family of Kanerkhed, for example, had served the Bahmani sultans as *siledars*, or cavalrymen who furnished their own horses. The Mane family of Mhasvad did the same for the sultans of Bijapur. Those rulers also made the Nimbalkar family of Nimlak and the Ghatge family of Malavdi *sardeshmukhs* – "heads of *deshmukhs*" – as rewards for their military service to them.[24] The rights to lands inherited by Shivaji Bhosle, founder of the Maratha kingdom, had initially been conferred on his father Shahji by the sultans of Ahmadnagar and Bijapur for his service to those states. At Shahji's request, too, the Bijapur court in 1626 made Tarabai's grandfather and his brother, Sambhaji and Dharoji Mohite, the *deshmukhs* of Talbid (in Satara district). In 1636, that court even conferred a robe of honor on one of her Mohite ancestors, and in 1660, just fifteen years before her birth, two others were given the honor of an audience with Sultan 'Ali 'Adil Shah II.[25]

Military service to one or the other of the sultanates thus meshed closely with the economies and societies of those states. But in the course of the seventeenth century, as first the Nizam Shahi sultanate of Ahmadnagar and then the 'Adil Shahi state of Bijapur disintegrated, the traditional patrons for Maratha service élites vanished. This did not mean an end to their employment, however. To the contrary, several new patrons emerged, which created a seller's market for *deshmukhs* having access to military labor. The Mughals were the first and wealthiest buyers of such labor. Since the 1630s imperial officers had been drawing Maratha *deshmukhs* to their service – and away from Nizam Shahi or 'Adil Shahi service – typically by offering them attractive salaries and high ranks.[26] As early as the 1640s, Shivaji recruited into his own political movement thousands of *mavalis*, the men inhabiting the jungles and ravines of the Sahyadri Mountains. But by the 1680s, the Mughals too were recruiting

---

[22] Stewart Gordon, *The Marathas, 1600–1818*. New Cambridge History of India, vol II.4 (Cambridge, 1993), 34.

[23] See Frank Perlin, "The Precolonial Indian State in History and Epistemology: a Reconstruction of Societal Formation in the Western Deccan from the Fifteenth to the Early Nineteenth Century," in *The Study of the State*, ed. Henry Claessen and Peter Skalnik (The Hague, 1981), 280.

[24] Günther-Dietz Sontheimer, *Pastoral Deities in Western India*, trans. Anne Feldhaus (Delhi, 1993), 163, 30, 158, 159.

[25] Pawar, *Tarabaikalina*, I: nos. 5, 7, 8, 16, 24.

[26] The Mughals managed to enroll into their imperial service nearly a hundred Maratha chiefs who had formed the core of Bijapur's forces. Jos Gommans, *Mughal Warfare: Indian Frontiers and High Roads to Empire, 1500–1700* (London and New York, 2002), 79.

mavalis, whom they deployed against the Maratha kingdom that Shivaji had founded only several years earlier.[27] In a sense, then, the Mughal–Maratha struggle amounted to a bidding war between Aurangzeb's officers and those of the Maratha kingdom over access to military labor proffered by local chieftains.[28] The competition grew in intensity as the number of bidders increased, for after 1708 it was no longer just Marathas and Mughals competing with one another to recruit such labor. Now Shahu was on the scene, bidding against Tarabai to recruit and employ local military talent.[29]

The seller's market for *deshmukhs* with access to military labor in turn drove up the rewards for such labor, with the result that Maratha society became ever more mobile and militarized. By the eighteenth century, warfare had become so lucrative that many enterprising men with no ties to land or prior *deshmukh* status emerged as chiefs (*sardar*) who enlisted villagers into their warbands. The character of Maratha armies was naturally affected by the influx of armed villagers who would spend half the year (May to October) working their fields and the other half (October to May) on campaign. As Rosalind O'Hanlon writes, from the mid-seventeenth century on, one finds "a loose agglomeration of armed lineages, small autochthonous gentry and mobile peasant cultivators doubling as military recruits during the campaigning season."[30]

By the mid-eighteenth century, villagers had become so prominent in warfare that to some members of the Mughal nobility, Maratha armies appeared as little more than rabble, albeit a rabble they had learned to respect. "Most of the men in the Mahratta army," noted Nawab Ibrahim Khan around 1740, "are unendowed with the excellence of noble and illustrious birth, and husbandmen, carpenters, and shopkeepers abound among their soldiery." And yet, he continued,

as they undergo all sorts of toil and fatigue in prosecuting a guerrilla warfare, they prove superior to the easy and effeminate troops of Hind [i.e., north India], who for the most part are of more honourable birth and calling.[31]

---

[27] Guha, *Environment and Ethnicity*, 85–86.
[28] *Deshmukhs* of the eastern periphery of Shivaji's kingdom, writes Muzaffar Alam, would "vacillate between the two powers, thus trying to use their antagonism to both to suit their own interests." Muzaffar Alam, "The Zamindars and Mughal Power in the Deccan, 1685–1712," *Indian Economic and Social History Review* 11, no. 1 (March 1974): 75. Yet the Mughals had considerable success enlisting Maratha *deshmukhs*. Between 1658 and 1707 the share of Marathas enrolled in imperial service increased from 5.5 percent to 16.7 percent of the total. Gommans, *Mughal Warfare*, 79.
[29] Gordon, *The Marathas*, 104.
[30] Rosalind O'Hanlon, *A Comparison between Women and Men: Tarabai Shinde and the Critique of Gender Relations in Colonial India* (Madras, 1994), 4.
[31] Nawab Ibrahim Khan Bahadur, *Tarikh-i Ibrahim Khan* (comp. 1786), in Elliot and Dowson, *History of India*, VIII:262–63.

In other words, Mughal and Maratha armies differed as much by class and culture as by styles of warfare. The Mughals, notes Dirk Kolff, were "so geared to the enlistment of foreign cavaliers as to be unable to admit into their armies more than a limited number of peasant-soldiers."[32] Again, this points to the relative ease with which the Mughals could recruit both warhorses and professional cavalrymen from markets in adjacent Central Asia. For the Mughals, as for "chivalrous" cultures anywhere in the premodern world, proper armies were composed of high-born professional archers, lancers, or swordsmen mounted on heavy steeds. That, in their own estimate, was what made a nobility noble, in contrast to the peasant-soldiers that Mughal officers encountered in the western Deccan.

One consequence of the militarization of Maratha society was ecological. As more patrons bid for the services of military labor, the military life became marginally more lucrative than agriculture itself. One sees this in the growing presence of villagers in Maratha armies, and also in the rising value of pasture relative to crop land in the Desh. "Under a local ruler," writes Günther-Dietz Sontheimer, referring to the period after 1674,

the land could be cultivated, but the more promising source of income was warfare, with its easily gained riches. For that purpose the *siledar* [i.e., cavalryman] had to put riders and horses at the king's disposal. Therefore, the pastures of the area were more profitable than was agriculture. For the farmers of the pastoral region, cattle were more valuable than was [crop] land, which was endangered by war or drought. Cattle could be driven into the forests during a drought, or, when threatened by enemies, they could be hidden in ravines.[33]

Here it is useful to note the different kinds of warhorses typically deployed by the Mughals and the Marathas. Since the pasturage of the Desh could not support the successful breeding of the heavy warhorses preferred by the Mughals or the sultans of the Deccan, such horses always had to be imported from beyond India. On the other hand, the pastures lying in the rainshadow of the Sahyadri Mountains, particularly in the Bhima valley, proved excellent for breeding and raising the smaller, lighter horses preferred by Maratha cavalrymen.[34]

The militarization of Maratha society was related to a second broad trend visible in Tarabai's day, namely, the changing meaning of "Maratha." From at least the fourteenth century the term seems to have carried multiple semantic registers. At one level, it referred simply to speakers of Marathi. Thus in 1342 the Moroccan traveler Ibn Battuta referred to all the native inhabitants

[32] Dirk H. A. Kolff, "The Polity and the Peasantry," in *Warfare and Weaponry in South Asia, 1000–1800*, ed. Jos J. L. Gommans and Dirk H. A. Kolff (New Delhi, 2001), 222.
[33] Sontheimer, *Pastoral Deities*, 164.   [34] Gommans, *Mughal Warfare*, 111–14.

of the Daulatabad region as belonging collectively to the "tribe" (*qabila*) of "Marhatas," whose élites included both Brahmins and *kshatriyas*.[35] But the term began to acquire another meaning only several years later when the Bahmani kings established independent rule in the Deccan. As we have just seen, those kings and their successors in the western Deccan, the sultans of Ahmadnagar and Bijapur, systematically employed military labor from amongst the native population. To the employers, "Marathas" referred to those Marathi-speaking chiefs and their warrior-clients who offered themselves for military service. In this way the term became associated with a martial ethos, in addition to its earlier association with members of a certain language community.

At the same time, villagers who were not Untouchables and who were not integrated into a sultanate's service élite – cultivators, artisans, petty merchants – identified themselves as "Kunbi."[36] What distinguished the "Maratha" from the "Kunbi," notes Gordon, was precisely the former's martial tradition, of which he was proud, and the rights to land control he received from the sultan in return for military service. Over time, being Maratha embraced patterns of dress, diet, and codes of "correct" behavior, so that the category gradually solidified and acquired social boundaries. In short, "Maratha" had become "a relational and interactional term that described a new emerging service élite."[37] But in the course of the eighteenth century, as villagers became ever more prominent in armies mobilized by the government of the Peshwas, they, too, began seeing themselves as Marathas. As this occurred, the distinction between Kunbi and Maratha became blurred; eventually, the categories would fuse into "Maratha-Kunbi."[38]

As a third trend in the social history of Tarabai's day, Brahmins entered all levels of eighteenth-century Maratha politics. This, too, was related to the growing militarization of Maharasthrian society.[39] Because *sardars*, or chieftains, paid their troops in cash, they would have to negotiate with bankers for cash loans at the beginning of a campaign season. These bankers were generally

---

[35] Ibn Battuta, *Travels in Asia and Africa, 1325–1354*, trans. H. A. R. Gibb (1929; reprint, Delhi, 1986), 227–28.

[36] We have seen that the poet Tukaram, whose family were village grocers and petty traders, identified himself as a Kunbi (chapter 6).

[37] Gordon, *The Marathas*, 15–17.

[38] See Satish Chandra, "Social Background to the Rise of the Maratha Movement during the 17th Century in India," *Indian Economic and Social History Review* 10, no. 3 (September 1973): 214–16.

[39] See Stewart Gordon, *Marathas, Marauders, and State Formation in Eighteenth-Century India* (Delhi, 1994), 43–44, 56–57; and Wink, *Land and Sovereignty*, 322–35, *passim*. I am indebted in this paragraph to a most useful discussion with Stewart Gordon on the question of militarization.

Brahmins. But the interest rates at which they made such loans depended on the fiscal stability of the area under a given chief's control. Evaluating the fiscal worth of a *sardar's* lands, and hence the value of his credit, were accountants (*kulkarnis*, *deshpandes*) who kept the local records. These men, too, were usually Brahmins. Banking and credit thus provided the hinge by which Brahmins acquired influence in the political system, whether as village money-lenders advancing cash to *sardars* and local headmen, or as great banking firms financing the Maratha government's fielding of whole peasant-armies.[40] In this way networks of Brahmin families involved in finance and banking contributed to the militarization of eighteenth-century Maratha society.[41]

By the 1720s, Brahmins were translating their financial power directly into political power. As we have seen, the process began in 1713 when Shahu appointed as his *peshwa* Balaji Vishvanath, who had already created a private army, the Huzarat ("King's Men"), by borrowing heavily from Brahmin money-lenders with whom he had close connections.[42] Once Balaji was in power, Brahmins belonging to his own caste, the Chitpavan, began migrating from their native Konkan coast up to Shahu's capital at Satara. There they served as tax-collectors, administrators, and especially as bankers loaning Shahu money to raise his armies. Upon Balaji's death in 1720, his son Baji Rao I was named by Shahu to succeed him, thereby launching a series of hereditary Brahmin Peshwas. The power of the Peshwa and the influence of Chitpavan Brahmins then continued to grow in tandem with one another. Moreover, as the political prominence of Chitpavan Brahmins rose, so did their sense of caste superiority – a classic instance of social rank rising with political fortune.[43]

A fourth theme of Tarabai's period was the Maratha state's intervention in the socio-ritual affairs of Hindu communities. According to a 1744 ruling, government permission was required before Brahmin priests could perform purification ceremonies. Violators of this ruling were deprived of their caste status, restorable only upon payment of a government fee. Or again, when groups of Brahmins disputed the proper order in which different parts of the Vedic scriptures should be recited, it was the government that ordered a meeting (*sabha*) to resolve the matter. In addition to formulating and enforcing codes

---

[40] Notes André Wink, "They were all brahmans who rose with the tide of Maratha expansion from the humble position of village accountant or money-lender." Wink, *Land and Sovereignty*, 337.

[41] Some historians have argued that the "decline" of the Mughal empire and "rise" of the Marathas in the eighteenth century were related, in part, to the fact that banking firms had diverted their resources from Mughal to Maratha forces. See Karen Leonard, "The 'Great Firm' Theory of the Decline of the Mughal Empire," *Comparative Studies in Society and History* 21 (1979): 152–65.

[42] Malgonkar, *Chhatrapatis of Kolhapur*, 91.

[43] Wink, *Land and Sovereignty*, 69.

of proper behavior for Brahmins, the government also forbade the lower castes to imitate the social or ritual practices of Brahmins, such as wearing the sacred thread.[44] These measures, ensuring as they did the protection of upper-caste interests in the social hierarchy, clearly reflect the influence of a government headed by Brahmin Peshwas. It is notable that such state intervention in the social order contrasted with the practices of the Deccan sultanates. Inheriting the secularist tradition of the sultanate form of polity, which separated the religious and political domains of life (see chapter 1), those kingdoms had adopted a hands-off policy with respect to the customs and rites of Hindu communities.[45]

Finally, while Tarabai remained confined in prison or under house arrest, the Peshwas of Satara, building on Tarabai's own earlier invasions of Gujarat, Khandesh, and Malwa, embarked on a stunning series of conquests that briefly encompassed the whole of north India.[46] Reaching their peak under the second Peshwa, Baji Rao I (1720–40), these conquests carried important ramifications for society back in Maharashtra. First, after 1735 Maratha armies began remaining in north India through the monsoon season without returning to Maharashtra. This, however, hindered agricultural operations in the Maratha heartland, since many of the soldiers were themselves cultivators (*mirasdars*). The government endeavored to compensate for this loss by mobilizing landless peasants (*uparis*) to cultivate state lands and wastelands. But this only reduced government revenues, since landless peasants paid little or no land taxes.[47] On the other hand, attempts to bring peasant-soldiers back to Maharashtra for agricultural purposes only left the armies in the north strapped for manpower. To meet that problem, the government enlisted non-Maratha mercenaries,

---

[44] Hiroshi Fukazawa, "The State and the Caste System (jati)," in his *The Medieval Deccan: Peasants, Social Systems and States, Sixteenth to Eighteenth Centuries* (Delhi, 1991), 97–98, 100–01, 104.

[45] There is evidence, however, that the Mughals were less inhibited in this respect. In the late seventeenth century, thousands of Untouchables of the Junnar region petitioned Aurangzeb to require Brahmins to officiate at their weddings, which the Brahmins had theretofore refused to do. After looking into the matter, the emperor reportedly turned down the request, upholding the position held by the Brahmins. This established a precedent that would be followed in Junnar throughout the eighteenth century. The ruling points to Aurangzeb's well-known conservative instincts: when faced with choosing between an open society and a more hierarchical order dominated by Brahmins, he favored the latter. But the incident also suggests that village populations, in their efforts to resolve their internal disputes, looked to whatever ruling body appeared to have effective power and legitimate authority in their locality. See Fukazawa, *Medieval Deccan*, 106.

[46] For modern perspectives, see the study in this series by Gordon, *The Marathas*, esp. chapters 4–7. See also Wink, *Land and Sovereignty*, chapters 1–3. The classic accounts remain G. S. Sardesai, *New History of the Marathas*, vol. 2: *The Expansion of the Maratha Power, 1707–1772* (Bombay, 1948), and V. G. Dighe, *Peshwa Bajirao I and Maratha Expansion* (Bombay, 1944).

[47] Fukazawa, *Medieval Deccan*, 183–89.

namely Pathans, Arabs, and both north and south Indians.[48] But this further altered the character of "Maratha" armies, as had happened earlier with their incorporation of peasant-soldiers.

Yet another consequence of the northern conquests was that, due to prolonged exposure to north India, members of the Maratha ruling élite acquired a taste for the refinements of Mughal culture. This in turn created a demand in urban Maharashtra for Kashmiri shawls, Bengali silks, ivory craft, metalwork in silver, copper, and brass, etc. Maratha administrators in Satara, and after 1750 in Pune, also patronized north Indian styles of painting and music.[49] It was hardly the first time that a conquering people assimilated the culture of the conquered.

THE RETURN OF TARABAI (1748–61)

Despite her long, thirty-four-year confinement, Tarabai was probably well aware of these developments taking place in Maratha society during the first half of the eighteenth century. Being by temperament publicly engaged, she would have found ways to keep informed on news from the outside world, especially political news.

She was certainly aware of the increasingly divergent fates of the two Maratha kingdoms, Kolhapur and Satara, each claiming to be the sole rightful successor to Shivaji's state. From Shahu's capital of Satara, some sixty-five miles north of Panhala, the Peshwas had sent armies over the whole of north India. Indeed, they had become de facto successors to the Mughals, propping up the same empire that Tarabai in her earlier years had so fiercely resisted. The state of Kolhapur, by contrast, had stagnated. In 1731, the kingdom's status as a separate but junior Maratha state in relation to Satara was formalized after a brief skirmish in which Shahu had bested Sambhaji of Kolhapur. The two royal cousins now reached an accord that demarcated the Varna River as the permanent boundary between their respective states. While stabilizing their mutual relations, however, the Treaty of Varna also had the effect of hemming in Kolhapur, leaving it landlocked and with nowhere to expand. Yet the Kolhapur princely state would endure for more than two centuries, until the departure of the British in 1947.

---

[48] As early as 1738, the Peshwas were seeking to recruit Arab soldiers into their armies. Guha, *Environment and Ethnicity*, 87n.
[49] Gordon, *The Marathas*, 145.

As another consequence of the confrontation between Shahu and Sambhaji, Kolhapur's royal women, including Tarabai, were taken to Shahu as prisoners of war. When given the choice of where she preferred to live as a prisoner, Panhala or Satara, Tarabai had claimed that it made no difference to her. But of course it did. She knew that even under conditions of house arrest, at Satara she would be at the heart of the more dynamic of the two Maratha states. She accordingly left Panhala and accompanied her nephew to Satara. Still, we hear little from her for another fifteen years, until 1748, when Shahu's favorite wife died. The king now became increasingly morose and reclusive, retiring for long stretches of time to a grass hut some distance from the capital. Most of all, being without a son, Shahu brooded over who might succeed him. He even considered adopting some distant Bhosle relative.

This was when Tarabai, now seventy-three years old and still under a rather loose house arrest, stepped out from behind the shadows. "Why adopt an outsider," she asked, "where there is a (direct) member of our own family?"[50] She then told an astonished court at Satara that, unknown to the public, she had a grandson named Ramraja who had been secretly raised in a village not far from Satara. Now twenty-two years old, Ramraja was very much available to succeed Shahu to the throne of Satara. This bombshell evoked different responses from members of the court. Shahu's senior wife Sakwar Bai, convinced that the story was a hoax, flew into a rage. For his part, Shahu was willing to accept the tale if it could be verified by some reliable party, which it duly was.

But in October 1749, the king's health began to fail. Shahu also grew anxious for the stability of the throne in view of the controversies swirling around the issue of his successor, and especially in view of Sakwar Bai's implacable opposition to Tarabai and to the planned succession of her grandson Ramraja. Under the circumstances, the ill and exasperated king turned to Nana Saheb, the third in a succession of hereditary Brahmin Peshwas who for several decades had been steadily gathering power while managing the Satara kingdom. Shahu drafted several orders effectively making the Peshwa sovereign and the king a mere figurehead. Then in December he died. By the end of the month, a delegation had retrieved the theretofore unknown Ramraja from his village, and in early January 1750 he was crowned king.[51]

Having so brazenly stepped back onto center stage, Tarabai now seemed intent on repeating what she had done a half-century earlier – govern the state through a puppet king. But rifts swiftly opened between her and both

---

[50] Cited in Malgonkar, *Chhatrapatis of Kolhapur*, 180.
[51] Kishore, *Tara Bai*, 168–78.

Ramraja and the Peshwa, Nana Saheb (1740–61). She certainly misjudged the resolution of her grandson, who soon let it be known that he wished to be his own man. Nana Saheb responded to this by washing his hands of Satara altogether and relocating in Pune, which now became the de facto capital of the Satara dynastic house and administrative center of the Maratha confederacy. Tarabai, on the other hand, responded to Ramraja's assertions of independence by having her men seize the hapless king and throw him into Satara's prison (November 1750). There he would remain for the rest of his life. Tarabai went further and publicly disavowed her earlier tale respecting Ramraja's origins, even denying that the king was her grandson after all. Instead, as she now claimed before a stunned court, he was a mere impostor. Yet she jealously guarded her ward; on learning that one of the fort's officers had plotted to free the imprisoned king, she ordered the man beheaded.[52] At the same time, she openly opposed Nana Saheb, exhorting the Peshwa's enemies, including even the Nizam of Hyderabad, to take up arms and remove him from power. But such pleas, transmitted to chiefs through her many agents scattered across the kingdom, proved mainly ineffectual.

Perhaps the most notable measure she took against the Peshwa was to raise the cry of caste. Aiming to draw support away from the Brahmin administrators who had attained such prominence during her confinement, Tarabai projected herself as the champion of Marathas against Brahmins in general, and against Nana Saheb and his network of Konkani Chitpavans in particular. She not only saw herself as a proud and true Maratha, but she characterized the Bhosle family, into which she had married, as "the best among the *kshatriyas*"[53] – a claim recalling her earlier insistence on having her son undergo a sacred thread ceremony that would confirm his claims to *kshatriya*, or warrior, status. Tarabai also appealed to the Maratha identity of men like Raghuji Bhosle and Fateh Singh Bhosle in an effort to rouse them to resist the Brahmin domination of the state.[54] Some of her most loyal supporters seem to have shared her chauvinistic sentiments. One of these was Mudhoji Naik Nimbalkar, who in October 1751 had been defending the fort of Nandgiri (in Satara district) from an assault by the Peshwa's army. Amidst the siege, Nimbalkar defiantly wrote the Brahmin Peshwa, "We Marathas will sacrifice our children defending a cause to which we have pledged our support. But we will not betray those whom we support."[55]

---

[52] Malgonkar, *Chhatrapatis of Kolhapur*, 198.   [53] Pawar, *Tarabaikalina*, III: no. 125.
[54] G. S. Sardesai, ed., *Selections from the Peshwa Daftar*, vol. 6: *Ramraja's Struggle for Power*, 148, 151. Cited in Brij Kishore, *Tara Bai*, 201.
[55] Pawar, *Tarabaikalina*, III: no. 25.

Even Ramraja, just seven months before his imprisonment, had complained that "Here [in Satara] the Peshwa is setting up Brahmin rule."[56]

But efforts to provoke an anti-Brahmin backlash came to nothing, and in the end, Tarabai and Nana Saheb reached a carefully choreographed compromise. The Peshwa agreed to show his loyalty to Ramraja and to obey the orders of the imprisoned king's spokeswoman, Tarabai, who in turn agreed to acknowledge Nana Saheb's right to govern the country.[57] At Tarabai's insistence, on September 14, 1752 the two solemnly confirmed their pact before the god Khandoba at Jejuri, thirty miles southeast of Pune.[58] In light of the Brahmin–Maratha cleavage that Tarabai sought to exploit, her insistence that the Brahmin Peshwa swear his loyalty before this particular deity, a Maharashtrian deity *par excellence*, is perhaps significant. Khandoba, writes Günther-Dietz Sontheimer, is "a god of war and the territorial guardian of Maharashtra," the high god for many pastoral tribes, especially the Dhangars, and "above all a god of the warring 'Maratha' groups – the Marathas in the broadest sense."[59]

From this point on, Tarabai settled into her life's final role – that of a powerful, quasi-sovereign dowager. At Satara she maintained a regular court and conducted business of state, issuing orders, conferring grants, and receiving Maratha *sardar*s, while the Peshwa at least publicly acquiesced to her will or sought her advice. On one occasion, for example, he had Tarabai write to Maratha chiefs to mobilize them against three hostile armies that had crossed the Narmada into Maharasthra. For her part, Tarabai conveyed to the Peshwa her support for the steps he had taken respecting Afghan invasions of the Punjab.[60] Moving to more mundane concerns, in 1752 she ordered a Maratha chief to supply fodder for the cavalry horses at specified rates.[61] The same year, the superintendent of Pratapgarh fort asked her to have some roofs in a temple compound rethatched.[62] And the next year, we find her settling a divorce case involving her Muslim maid.[63]

Meanwhile, by the late 1750s the Marathas, now the protectors of the Mughal emperor, had become inextricably enmeshed in north Indian affairs. On behalf of their imperial clients, Maratha generals were now negotiating with Ahmad Shah Abdali, whose Afghan army had entered the Punjab in 1759 to make good on their territorial claims on that province. As a major showdown between Marathas and Afghans was brewing, Nana Saheb in December 1760

[56] Cited in Malgonkar, *Chhatrapatis of Kolhapur*, 188.
[57] Pawar, *Tarabaikalina*, III: no. 81.   [58] Kishore, *Tara Bai*, 211.
[59] Sontheimer, *Pastoral Deities*, 125, 164.   [60] Pawar, *Tarabaikalina*, III: nos. 44, 119.
[61] G. S. Sardesai, ed., *Selections from the Peshwa Daftar*, vol. 26: *Tarabai and Sambhaji, 1738–1761* (Bombay, 1932), no. 190.
[62] *Ibid.*, no. 193.   [63] Pawar, *Tarabaikalina*, III: no. 70.

began moving his own army north with a view to joining the main Maratha force then camped at Panipat, north of Delhi. But he never reached the famous battlefield. On January 14, 1761 an estimated 50,000 Marathas were slaughtered at Panipat in one of the greatest military debacles in Indian history.[64] For Nana Saheb personally, the disaster represented an indictment of decades of his and his predecessors' northern policy. Upon hearing the news while still en route to join the battle, the Peshwa turned around and headed back to Pune, a disillusioned and broken man. Within six months he was dead.

How did Tarabai respond to news of the debacle? After all, six decades earlier she herself had launched the policy of northern expansion that ultimately led to Panipat. One view is that she derived satisfaction at seeing her old adversary, the Peshwa, discomfited by the disaster. According to Grant Duff, "to the last moment of her existence" she harbored such hostility toward both Nana Saheb and his cousin Sadashiv Rao, who was killed at Panipat, "that she expired contented, having lived to hear of their misfortunes and death."[65] But it has also been suggested that, because Tarabai had assured the Peshwa of her full confidence in him shortly after Panipat, she must have sympathized with his grief over the defeat.[66] The problem with this argument, however, is that for the previous eight years these two master politicians, each of them well acquainted with the other's weaknesses, had been playing an intricate game of charades. Nana Saheb would outwardly submit to Tarabai, who in return would outwardly congratulate the Peshwa for his victories or ply him with gifts.[67] In this light, one could imagine her outwardly commiserating with the Peshwa over the Panipat disaster, while inwardly harboring feelings of *schadenfreude*, or delight at another's misfortune.

In any event, within six months of Nana Saheb's death, on December 9, 1761, Tarabai herself had died of old age. She was eighty-six. Revealing her characteristic zeal for administration, she bestowed a village on a recipient just a week before her death, on the occasion of a lunar eclipse.[68]

SUMMARY

Tarabai's career divides into three distinct periods. In the first (age nineteen to thirty-nine), comprising the twenty years between her flight to Jinji and her

---

[64] Gordon, *The Marathas*, 153. Sardesai estimates that the casualties reached 75,000. Sardesai, *New History*, ii:459.

[65] Grant Duff, *History*, i:412.   [66] Kishore, *Tara Bai*, 215.

[67] On the very day he died, the Peshwa received a gift of mangoes and jams that Tarabai had specially prepared and sent to him several days earlier. *Ibid.*, 215.

[68] Pawar, *Tarabaikalina*, iii: no. 163.

imprisonment in Panhala, she appears as an active administrator ably coordinating the defense of Shivaji's fledgling kingdom against the might of the imperial Mughals. She governed as regent for her minor son because Maratha political culture barred a woman from assuming the symbols of royalty for herself. Yet Portuguese onlookers in those years did not hesitate to call her *a rainha dos Marathas*, or the Queen of the Marathas. The characterization confirms what we know from other sources, namely, that her gender in no way limited her ability to exercise the functions of an absolute monarch.

The second period of Tarabai's career (age thirty-nine to seventy-three) encompassed thirty-four years when, being either imprisoned or confined, she simply disappeared from public view. In the third period (age seventy-three to eighty-six), she emerged for thirteen more years in the public spotlight as a powerful dowager. Already by 1750 we find her carrying on vigorous correspondence, both administrative and political, with commanders and *sardars* throughout Maharashtra. Yet many of her correspondents were men who could not have been active during her earlier career. It might seem surprising that she so readily re-entered active public life after three-and-a-half decades of apparent obscurity. It is most likely that she maintained covert correspondence with Maratha chieftains throughout her confinement, but that such correspondence never got included in official records such as the *Peshwa Daftar*.

Maharashtrian society passed through momentous changes during Tarabai's lifetime. Some of these derived from the Marathas' military drive into Mughal north India, a policy that she herself had pioneered and which the Peshwas vigorously pursued during and after her confinement. Another was a broadening scope of the term "Maratha." While at one level referring to any speaker of Marathi, from the fourteenth century on the term had taken on a distinctly military ethos, referring to those élite Marathi-speakers who themselves or whose ancestors had received land assignments (*watan*) in return for rendering military service to one or another of the sultanates of the western Deccan. That historical connection would explain how Muslim domestic practices such as the seclusion of women or eating from a single dish with fellow members of one's caste became assimilated to Maratha identity.[69]

In the eighteenth century, however, owing to the rise of new classes of military men from families having no history of military service, there was uncertainty as to the rank of Marathas in the four-fold *varna* system.[70] During Tarabai's long confinement, Brahmin Peshwas had promoted a new

---

[69] Rosalind O'Hanlon, *Caste, Conflict, and Ideology: Mahatma Jotirao Phule and Low Caste Protest in Nineteenth-Century Western India* (Cambridge, 1985), 19.
[70] Chandra, "Social Background," 216.

generation of chieftains (*sardars*) who, unlike Tarabai herself, were not descended from older families of *deshmukhs*. That is, they lacked ties to hereditary lands (*watans*) that the sultans of the Deccan had conferred on those older families. Yet despite their humble origins, these chieftains' association with military careers nonetheless conferred on them a Maratha identity. For example, Malhar Rao Holkar, who led successful expeditions north of the Narmada River between the 1720s and 1760s, became celebrated as a great Maratha, even an arch-Maratha, although he had come from a community of Dhangars, or shepherds. Similarly, as Kunbi villagers increasingly participated in the armies of the eighteenth century, the idea gained currency that Kunbis, too, were Marathas.[71] In short, during the eighteenth century, the term had become flexible and open to appropriation by anyone associated with military prowess.

In the course of the nineteenth century, by contrast, the term became identified with a more bounded and exclusive community, especially in relation to Maharashtrian Brahmins.[72] While this latter phenomenon has been traced to the advent of British rule,[73] Tarabai's attempt to mobilize Marathas *as Marathas* against the Brahmin Peshwa nonetheless anticipated that later development. This, in turn, has cost Tarabai dearly in the estimate of those historians who have traced more recent Maratha–Brahmin tensions back to this "evil genius of Maharashtra."[74] But Tarabai did not oppose the Peshwa solely or even primarily because he was a Brahmin. There were other issues. Whereas Tarabai's ancestors were rooted in landholding and military service, the Peshwas' ancestors were rooted in finance and banking. Whereas her forebears had been bred in the dry, upland Desh, with its distinctive speech, diet, and customs, the Peshwas had come from the low, wet Konkan coast with its own distinctive culture. Perhaps most importantly, Tarabai felt that the Peshwas had appropriated powers that her own father-in-law, Shivaji, had invested only in the Maratha *chhatrapati*, or king.

This outcome was deeply ironic, however, inasmuch as the Peshwas' rise to supreme power, which Tarabai so resented, was linked in part to her own

---

[71] After the British pacification of India in the nineteenth century, economic prosperity seems to have replaced warrior prowess as the key criterion for Maratha status. This is suggested in the Marathi proverb, "when a kunbi prospers, he becomes a Maratha." O'Hanlon, *Caste, Conflict, and Ideology*, 18.

[72] See Prachi Deshpande, "Caste as Maratha: Social Categories, Colonial Policy, and Identity in Early Twentieth-Century Maharashtra," *Indian Economic and Social History Review* 41, no. 1 (2004): 7–32.

[73] O'Hanlon, *Caste, Conflict, and Ideology*, 24–41; Deshpande, "Caste as Maratha."

[74] Kishore, *Tara Bai*, 218. Referring to her years after 1707, the historians S. M. Garge, G. S. Sardesai, and Brij Kishore have characterized Tarabai as selfish, unscrupulous, high-handed, unpatriotic, and power-greedy. See Patil, *Maharini Tarabai*, 1.

actions. In 1749 Shahu voluntarily delegated considerable power to Nana Saheb because of the fierce opposition of his senior wife, Sakwar Bai, to Tarabai and to the latter's plans to place her grandson on the Maratha throne. After Shahu's death, Tarabai took several measures that further undermined the king's authority, which by default enhanced that of the Peshwa. First, she imprisoned her reputed grandson not long after his coronation, rendering him ineffectual. Then she denied he was her grandson after all, depriving him of a legitimate claim to the throne. Even the Peshwa wrote that should Ramraja prove to be false, he could not respect him.[75]

In the last analysis, Tarabai's long life spanned three distinct eras in the history of the western Deccan – the late medieval era of the Bijapur sultans, the early modern era of the Maratha kingdom, and the modern era of European imperial domination. She was deeply immersed in all three eras. Her family had enjoyed *deshmukh* status and had held hereditary lands (*watans*) since 1626, thanks to the patronage of the sultans of Bijapur. And her ties to that sultanate persisted through her long association with Panhala, of all Maharashtrian forts the most imbued with the history and architectural vision of the sultanate of Bijapur (see Plate 16). As for the second era, it is doubtful that without Tarabai's exertions the fledgling Maratha kingdom founded by her famous father-in-law would have survived the reign of Aurangzeb. Her bold military initiatives anticipated the Marathas' fateful policy of advancing deep into north India. And her early struggles with Shahu, combined with her subsequent imprisonment of her sovereign "grandson," contributed to the emergence of an alternate hub of power in the kingdom – a hereditary line of Brahmin Peshwas.

Tarabai's connection with the third, or European, era is symbolized by an incident that occurred just three years before her death. In late 1715 her former chief adviser, Ramchandra Nilkanth, had completed a political treatise, the *Ajnapatra*, that discussed among other topics the arrival of Europeans in the western Deccan. He called them "hat-wearers." Although these newcomers might appear to be ordinary merchants, warned the author,

they are not like other merchants. Their masters, every one of them, are ruling kings . . . These hat-wearers have full ambition to enter into these provinces to increase their territories, and to establish their own opinions (religion).[76]

During the five decades following the writing of these prescient words, "hat-wearers" had been swarming along India's shores like locusts. Some had already

---

[75] Pawar, *Tarabaikalina*, III, no. 85.
[76] S. V. Puntambeker, "The *Ajnapatra* or Royal Edict Relating to the Principles of Maratha State Policy," *Journal of Indian History* 8, no. 2 (August 1929): 212.

begun nibbling at Indian territory, typically by marketing their weapons to political players in the interior. In April 1758, the acting governor of Portuguese Goa wrote to Tarabai, now eighty-three years old, to say that he would be pleased to supply her with the 2,000 guns she had ordered, provided she paid for them before delivery.[77]

The era of the "hat-wearers" had dawned.

[77] Pawar, *Tarabaikalina*, III: no. 122.

SELECT BIBLIOGRAPHY

Primary sources

Abbott, Justin E., trans. *Life of Tukaram: Translation from Mahipati's* Bhaktalilamrita, *Chapter 25 to 40*. 1930. Reprint. Delhi, 2000.

'Afif, Shams-i Siraj. *Tarikh-i Firuz Shahi*. Extracts translated and edited by H. M. Elliot and John Dowson in *History of India as Told by its Own Historians*. III:269–373. 8 vols. Allahabad, 1964.

Alvares, Francisco. *The Prester John of the Indies: a True Relation of the Lands of the Prester John, being the Narrative of the Portuguese Embassy to Ethiopia in 1520*. Translated by Lord Stanley of Alderley. Revised and edited by C. F. Beckingham and G. W. B. Huntingford. 2 vols. Cambridge, 1961.

Amir Khusrau. *Nuh Sipihr*. Edited by Mohammad Wahid Mirza. Islamic Research Association series no. 12. London, 1950. Extracts translated and edited by H. M. Elliot and John Dowson in *The History of India as Told by its Own Historians*. III: 557–66. 8 vols. Allahabad, 1964.

Anonymous. *Tarikh-i Muhammad Qutb Shah*. Translated by John Briggs under the title *History of the Rise of the Mahomedan Power in India*. III: 202–92. 4 vols. 1829. Reprint. Calcutta, 1966.

Barani, Zia al-Din. *Tarikh-i Firuz Shahi*. Extracts translated and edited by H. M. Elliot and John Dowson in *The History of India as Told by its Own Historians*. III:93–268. 8 vols. Allahabad, 1964.

Beckingham, C. F. and G. W. B. Huntingford, ed. and trans. *Some Records of Ethiopia, 1593–1646: being Extracts from* The History of High Ethiopia or Abassia *by Manoel de Albeida*. London, 1954.

Chitre, Dilip, trans. *Says Tuka: Selected Poetry of Tukaram*. New Delhi, 1991.

Coolhaas, W. Ph., ed. *Pieter Van den Broecke in Azië*. 2 vols. The Hague, 1962.

Desai, P. B., trans. "Kalyana Inscription of Sultan Muhammad, Saka 1248," *Epigraphia Indica* 32 (1957–58): 165–68.

Desai, Ziyaud-Din A. *Arabic, Persian and Urdu Inscriptions of West India, a Topographical List*. New Delhi, 1999.

—. *A Topographical List of Arabic, Persian and Urdu Inscriptions of South India*. New Delhi, 1989.

Federici, Cesare. "Extracts of Master Caesar Frederike his Eighteene Yeeres Indian Observations." In *Hakluytus Posthumus, or Purchas his Pilgrimes*, by Samuel Purchas. X: 83–143. 20 vols. 1625. Glasgow, 1905.

Filliozat, Pierre-Sylvan, trans. *Le Prataparudriya de Vidyanatha*. Pondicherry, 1963.

Filliozat, Vasundhara. *l'Épigraphie de Vijayanagara du début à 1377*. Paris, 1973.

Firishta, Muhammad Qasim. *Tarikh-i Firishta* (completed 1611). 2 vols. Lucknow, 1864–65. Translated by John Briggs under the title *History of the Rise of the Mahomedan Power in India.* London, 1829. 4 vols. Reprint. 3 vols. Calcutta, 1966.

Foster, William, ed. *Early Travels in India, 1583–1619.* New Delhi, 1968.

Fryer, John. *A New Account of East India and Persia, being Nine Years' Travels, 1672–1681.* Edited by William Crooke. 2 vols. London, 1912.

Gawan, Khwaja 'Imad al-Din Mahmud. *Riyad al-insha'.* Edited by Shaikh Chand bin Husain. Hyderabad, 1948.

Goron, Stan and J. P. Goenka. *The Coins of the Indian Sultanates.* New Delhi, 2001.

Ibn Battuta. *The Rehla of Ibn Battuta.* Translated by Mahdi Husain. Baroda, 1953.

— *Travels in Asia and Africa, 1325–1354.* Translated by H. A. R. Gibb. Reprint. New Delhi, 1986.

'Isami, 'Abd al-Malik. *Futuhus-salatin.* Text edited by A. S. Usha. Madras, 1948. Edited and translated by Agha Mahdi Husain under the title *Futuhu's Salatin.* 3 vols. London, 1967.

Jahangir (Emperor). *The Tuzuk-i-Jahangiri, or Memoirs of Jahangir.* Translated by Alexander Rogers, edited by Henry Beveridge. 1909–14. 2 vols. Reprint. Delhi, 1968.

Kadiri, A. A. "Inscriptions of the Sidi Chiefs of Janjira." *Epigraphia Indica, Arabic and Persian Supplement* (1966): 55–76.

Khafi Khan. *Muntakhab al-lubab.* Calcutta, 1874. Extracts translated and edited by H. M. Elliot and John Dowson in *History of India as Told by its Own Historians.* VII:207–533. 8 vols. Allahabad, 1964.

Khobrekar, V. G., ed. *Tarikh-i-Dilkasha (Memoirs of Bhimsen Relating to Aurangzib's Deccan Campaigns).* Translated by Jadunath Sarkar. Bombay, 1972.

Krishnaswami Aiyangar, S., ed. *Sources of Vijayanagar History.* 1919. Reprint. Delhi, 1986.

Kulkarni, G. T. and M. S. Mate, ed. and trans. *Tarif-i-Husain Shah Badshah Dakhan.* Pune, 1987.

Leach, Linda York. *Mughal and Other Indian Paintings from the Chester Beatty Library.* 2 vols. London, 1995.

Mu'tamad Khan. *Iqbal-nama-yi Jahangiri.* Extracts translated and edited by H. M. Elliot and John Dowson in *History of India as Told by its Own Historians.* VI:400–38. 8 vols. Allahabad, 1964.

Nikitin, Athanasius [Afanasy]. "The Travels of Athanasius Nikitin of Twer." Translated by Count Wielhorsky. In *India in the Fifteenth Century,* edited by R. H. Major, 1–32. Hakluyt Society, First Series no. 22. Reprint. New York, 1970.

Omvedt, Gail and Bharat Patankar, trans. *The Revolutionary Abhangs of Tukaram.* Forthcoming.

Pawar, Appasaheb, ed. *Tarabaikalina Kagadpatre.* 3 vols. Kolhapur, 1969.

Pires, Tomé. *The Suma Oriental of Tomé Pires: an Account of the East, from the Red Sea to Japan, Written in Malacca and India in 1512–1515.* Translated by Armando Cortesão. 2 vols. London, 1944. Reprint. New Delhi, 1990.

van Ravesteijn, Pieter Gielis. "Journal, May 1615 to Feb. 1616." In Heert Terpstra, *De opkomst der Westerkwartieren van de Oost – Indische Compagnie (Suratte, Arabië, Perzië)*, 174–203. The Hague, 1918.

Samani, Muhammad ʿAli. *Siyar al-Muhammadi* [composed 1427]. Edited by S. N. Ahmad Qadri. Hyderabad, 1969.

Sardesai, G. S., ed. *Selections from the Peshwa Daftar*. Vol. 6: *Ramraja's Struggle for Power*. Vol. 26: *Tarabai and Sambhaji (1738–1761)*. Bombay, 1932.

Shirazi, Rafiʿ al-Din. *Tadhkirat al-muluk* (completed 1608). Extracts translated by J. S. King, "History of the Bahmani Dynasty." *Indian Antiquary* 28 (June 1899): 153–55, 182, 191–92, 218–19, 242–47.

Tabataba, ʿAli. *Burhan-i maʾathir* (completed 1591). Delhi, 1936. Extracts translated by J. S. King, "History of the Bahmani Dynasty." *Indian Antiquary* vol. 28 (1899): 119–38, 141–53, 180–81, 182–91, 209–17, 235–42, 277–92, 305–23. Extracts translated by T. W. Haig, "The History of the Nizam Shahi Kings of Ahmadnagar," *Indian Antiquary* vol. 49 (1920): 67–75, 84–91, 102–08, 123–28, 157–67, 177–88, 197–204, 217–24; vol. 50 (1921): 1–8, 25–31, 73–80, 101–06, 141–46, 193–98, 205–10, 229–34, 261–68, 277–83, 321–28; vol. 51 (1922): 29–36, 66–73, 125–31, 198–203, 235–42; vol. 52 (1923): 29–39, 159–62, 250–62, 287–300, 331–46.

Wagoner, Phillip B. *Tidings of the King: a Translation and Ethnohistorical Analysis of the Rayavacakamu*. Honolulu, 1993.

Wright, H. Nelson. *The Coinage and Metrology of the Sultans of Delhi*. Delhi, 1936.

Secondary sources

Alam, S. M. "The Historic Deccan – a Geographical Appraisal." In *Aspects of Deccan History*, edited by V. K. Bawa, 16–31. Hyderabad, 1975.

Chandra, Satish. "Social Background to the Rise of the Maratha Movement during the 17th Century in India." *Indian Economic and Social History Review* 10, no. 3 (September 1973): 209–17.

Chowdhuri, Jogindra Nath. *Malik Ambar: a Biography Based on Original Sources*. Calcutta, *c.* 1933.

Dallapiccola, Anna L., ed. *Vijayanagara – City and Empire: New Currents of Research*. Stuttgart, 1985.

Deleury, G. A. *The Cult of Vithoba*. Poona, 1960.

Deshpande, Prachi. "Caste as Maratha: Social Categories, Colonial Policy, and Identity in Early Twentieth-Century Maharashtra." *Indian Economic and Social History Review* 41, no. 1 (2004): 7–32.

Digby, Simon. "The Sufi *Shaykh* and the Sultan: a Conflict of Claims to Authority in Medieval India." *Iran* 28 (1990): 71–81.

—. "*Tabarrukat* and Succession among the Great Chishti Shaykhs of the Delhi Sultanate." In *Delhi through the Ages*, edited by R. E. Frykenberg, 63–103. New York, 1986.

Eaton, Richard M. *Sufis of Bijapur, 1300–1700: Social Roles of Sufis in Medieval India*. Princeton, 1978.

Ernst, Carl W. *Eternal Garden: Mysticism, History, and Politics at a South Asian Sufi Center.* Albany, 1992.

Faruqi, Shamsur Rahman. "A Long History of Urdu Literary Culture, Part I: Naming and Placing a Literary Culture." In *Literary Cultures in History: Reconstructions from South Asia,* edited by Sheldon Pollock, 805–63. Berkeley, 2003.

Feldhaus, Anne. "Maharashtra as a Holy Land: a Sectarian Tradition." *Bulletin of the School of Oriental and African Studies* 49 (1986): 532–48.

Fukazawa, Hiroshi. *The Medieval Deccan: Peasants, Social Systems and States, Sixteenth to Eighteenth Centuries.* Delhi, 1991.

Gordon, Stewart. *The Marathas, 1600–1818.* New Cambridge History of India, vol. II.4. Cambridge, 1993.

—. *Marathas, Marauders, and State Formation in Eighteenth-Century India.* Delhi, 1994.

Graham, Terry. "Shah Ni'matullah Wali: Founder of the Ni'matullahi Sufi Order." In *The Heritage of Sufism,* edited by Leonard Lewisohn. Vol. 2: *Legacy of Medieval Persian Sufism (1150–1500),* 173–90. Oxford, 1999.

Grant Duff, James. *History of the Mahrattas.* Edited by J. P. Guha. 2 vols. New Delhi, 1971.

Guha, Sumit. "Speaking Historically: the Changing Voices of Historical Narrative in Western India, 1400–1900," *American Historical Review* 109, no. 4 (October 2004): 1084–1103.

Gune, V. T. *Judicial System of the Marathas.* Poona, 1953.

Heras, Henry. *The Aravidu Dynasty of Vijayanagar.* Madras, 1927.

Husain, Mahdi. *Tughluq Empire.* New Delhi, 1976.

Hussaini, Syed Shah Khusro. "Gisudaraz on *Wahdat al-wujud.*" *Studies in Islam* (October 1982): 233–45.

Israel, Milton and N. K. Wagle, eds. *Religion and Society in Maharashtra.* Toronto, 1987.

Jayasuriya, Shihan de Silva and Richard Pankhurst, eds. *The African Diaspora in the Indian Ocean.* Trenton, 2003.

Karashima, Noboru. *Towards a New Formation: South Indian Society under Vijayanagar Rule.* New Delhi, 1992.

Kishore, Brij. *Tara Bai and her Times.* Bombay, 1963.

Kulkarnee, Narayan H. "Medieval Maharashtra and Muslim Saint-Poets." In *Medieval Bhakti Movements in India,* edited by N. N. Bhattacharyya, 198–231. New Delhi, 1989.

Kulkarni, A. R. "Social Relations in the Maratha Country in the Medieval Period." *Indian History Congress.* Proceedings of the 32nd Session, Jabalpur (1970): 231–69.

Kulke, Hermann. "Maharajas, Mahants and Historians: Reflections on the Historiography of Early Vijayanagara and Sringeri." In *Vijayanagara – City and Empire: New Currents of Research,* edited by Anna L. Dallapiccola, 1:120–43. 2 vols. Stuttgart, 1985.

Mahalingam, T. V. *Administration and Social Life under Vijayanagar.* 2nd edn. Madras, 1975.

Malgonkar, Manohar. *Chhatrapatis of Kolhapur.* Bombay, 1971.

Matthews, D. J. "Eighty Years of Dakani Scholarship." *Annual of Urdu Studies* 8 (1993): 91–108.

Michell, George. *Architecture and Art of Southern India: Vijayanagara and the Successor States*. New Cambridge History of India, vol. I:6. Cambridge, 1995.

— and Richard Eaton *Firuzabad: Palace City of the Deccan*. Oxford, 1992.

— and Mark Zebrowski. *Architecture and Art of the Deccan Sultanates*. New Cambridge History of India, vol. I:7. Cambridge, 1999.

Morrison, Kathleen D. *Fields of Victory: Vijayanagara and the Course of Intensification*. Contributions of the University of California Archaeological Research Facility, Berkeley, No. 53. Berkeley, 1995.

—. "Naturalizing Disaster: from Drought to Famine in Southern India." In *Environmental Disaster and the Archaeology of Human Response*, edited by Garth Bawden and Richard M. Reycraft, 21–34. Albuquerque, 2000.

Murty, M. L. K. and Günther-Dietz Sontheimer. "Prehistoric Background to Pastoralism in the Southern Deccan in the Light of Oral Traditions and Cults of Some Pastoral Communities." *Anthropos* 75 (1980): 163–84.

Narayana Rao, Velcheru. "Epics and Ideologies: Six Telugu Folk Epics." In *Another Harmony: New Essays on the Folklore of India*, edited by Stuart H. Blackburn and A. K. Ramanujan, 131–64. Berkeley, 1986.

—. "Kings, Gods and Poets: Ideologies of Patronage in Medieval Andhra." In *Powers of Art*, edited by Barbara S. Miller, 142–59. Delhi, 1992.

Nayeem, M. A. "Foreign Cultural Relations of the Bahmanis (1461–81 A.D.) (Gleanings from Mahmud Gawan's *Riyazul Insha*)." In *Studies in the Foreign Relations of India*, edited by P. M. Joshi and M. A. Nayeem, 394–400. Hyderabad, 1975.

O'Hanlon, Rosalind. *Caste, Conflict, and Ideology: Mahatma Jotirao Phule and Low Caste Protest in Nineteenth-Century Western India*. Cambridge, 1985.

Parabrahma Sastry, P. V. *The Kakatiyas of Warangal*. Hyderabad, 1978.

Patil, Shalini V. *Maharani Tarabai of Kolhapur (c. 1675–1761)*. New Delhi, 1987.

Pawar, A. G. "Palace Revolution at Kolhapur, 1714." In *Studies in Indology and Medieval History*, edited by M. S. Mate and G. T. Kulkarni, 159–70. Poona, 1974.

Petievich, Carla. "The Feminine and Cultural Syncretism in Early Dakani Poetry." *The Annual of Urdu Studies* 8 (Madison, 1993): 119–30.

Ramaswamy, Vijaya. "Artisans in Vijayanagar Society." *Indian Economic and Social History Review* 22, no. 4 (1985): 417–44.

—. "Women 'In', Women 'Out': Women within the Mahanubhava, Warkari, and Ramdas Panths." In *Organizational and Institutional Aspects of Indian Religious Movements*, edited by Joseph T. O'Connell, 240–72. Shimla, 1999.

Richards, J. F. *Mughal Administration in Golconda*. Oxford, 1975.

— and V. Narayana Rao, "Banditry in Mughal India: Historical and Folk Perceptions." In *The Mughal State, 1526–1750*, edited by Muzaffar Alam and Sanjay Subrahmanyam, 491–519. New Delhi, 1998.

Saksena, Banarasi Prasad. "A Few Unnoticed Facts about the Early Life of Malik Amber." *Proceedings, Indian History Congress* 5 (1941): 601–03.

Sardesai, Govind Sakharam. *New History of the Marathas*. 3 vols. Bombay, 1971.

Sarkar, Jadunath. *House of Shivaji (Studies and Documents on Maratha History, Royal Period)*. 3rd edn. Calcutta, 1955.

Schwartzberg, Joseph E., ed. *A Historical Atlas of South Asia*. Chicago, 1978.

Seth, D. R. "The Life and Times of Malik Ambar." *Islamic Culture* 31 (1957): 142–55.

Sewell, Robert. *A Forgotten Empire (Vijayanagara): a Contribution to the History of India*. 1900. Reprint. Delhi, 1962.

Sherwani, Haroon Khan. *The Bahmanis of the Deccan*. 2nd edn. 1977. Reprint. New Delhi, 1985.

—. *Mahmud Gawan, the Great Bahmani Wazir*. Allahabad, 1942.

— and P. M. Joshi, eds. *History of Medieval Deccan (1295–1724)*. 2 vols. Vol 1: Hyderabad, 1973; vol. 2: Hyderabad, 1974.

Shyam, Radhey. *The Kingdom of Ahmadnagar*. Delhi, 1966.

—. *Life and Times of Malik Ambar*. New Delhi, 1968.

Siddiqi, Muhammad Suleman. *The Bahmani Sufis*. Delhi, 1989.

—. "Ethnic Change in the Bahmanid Society at Bidar, 1422–1538." *Islamic Culture* 60, no. 3 (July 1986): 61–80.

Sinha, H. N. *The Rise of the Peshwas*. Allahabad, 1954.

Smith, Graham and J. Duncan M. Derrett. "Hindu Judicial Administration in Pre-British Times and its Lesson for Today." *Journal of the American Oriental Society* 95, no. 3 (July–September 1975): 417–23.

Stein, Burton. *Vijayanagara*. New Cambridge History of India, vol. I:2. Cambridge, 1989.

Sontheimer, Günther-Dietz. "Hero and Sati-Stones of Maharashtra." In *Memorial Stones: a Study of their Origin, Significance, and Variety*, edited by S. Settar and Gunther D. Sontheimer, 261–81. Dharwad, 1982.

—. *Pastoral Deities in Western India*. Translated by Anne Feldhaus. Delhi, 1993.

Subrahmanyam, Sanjay. "The Port City of Masulipatnam, 1550–1750: a Bird's Eye View." In *Craftsmen and Merchants: Essays in South Indian Urbanism*, edited by Narayani Gupta, 47–74. Chandigarh, 1993.

Talbot, Cynthia. *Precolonial India in Practice: Society, Region, and Identity in Medieval Andhra*. Oxford, 2001.

—. "Inscribing the Other, Inscribing the Self: Hindu–Muslim Identities in Pre-Colonial India." *Comparative Studies in Society and History* 37, no. 4 (October 1995): 692–722.

—. "Political Intermediaries in Kakatiya Andhra, 1175–1325." *Indian Economic and Social History Review* 31, no. 3 (1994): 261–89.

—. "The Story of Prataparudra: Hindu Historiography on the Deccan Frontier." In *Beyond Turk and Hindu: Rethinking Religious Identities in Islamicate South Asia*, edited by David Gilmartin and Bruce B. Lawrence, 282–99. Gainesville FL, 2000.

Tamaskar, B. G. *The Life and Work of Malik Ambar*. Delhi, 1978.

Toru, Miura and John Edward Philips, eds. *Slave Elites in the Middle East and Africa: a Comparative Study*. London and New York, 2000.

Tulpule, S. G. "Eknath's Treatment of the *Ramayana* as a Socio-Political Metaphor." In *Ramayana and Ramayanas*, edited by Monika Thiel-Horstmann, 139–52. Wiesbaden, 1991.

Varadarajan, Lotika. "Konkan Ports and Medieval Trade." *Indica* 22, no. 1 (March 1985): 9–16.

Vaudeville, Charlotte. *Myths, Saints and Legends in Medieval India,* compiled by Vasudha Dalmia. Delhi, 1996.

Verghese, Anila. *Archaeology, Art and Religion: New Perspectives on Vijayanagara.* New Delhi, 2000.

—. *Religious Traditions at Vijayanagara, as Revealed through its Monuments.* New Delhi, 1995.

—. "Court Attire of Vijayanagara (From a Study of Monuments)." *Quarterly Journal of the Mythic Society* 82 (1991): 43–61.

Wagoner, Phillip B. "Architecture and Royal Authority under the Early Sangamas." In *New Light on Hampi: Recent Research at Vijayanagara,* edited by John M. Fritz and George Michell, 12–23. Mumbai, 2001.

—. "Delhi, Warangal, and Kakatiya Historical Memory." *Deccan Studies* [Journal of the Centre for Deccan Studies, Hyderabad] 1, no. 1 (2002): 17–38.

—. "Fortuitous Convergences and Essential Ambiguities: Transcultural Political Élites in the Medieval Deccan." *International Journal of Hindu Studies* 3, no. 3 (December 1999): 241–64.

—. "From 'Pampa's Crossing' to 'The Place of Lord Virupaksa': Architecture, Cult, and Patronage at Hampi before the Founding of Vijayanagara." In *Vijayanagara: Progress of Research, 1988–1991,* edited by D. Devaraj and C. S. Patil, 141–74. Mysore, 1996.

—. "Harihara, Bukka, and the Sultan: the Delhi Sultanate in the Political Imagination of Vijayanagara." In *Beyond Turk and Hindu: Rethinking Religious Identities in Islamicate South Asia,* edited by David Gilmartin and Bruce B. Lawrence, 300–26. Gainesville FL, 2000.

—. "'Sultan among Hindu Kings': Dress, Titles, and the Islamicization of Hindu Culture at Vijayanagara." *Journal of Asian Studies* 55, no. 4 (November 1996): 851–80.

— and John Henry Rice "From Delhi to the Deccan: Newly Discovered Tughluq Monuments at Warangal-Sultanpur and the Beginnings of Indo-Islamic Architecture in Southern India." *Artibus Asiae* 61, no. 1 (2001): 77–117.

Wink, André. *al-Hind: the Making of the Indo-Islamic World.* Vol. 2: *The Slave Kings and the Islamic Conquest, 11th–13th Centuries.* Leiden, 1997.

—. *Land and Sovereignty in India: Agrarian Society and Politics under the Eighteenth-century Maratha Svarajya.* Cambridge, 1986.

Yazdani, G. *Bidar: its History and Monuments.* Oxford, 1947.

INDEX

INDEX

Iranian plateau
  source of military technology, 19
  source of personnel, 61
  source of political culture, 22
  ties with Deccan, 9, 11
Iranians
  recruited to the Deccan, 60–62
  withdraw from Golkonda, 159
  see also Westerner
'Isami, 'Abd al-Malik (historian), 39, 45–46

Jahangir (Mughal emperor), 125
  obsession with Malik Ambar, 118, 121–22
Jahangir Khan (general), 96–97
Jami, 'Abd al-Rahman (poet), 66
Janjira (sea-fort), 127
Jejuri (town), 197
Jinji (fort), 180
Jnanadev (poet-saint), 131, 132, 151
Junaidi
  see Siraj al-Din Junaidi
Junnar (fort), 97, 118, 129

Kabul, 79
Kakatiya (dynasty), 9, 88, 99, 156
  emergence, 13
  growth and dynamic character, 14–16, 138
  tributary relations with Delhi, 25
  Tughluq conquest, 20–21
Kalyana (city)
  Chalukya imperial capital, 94
  control passes from Bidar to Bijapur to
    Ahmadnagar, 96
  identified with Rama Raya's family, 94–95
  nexus of linguistic frontiers,
    64, 99
  Rama Raya as sovereign of, 95, 97
  temple repaired by Tughluqs, 24
Kam Bakhsh (son of Aurangzeb), 164, 166,
    184
Kambata (region of Ethiopia), 105, 108
Kampamna (son of Sangama), 38
Kampili (kingdom), 39
Kanchipuram (city), 18
Kanhoji Angria (coastal lord), 186
Kannada (language)
  and Chalukya inscriptions, 13
  and Vijayanagara inscriptions, 82, 104
  used by Rama Raya, 97
Kapaya Nayaka (chieftain), 50
Karimi (mercantile group), 75
Karnataka, 6
  and Kannada language, 13
  as Sangama base, 42, 50
Karve, Irawati, 152
Kaulas (fort), 162

Kaveri delta
  tax rebellion, 86
  textile production, 85
Khafi Khan (*Muntakhab al-lubab*), 155, 160,
    162, 163, 171, 172, 177, 182, 183
Khalji (Delhi dynasty), 20, 24, 40–41
  see also 'Ala al-Din Khalji, Khusrau Khan,
    Malik Kafur
Khandesh (region)
  invaded by Tarabai, 183
  relations with Bahmanis, 74
Khandoba (deity), 197
Khed (town), 185
khil'at (robe of honor), 18
Khirki (Aurangabad), 123
Khuldabad (necropolis), 46
Khurasan (northeastern Iranian plateau),
    61, 63
Khush Mahal (palace), 21, 50
Khusrau Khan (Khalji general), 19
Koilkonda (fort), 88
Kolff, Dirk, 190
Kolhapur (city), 182
Kolhapur (state), 194
Kondapalli (fort), 88
Kondavidu (fort), 88, 95
Konerunatha Kavi (poet), 94
Konkan coast, 61, 62, 67–68, 71, 127, 179
  Bahmani trade, 74–75
  Chitpavan Brahmins of, 192
  economy, 137
  Kanhoji Angria lord of, 186
  Mahmud Gawan's campaign, 71, 72
  pirates, 71
  slave trade, 106
Krishna delta, 13, 88
Krishna Raya (Vijayanagara king), 79, 90
  claims to pan-Deccan sovereignty,
    89–90
  coinage under, 84
  military successes, 88–90
Krishna River, 37, 38, 40, 152
  and Battle of Talikota, 98
  dividing a Muslim north and Hindu south,
    78, 87
  dividing Bahmani and Sangama states, 42
kshatriya (class), 15, 191
  and Bhosle family, 196
  and Pratapa Rudra, 16, 27
  and Tarabai's son, 181
Kulpak (town), 162, 172
Kunbi (caste)
  demographic ascendance as farmers, 137
  identity merging with Marathas, 191, 200
  Tukaram, 133, 140
Kurnool (fort), 91

214

THE NEW CAMBRIDGE HISTORY OF INDIA

I The Mughals and Their Contemporaries

*M. N. PEARSON, *The Portuguese in India*
*BURTON STEIN, *Vijayanagara*
*MILO CLEVELAND BEACH, *Mughal and Rajput painting*
*CATHERINE ASHER, *Architecture of Mughal India*
*JOHN F. RICHARDS, *The Mughal empire*
*GEORGE MICHELL, *Architecture and art of southern India*
*GEORGE MICHELL and MARK ZEBROWSKI, *Architecture and art of the Deccan sultanates*
*RICHARD M. EATON, *A social history of the Deccan, 1300–1761: eight Indian lives*

II Indian States and the Transition to Colonialism

*C. A. BAYLY, *Indian society and the making of the British Empire*
*P. J. MARSHALL, *Bengal: the British bridgehead: eastern India 1740–1828*
*J. S. GREWAL, *The Sikhs of the Punjab: revised edition*
*STEWART GORDON, *The Marathas 1600–1818*
*OM PRAKASH, *European commercial enterprise in pre-colonial India*

III The Indian Empire and the Beginnings of Modern Society

*KENNETH W. JONES, *Socio-religious reform movements in British India*
*SUGATA BOSE, *Peasant labour and colonial capital: rural Bengal since 1770*
*B. R. TOMLINSON, *The economy of modern India, 1860–1970*
*THOMAS R. METCALF, *Ideologies of the Raj*
*DAVID ARNOLD, *Science, technology and medicine in Colonial India*
*BARBARA N. RAMUSACK, *The Indian princes and their states*
GORDON JOHNSON, *Government and politics in India*

IV The Evolution of Contemporary South Asia

*PAUL R. BRASS, *The politics of India since Independence: second edition*
*GERALDINE FORBES, *Women in modern India*
*SUSAN BAYLY, *Caste, society and politics in India from the eighteenth century to the modern age*
*DAVID LUDDEN, *An agrarian history of South Asia*
FRANCIS ROBINSON, *Islam in South Asia*
ANIL SEAL, *The transfer of power and the partition of India*

*Already published